LIVING IN THE LIONS' DEN WITHOUT BEING EATEN

LIVING in the LIONS' DEN without BEING EATEN

WILLIAM CARR PEEL

NAVPRESS ▲

BRINGING TRUTH TO LIFE
NavPress Publishing Group
P.O. Box 35001, Colorado Springs, Colorado 80935

The Navigators is an international Christian organization. Jesus Christ gave His followers the Great Commission to go and make disciples (Matthew 28:19). The aim of The Navigators is to help fulfill that commission by multiplying laborers for Christ in every nation.

NavPress is the publishing ministry of The Navigators. NavPress publications are tools to help Christians grow. Although publications alone cannot make disciples or change lives, they can help believers learn biblical discipleship, and apply what they learn to their lives and ministries.

© 1994 by William Carr Peel

Library of Congress Catalog Card Number:
    94-11890
ISBN 08910-97945

Some of the anecdotal illustrations in this book are true to life and are included with the permission of the persons involved. All other illustrations are composites of real situations, and any resemblance to people living or dead is coincidental.

Unless otherwise identified, all Scripture quotations in this publication are taken from the *HOLY BIBLE: NEW INTERNATIONAL VERSION*® (NIV®). Copyright ©1973, 1978, 1984 by International Bible Society. Used by permission of Zondervan Publishing House. All rights reserved. Other versions used include: the *New American Standard Bible* (NASB), ©The Lockman Foundation 1960, 1962, 1963, 1968, 1971, 1972, 1973, 1975, 1977; *The Living Bible* (TLB) © 1971, used by permission of Tyndale House Publishers, Inc., Wheaton, IL; *The Message: The New Testament in Contemporary English*, copyright © 1993 by Eugene H. Peterson, all rights reserved, used by permission of NavPress Publishing Group; and the *King James Version* (KJV).

Peel, William Carr.
    Living in the lions' den without being eaten / William Carr Peel.
        p.   cm.
    Includes bibliographical references.
    ISBN 0-89109-794-5
    1. Conduct of life. 2. Daniel (Biblical character). 3. Americans—Religious life. I. Title.
BJ1581.2.P4228   1994
248.4—dc20   94-11890
                                                            CIP

Printed in the United States of America

FOR A FREE CATALOG OF
NAVPRESS BOOKS & BIBLE STUDIES,
CALL 1-800-366-7788 (USA)
or 1-416-499-4615 (CANADA)

Contents

✤

To Kathy,
for living with me
in the lions' den
for twenty-three years

Acknowledgments

❖

When you write a book on impact, you naturally think back to the people who have influenced your life. Numerous people have played Daniel's part in my life. Though their names escape the headlines, most readers could care less, and many of them will be surprised to find their names here, I nonetheless feel an obligation to publicly acknowledge their contribution to my life and thus to this book. They are:

- ◆ my parents, Carr and Margery Peel, who taught me right from wrong
- ◆ my fourth grade teacher, Jean Pigot, who helped me survive a move to a new city and school
- ◆ my seventh grade coach, Charles Spano, who taught me the meaning of intestinal fortitude when I wanted to quit
- ◆ Tim Hill and Winston Cook, fellow students at SMU whose enthusiasm for Christ lured me to faith
- ◆ Bill McRae, who led me to love God's Word
- ◆ Bill Garrison, who showed me that God's heroes are laypeople
- ◆ Morris Weeks, my father-in-law, who is one of the most persistent men I know

- ◆ John Breedlove and Brad Harvey, who taught their small-group leader the importance of a small group of peers in a time of crisis
- ◆ Steve Keuer, who models a life of excellence and integrity in medicine
- ◆ Frank and Sue Pillsbury, who showed me how to influence the next generation as grandparents
- ◆ Harold Smotherman, who demonstrated that you don't have to put your brain on the shelf after you reach retirement age
- ◆ Watson Simons, who has a contagious belief in the power of prayer

Many times unknowingly, these people marked my life for good. The most influential person in my life, however, is my wife of twenty-three years (as of this writing). Kathy is passionate not only about her family, but about encouraging every woman in North America to be all God created her to be. She teaches me to dream—big!

Introduction

*In times like these,
it helps to recall that there have always been
times like these.*
PAUL HARVEY

October 22, 1962. Y. A. Tittle amazed us by throwing passes for the New York Giants at the ancient age of thirty-six. John Wayne was throwing punches in *North to Alaska* at the theater. Telstar was beaming live television signals across the Atlantic. Every girl at my school wanted a Barbie doll for Christmas. And James Meredith walked the campus of the University of Mississippi—the first black enrolled in the formerly all-white school. Normally, I would have been watching "The Andy Griffith Show." But this night was different.

I sat speechless in front of our black and white television in Houston, Texas, and anxiously listened as President Kennedy informed the nation about the Cuban missile crisis. Houston lay within easy range of Castro's forty-two missiles, and the myriad of oil refineries in the Houston area made us a prime target for an early strike.

From my earliest days, the "evil empire" of communism posed a threat in my mind. I wondered what would become of our freedom if Russia conquered America. Feelings of anger, mingled with childlike fear, still flood my memory as I recall round-faced Nikita Khrushchev hammering the podium with his shoe at the United Nations. He belligerently proclaimed, "We will bury you!" To a thirteen-year-old boy, this man was evil incarnate.

Thankfully, Khrushchev was wrong. In November of 1989, twenty-seven years later, the Berlin wall fell, signaling the collapse of most of the communist regimes of eastern Europe. Millions of Americans celebrated the beginning of the end of communism. At last, our freedom was safe. Or was it?

While Russia devoured itself from the inside out, America was changing as well—and not for the better. In early 1993, Alexander Solzhenitsyn addressed the problem: "The West . . . has been undergoing an erosion and obscuring of high moral and ethical ideals. The spiritual axis of life has grown dim."[1] When novelist Walker Percy was asked what concerned him most about America's future, he replied, "Probably the fear of seeing America, with all its strength and beauty and freedom . . . gradually subside into decay through default and be defeated, not by the Communist movement, demonstrably a bankrupt system, but from within by weariness, boredom, cynicism, greed, and in the end helplessness before its problems."[2] Not a pretty picture.

Unfortunately, night after night the evening news updates Percy's prophetic words—lived out before our eyes. Since the early 1960s we have seen these changes in the U.S.:

- ◆ Birth rates for unwed girls skyrocketed 400 percent.
- ◆ Violent crime increased 500 percent.
- ◆ Incidents of sexually transmitted disease, which had been on a steady decrease, showed almost a 400 percent increase from 1963 to 1975.
- ◆ Divorce rates quadrupled.
- ◆ The percentage of children living in single-parent homes tripled.
- ◆ The teen suicide rate doubled.
- ◆ Scholastic Aptitude Test score averages, which had been steadily climbing, plummeted 90 points in ten years.
- ◆ American business has shown a decrease in productivity.

It seems the country that led the world in almost every area now leads the world in decline. It is obvious what we are doing is not working any more.

As a person, I am concerned about surviving. I feel uneasy about the deadlines that are relentlessly approaching—deadlines in the areas of environment, education, politics, family values, and health, among many. Things simply cannot go on the way they're going. I can no longer turn my head and say, "I just can't think about these things." I am bracing myself for impact. I want to know if there is any hope of surviving and where I can find safety.

As a member of the baby boom generation I am concerned about what I can do to change things. The rosy future I was told to expect is not squaring with reality. Our country is coming apart at the seams, and I am part of a generation that doesn't want to sit back and watch it happen. Doing good is no longer an option—it is an obligation. I want to know if it is possible to change the future. I want to know if I can make a difference, and what I can do to make my world a better place.

As a parent, I am concerned for my children. No one knows what they will face in their future, but I would be a fool not to be concerned for their welfare. I want to know how I can prepare them for the challenges ahead without destroying their hope. I want to know how to challenge them to be the cultural change agents of tomorrow.

As a Christian, I am concerned about the moral and spiritual deadlines that are fueling other crises. I wonder if it's possible to reverse the social erosion and moral decay of our culture. I'm confused about how to respond to a cultural environment that is increasingly hostile to the Christian faith. Do I isolate myself and associate only with other like-minded individuals? Walk the picket lines? Retreat within the shelter of my cocoon and pray for the Lord's return? Or should I just give up, take the path of least resistance, and capitulate to the enemy's mindset—hoping God will understand how hard it is to stand up for what is right at this particular time in history?

What exactly does God expect of Christians living in a godless culture?

A PROVEN PARADIGM FOR OUR DAY

Every generation is accountable for its own impact on society, and this isn't the first time God's people have fought an uphill battle

Jesus is my MODEL, EXAMPLE, PATTERN
(WORD)   my STANDARD

against a godless culture. Others have lived when things have been just has hopeless, and deadlines just as daunting as those we face.

Quite frankly, it's been worse.

Take Daniel, for example. Ripped from his home at age fourteen and taken eight hundred miles to Babylon, Daniel was thrust into a culture totally dominated by pagan thought. He faced educational indoctrination, pressure to compromise his loyalty to God, jealousy from his peers, threat of physical violence, and the hazard of an untimely death throughout his lifetime. Yet in the midst of daily struggles, Daniel remained committed to God. As a result, God used him to profoundly impact the culture of his day.

WHEN THINGS DON'T WORK ANYMORE, YOU NEED A NEW PARADIGM

Paradigm comes from the Greek word meaning "model, pattern, example."

A paradigm is a shared set of assumptions and regulations (written or unwritten). It is a model of how things are done. It helps us explain our world and predict its behavior. In other words, it helps us explain why one person is successful, and another is not.

Daniel's life provides us with the paradigm—a model, pattern, formula, or example—to live successfully in the U.S. today. Whether we're trying to cope with our everyday lives or crusading to save our culture, it is critical that we grasp the paradigm defined by Daniel's life.

Many Christians throughout history have followed Daniel's paradigm with remarkable results: the first-century Church grew from a handful to a half million persons in less than sixty years; William Wilberforce, member of the English parliament, saw slavery abolished in the British empire; Jeremiah Lanphier saw millions come to Christ in the last century by calling a few to prayer.

Sound incredible? Could things like this happen again? Without a doubt. What God has done before, He can do again—and His method will be very much the same. He will look for faithful men and women who choose to follow Him. They will not be clergymen, for the most part, but ordinary individuals who let their faith influence every area of their lives. They will be the salt and light God will use to change our culture.

But what exactly do we do to change our culture? Some believe we have to follow a paradigm that emphasizes political power. It's important, as Americans and as Christians, that we do what we can to bring about change through the political rights given to every

ALL IT TAKES FOR EVIL TO TRIUMPH IS FOR Good men to do Nothing

American. But in all of our politicking and protesting during the last decade, it seems many have forgotten that Jesus Christ called us first to be salt and light in society through the demonstration of personal righteousness. All the political action and banner waving we can muster will not serve the cause of cultural change if people cannot see the grace of God in our lives.

Small wonder resentment is growing toward evangelical Christians. Over the past two decades, instead of leading lives that attract people toward a higher realm of existence, many have tried to force their value system on unbelievers. To a growing number of Americans, Christians simply look like another special interest group grabbing for power to pad their nest at the expense of someone else.

But Christians who complacently sit on the sidelines, play it safe, and do nothing are at fault as well. It's been said that all it takes for evil to triumph is for good men to do nothing.

So what does a person do when he or she knows things need to change? If you're a person who craves to bring about positive change in our society, or someone who is searching for a new paradigm of what it means to be a faithful Christian, this book is for you. If you feel helpless, yet you're not content to sit idly by watching the demise of America chronicled on the evening news, Daniel's life reveals a powerful paradigm that yields practical help in understanding how to do the following:

- Survive when the bottom drops out.
- Find the safest shelter in the severest storm.
- Impact your culture beginning right where you are.
- Seek divine guidance while in the trenches.
- Develop a culture-changing faith.
- Recognize opportunities in negative circumstances.
- Maintain a relationship with God when everyone else is compromising.
- Stand up for what is right when everyone else is giving in.
- Hold up under persecution and attack.
- Appeal to authority for change.
- Attract others to Christ without a pulpit.
- Remain a man or woman of integrity and survive the test of success.

◆ Develop and use the most powerful means for change in a culture.

This book is not for heroes, but for the millions of ordinary men and women like you and me. As we follow Daniel's example and are faithful to God in the ordinary course of our daily lives, we will attract others to our gracious Savior. In a few cases, God will give some of us recognition and extensive influence. Most of us, though, will remain as anonymous as the countless men and women who spread the gospel to millions around the Mediterranean during the first century.

If the Christian faith is to move from ridicule to respect again in our culture, it will be because you and I undergo a major paradigm shift. We must return to the biblical model of cultural impact. History pivots on the actions of individuals, and we never know what unconscious act of character, minor act of courage, or unconscious act of heroism might tip the balance and change the world. Such is the potential of any ordinary man or woman who desires to be faithful to God.

CHAPTER ONE

Opportunity Knocks
DANIEL 1:1-7

If Charles Dupee Blake were alive today, I doubt that children's rights activists would vote him one of their top-ten Most Admired People. Think about the words to his famous nineteenth-century nursery rhyme and you'll understand why.

> Rock-a-bye baby in the tree top.
> When the wind blows the cradle will rock,
> When the bough breaks the cradle will fall,
> And down will come baby, cradle and all.

The thought of hanging an innocent baby in a cradle at the top of a tree is ludicrous, and anyone caught in the act can expect a visit not only from the child welfare office, but from the police as well. It's completely irresponsible to place something as valuable as the life of a helpless child in such a precarious position—waiting for disaster when the wind blows.

In a similar way, many of us commit this same irresponsible act with our own lives. We hang our feelings of peace, significance, well-being, and security on some frightfully fragile boughs such as our circumstances, social status, physical health, and checkbook balance—branches that easily break if the gale-force winds of life blow against us.

I feel at peace if my life is stress-free. I hang my feelings of self-worth on the fragile bough of how people respond to me. I feel safe if my cholesterol level is normal. And I base my sense of security on the size of my bank account. Pretty dangerous!

Quite frankly, the question is not *if* gale-force winds will blow against us, but *when* they'll blow against us. Just as surely as a Colorado weather forecaster can predict snow in January, I can predict that piercing and powerful winds of life will break some boughs and produce pain in my life and yours.

Pain interrupts our lives. It doesn't matter whether it's physical, emotional, mental, or spiritual pain. It arrests our hopes, postpones our plans, and disturbs our dreams. Pain is the gift no one wants. I call it a gift because it always comes bundled with something of immense value. Pain always brings with it opportunities—not only the opportunity to choose between bitterness and growth, but often the opportunity for greater influence in our culture. How we respond to pain makes the difference—whether the size of our heart and the size of our impact grow or shrink.

Twenty years ago Tim Hansel fell and broke his back while on a high-country expedition and now lives with severe physical pain every day of his life. In his book *You Gotta Keep Dancin'* he writes from experience: "Pain is inevitable; misery is optional."[1] The same calamity that produces a deeper life and richer relationship with God in one person engenders deep bitterness in another. What makes the difference? George McDonald explains it like this:

> Sometimes a thunderbolt will shoot from a clear sky; and sometimes into the life of a peaceful individual, without warning of gathering storm, something terrible will fall. And from that moment everything is changed. That life is no more what it was. Better it ought to be, worse it may be. The result depends on the life itself and its response to the invading storm of trouble. Forever after, its spiritual weather is altered. But for the one who believes in God, such rending and frightful catastrophes never come but where they are turned around for good in his own life and in other lives he touches.[2]

No matter what we face in the unpredictable 1990s, as cultural, political, and spiritual deadlines approach us at mach speed, few of us will experience the intense, painful opportunities that a man named Daniel faced. Though his story is twenty-five hundred years old, the message is as contemporary as today's headlines. The cultural deadlines of his day came with devastating results. But Daniel found opportunity in every event, and God used him to influence his world for seven decades. Daniel's message rings clear in today's cacophony of voices, and I, for one, stand to learn a lot from the sermon of his life.

WHO WAS DANIEL?

Daniel had everything going for him. He was one of the privileged elite of his day, and had a lot to lose in the storms that blew his way.

Today he would be known as a "Renaissance man." In the first chapter of Daniel, we learn that he was intellectually superior—"quick to understand." But unlike some bright students who coast through their studies content with just a passing grade, Daniel applied himself. He worked hard at his own personal development, "showing aptitude in every kind of learning." Daniel was also "well informed" of the latest developments in his world—scientifically, socially, spiritually, and politically. He was a teacher's dream.

But Daniel not only had a brilliant mind, he also had a healthy body. On a high school campus today Daniel would be a stud—a handsome young man and fine physical specimen because he took excellent care of his body. He was a coach's dream.

Socially, Daniel was well-bred. He was nobility, a relative of the king of Judah, raised with all of the privileges and status of royalty—wealth, power, and education. More than likely, Daniel conversed with kings and dignitaries, and traveled throughout the Eastern Mediterranean world. His family probably had a host of servants at its disposal, and Daniel may have had his personal valet. Today's women would classify him as a "good catch." He was every mother-in-law's dream.

Incredibly, this life of power, position, and perks did not give Daniel a fat head. He was not proud or arrogant. Neither was he lazy and self-indulgent like many people with similar privileges. Daniel was a young man of character—the kind of son parents would love to call their own. He was absolutely committed to God and refused to compromise himself in any area.

To sum it up, Daniel was a young man with a future. If there ever was a person who could say God owed him favor and blessing as a reward for being such a good guy, it was Daniel. A prime candidate for "Most Likely to Succeed," Daniel had his whole life before him.

Then the winds blew, and the cradle of Jewish culture rocked and fell. Incredible as it may seem, the Jewish culture of Daniel's day was far from spiritually friendly. After generations of warning, God said "Enough!" and brought judgment on the nation of Judah. In the face of untold privilege and blessing, God's people chose to ignore Him. In the warmth of God's best, they grew cold and indifferent. They took His blessings for granted, feeling entitled to them. They wanted to enjoy the privileges of being God's chosen people without accepting the responsibilities that came with the relationship. God brought this biting accusation against His people: "When I fed them, they were satisfied; when they were satisfied, they became proud; then they forgot me" (Hosea 13:6).

Repeatedly God sent His prophets—Isaiah, Jeremiah, Zephaniah, Habakkuk, and others—to graciously warn and plead with His people to return to Him. Undaunted, they continued to live in sin. Finally, the deadline came for Judah. In 605 BC God unleashed the ancient Near Eastern superpower of the day on Judah and Jerusalem—Nebuchadnezzar and his Babylonian armies. In a short time Jerusalem fell to their siege, and God delivered King Jehoiakim of Judah into the hands of his enemies.

Before returning to Babylon, Nebuchadnezzar set up a puppet government in Jerusalem and required heavy tribute from the Jews. As insurance against further rebellion, Nebuchadnezzar took members of the royal family back to Babylon as captives. He confiscated precious articles from the Temple and took Judah's next generation of leaders to grace his court and to remind him of his great victory over the Jews and their God.

Daniel was one of the young hostages selected. Unlike current Near Eastern hostages who are kept in confinement, Nebuchadnezzar's plans called for Daniel and his friends to be rigorously trained and indoctrinated for three years. Then at the age of seventeen, they would enter the king's service.

Trust me, this was not in Daniel's original game plan for his life. In one moment his entire world was turned upside-down. He would never see his family or set foot in his blessed homeland again. He would never worship in the Temple again—losing not only his spiritual mentors, but even access to the Scriptures for a time. Daniel was taken captive to a land where his God was mocked. He would be the servant of an unreasonable tyrant who could take his life at the smallest provocation. Daniel would suffer the pain and humiliation of castration and never be able to father children. Every dream a young Jewish boy could visualize evaporated under the Mesopotamian sun as Daniel and his fellow captives trudged 800 miles to their new home on the banks of the Euphrates River.

"THIS ISN'T THE WAY LIFE IS SUPPOSED TO BE!"

Life doesn't turn out the way most of us plan it. But few of us can imagine the severity of the sudden changes that interrupted Daniel's plans. Why did something like this happen? Was it because Daniel sinned in some way and deserved this kind of judgment? I don't think so. Although every human being, including Daniel, is guilty of violating God's standards, there was nothing in Daniel's life that singled him out as more guilty than his fellow countrymen. In fact, the opposite is true. If anyone deserved to be singled out as not deserving this judgment, it was Daniel.

Did Daniel's difficult circumstances occur because his parents sinned? It's doubtful. As far as we know, there is nothing to indicate a connection between Daniel's parents and his adversity. Instead, the opposite is probably true. Since Daniel had to receive his spiritual nurturing and convictions from someone, the logical presumption is that he received this from his parents. More than likely his father and mother were part of a national revival that turned many lives from idolatry to God during the reign of King Josiah, a generation earlier.

There were, no doubt, countless people in Judah who deserved the calamity Daniel suffered. We wonder why God seemed to be so cruel to this young man. The answer is clear: because of the sin of his nation. When a nation wallows in sin, everyone suffers. Even the righteous. As long as sin dominates the world, bad things will continue to happen to good people. Even Christ, the perfectly righteous Son of God, felt the pain of humanity brought on by sin. Oxford professor Dorothy Sayers writes,

> For whatever reason, God chose to make man as he is—limited and suffering and subject to sorrows and death—He had the honesty and courage to take His own medicine. Whatever game He is playing with His creation, He has kept His own rules and played fair. He can exact nothing from man that He had not exacted from Himself. He has Himself gone through the whole of human experience, from the trivial irritations of family life and the cramping restrictions of hard work and lack of money to the worst horrors of pain and humiliation, defeat, despair, and death. When He was a man, He played the man. He was born in poverty and died in disgrace and thought it well worthwhile.[3]

But there's another reason why Daniel was on his way to Babylon—one we know from both history and revelation. It's a reason Daniel probably couldn't fathom even by faith: that God's ultimate plan for him was to influence the highest seats of power in the ancient world. That meant relocation. Behind the scenes, working silently and invisibly, God was preparing a faithful man to occupy a place of international prominence and to play a key role in the preservation and restoration of His people.

As he walked the dusty road toward Babylon, Daniel couldn't see that over the course of his seventy-year captivity, he would climb to the highest positions in the courts of Babylon and Persia. Then, in the last years of his life, Daniel would exercise more power than any other member of the Jewish race has ever known. He would also have the great privilege of leading his nation in repentance and seeing his people turn back to God and return to their homeland according to God's promise. God had a greater plan for Daniel than he had for himself. Had Daniel known this, I imagine he would have gladly gone.

HOW DID DANIEL RESPOND?

With no way of knowing what God was doing behind the scenes, Daniel could only hope that God had a good reason for the pain. Unlike many of us, Daniel never blamed God for his circumstances. Interestingly, we never read of Daniel blaming his unfaithful fellow countrymen either. Surely it would have been easy to rationalize placing himself at a distance from his fellow Jews and just taking care of himself. After all, it was their fault he was there. Instead, Daniel committed himself to his faithful Creator and continued to do good. Because he responded in this manner, he discovered that there is opportunity in catastrophe. So can we.

[handwritten margin note: DON'T REPAY EVIL FOR EVIL]

WALKING THROUGH THE DOOR OF OPPORTUNITY

The quickest way to lose perspective in life is to focus on the problem rather than on the Problem Solver. No matter how big the calamity, God's power and grace are bigger still. How should we respond when faced with an open door? Here are five suggestions from the life of Daniel.

[handwritten margin note: God's GRACE & POWER ARE Bigger]

Accept the Inevitable Interruptions of Life

You may not totally agree with Rabbi Harold Kushner, but he touched a nerve in his best-selling book, *When Bad Things Happen to Good People*. We writes, "Life is not fair. The wrong people get sick. And the wrong people get robbed. And the wrong people get killed in wars and in accidents. Some people see life's unfairness and decide 'There is no God; the world is nothing but chaos.'"[4]

It's true. Life is no Disneyland. The world we live in is fallen. It is no longer the paradise that God created. Sin and the usurping ruler of this age, Satan, have devastated God's creation. Everyone who comes to dwell here tastes the bitterness of life sometimes. Some more—some less. God does not shelter anyone from the results of the ongoing rebellion that dominates our planet. Even Christ, God's sinless, perfect Son, suffered as a man during His visit to earth.

In my experience, I can't count how many times I've heard men and women in the grip of some painful experience say, "This is not the way life is supposed to be" or "This isn't the way I planned my life." They are right! This isn't the way it's supposed to be. God created a flawless world and a faultless race to dwell in it. Had man not chosen to rebel against God's rule, we would experience the longing of our heart—to know God fully and rule His world in peace and harmony.

As long as Satan remains the prince of this world, every human being can expect pain—especially those who follow Christ. Just before the Lord Jesus returned to Heaven, He reminded the disciples,

> "If the world hates you, keep in mind that it hated me first. If you belonged to the world, it would love you as its own. As it is, you do not belong to the world, but I have chosen you out of the world. That is why the world hates you. Remember the words I spoke to you: 'No servant is greater than his master.' If they persecuted me, they will persecute you also." (John 15:18-20)

Not until Jesus Christ overthrows Satan and restores His earthly throne will our planet know lasting peace. One day this longing for a perfect world will be fulfilled, but not by politicians, Green Peace, or even the Church. At the end of his life, John received a revelation from God of things to come. Describing Christ's future rule, John wrote,

> And I heard a loud voice from the throne saying, "Now the dwelling of God is with men, and he will live with them. They will be his people, and God himself will be with them and be their God. He will wipe every tear from their eyes. There will be no more death or mourning or crying or pain, for the old order of things has passed away." He who was seated on the throne said, "I am making everything new!" (Revelation 21:3-5)

What a beautiful picture! Every human being I know longs for a day like that. Under Christ's rule there is no cause for pain, for all is right. But until that blessed time, we need to take Peter's advice:

"Dear friends, do not be surprised at the painful trial you are suffering, as though something strange were happening to you" (1 Peter 4:12). Given the spiritual situation, it would be strange if we didn't suffer in some way.

Don't Get Hung Up About the Source of Your Situation

Thoughtful men and women have argued this question for centuries: Do bad things come from God or Satan? Frankly, Scripture never gives us a satisfactory formula for determining the answer to that question in specific cases. What we do know is that both God and Satan are present in every difficulty we encounter, each with a different purpose in mind.

We see an example of this in the book of Genesis. Speaking to his brothers who sold him into slavery, Joseph explained, "You intended to harm me, but God intended it for good to accomplish what is now being done, the saving of many lives" (Genesis 50:20). Joseph's jealous brothers wanted him out of the picture. The natural thing for Joseph to do would be to retaliate, but he chose to see a bigger picture. God had placed Joseph in a position to save his family (and all of Egypt) during a famine. Rather than succumb to the temptation to retaliate, he chose to take advantage of the opportunity to honor God and serve his fellow man.

In every difficulty there is an opportunity to sin—Satan's desire, and an opportunity to live by faith—God's desire. Even in the New Testament the word that is used for Satan's temptations and God's tests is the same word. In every temptation there is a test, and in every test there is a temptation. The question is not so much where it came from, but what you are going to do now that it is here. In 1 Corinthians 10:13 Paul wrote,

> No temptation [or test] has seized you except what is common to man. And God is faithful; he will not let you be tempted [or tested] beyond what you can bear. But when you are tempted [tested], he will also provide a way out so that you can stand up under it.

If God brings a painful experience into my life, I can be sure that it is for my growth and spiritual development. In this case,

Romns 8

Be lED by the Spirit so I won't fulfill the lust of the Flesh (retaliate)

God's agenda= Total Renovation

Satan desires to twist my pain into bitterness. If Satan initiates the problem, he wants, of course, to destroy me or to tempt me toward an evil course. In this instance God gives me the grace to endure the pain and provides an opportunity to escape, discovering in a more intimate way the riches of Christ and moving toward my destiny. Paul reminds us "that in all things God works for good of those who love him, who have been called according to his purpose. For those God foreknew he also predestined to be conformed to the likeness of his Son" (Romans 8:28).

God's agenda is actually much more aggressive than ours. We're not talking about a minor remodeling job, but a total renovation. His plan—past, present, and future—is to make us like Christ. That's our destiny. Small thinkers that we are, we would be satisfied with less, especially if it meant less pain. C.S. Lewis put it like this:

> I think that many of us, when Christ has enabled us to overcome one or two sins that were an obvious nuisance, are inclined to feel (though we do not put it into words) that we are now good enough. He has done all we wanted him to do, and we should be obliged if he would leave us alone. As we say, "I never expected to be a saint, I only wanted to be a decent ordinary chap." . . .
>
> But the question is not what we intend ourselves to be, but what he intended us to be when he made us. . . .
>
> Imagine yourself as a living house. God comes in to rebuild that house. At first, perhaps, you can understand what he is doing. He is getting the drains right and stopping the leaks in the roof and so on: you knew that those jobs needed doing and so you are not surprised. But presently he starts knocking the house about in a way that hurts abominably and does not seem to make sense. What on earth is he up to? The explanation is that he is building quite a different house from the one you thought of—throwing out a new wing here, putting on an extra floor there, running up towers, making courtyards. You thought you were going to be made into a decent little cottage: but he is building a palace. He intends to come and live in it himself.[5]

Is 54

Enlarge your tent stretch your cords strengthen your stakes

When men and women chose to fulfill themselves in this world apart from God's rule, He allowed them to partially experience the consequences of their choices. He withdrew the full benefits of His rule, allowing the creation to fall into chaos, leaving us scrambling to find satisfaction and fulfillment apart from Him. Not only have we lost control of our world, we find that when we do get what we want, the fulfillment is fleeting.

The pain that this emptiness brings into our lives, whether physical or emotional, is a measure of God's grace. It shouts, "Something is drastically wrong down here." Satan loves to inflict pain. God allows it as the natural consequence of sin in order to drive us to Him. George Mueller reminds us,

> God delights to increase the faith of His children. We ought, instead of wanting no trials before victory, no exercise for patience, to be willing to take them from God's hand as a means. I say—and say it deliberately—trials, obstacles, difficulties, and sometimes defeats, are the very food of faith.

Resist the Belief That You Are Entitled to "the Good Life"

In the mid-1980s, McDonald's began luring us with the ad "You deserve a break today." Today entitlement is a federal budget issue and a major cultural trend. We say "I deserve a little happiness" to justify everything from indulging in a Haagen Daz ice cream bar to dumping a mate of fifteen or twenty years for a newer model. When someone gets less than they think they are "entitled to," I often hear, "This isn't fair. Why has God done this to me?"

A longstanding lie has circulated the globe with devastating results. It goes like this: "If I live a good, moral life and obey God, He will bless me and I can avoid the problems of life." In reality, most people who live by this falsehood are trying to put God in a position where He has to give them the life they want. Sometimes dubbed "prosperity theology," this way of thinking overlooks some rather significant figures in history—figures like Jesus Christ, for example.

The phone call devastated me. Debbie called to tell me that she and Bob were getting a divorce. As I probed for answers, I discovered that Bob had committed adultery several times over the last two years and had filed for divorce. He was one of the most godly young men I had ever worked with. I met him the summer before his senior year in high school. From everything I knew about him, he was sold out to Jesus. He was a leader. He led kids to Christ and even taught a Sunday school class while he was in college. He was a model disciple. He met Debbie at church, and they married a year after graduation. Bob was committed to pleasing God. He and Debbie were careful to maintain their purity while they dated. If ever there was a storybook marriage, this should have been it. Things didn't work out that way, however.

Soon after the honeymoon, Bob began to feel a coldness growing between him and Debbie whenever he touched her. She became increasingly uncomfortable with sex and tried to avoid the issue by retiring early. Bob was understanding at first, but things didn't get better. After two years of marriage, they were living isolated lives. Neither wanted counseling because they didn't want to admit they had a problem. After all, they were Christians.

After five years of disappointment, Bob took a tragic turn on a business trip. An attractive associate came on to him. He resisted the first night, but his physical longing was stronger than his strained relationship with God could control. Bob found himself unable to say no the next night.

When I talked to Bob numerous affairs later, he was a bitter man. Both his wife and God had disappointed him. "I kept my end of the bargain!" he said angrily. "I resisted temptation and kept myself pure before marriage. It's not fair!" Somewhere along the way Bob had acquired the belief that God would bless him with a sexually fulfilling marriage if he remained pure before marriage. God had let him down.

Believing the lie that we are entitled to some earthly peace and pleasure because we have been obedient will have devastating results in our life—just as it did Bob's. No human being, Christian or not, is in a position to bargain with God. We cannot put Him in a place where He owes us anything but judgment. A.W. Tozer warned us, "Whoever seeks God as a means toward desired ends will not find God. God will not be used."

When I take an honest look at my life, I must admit that I really don't want God to be fair. I do not want what I deserve. I may have some areas that seem to be under control, but there are plenty of other daily struggles that often end in behaviors that are displeasing to God. No, I really don't want God to be fair, because that would invite judgment. Instead, I want and need mercy and grace.

Thankfully, He doesn't give me what I deserve—eternal separation. Instead, He graciously pours out the riches of Heaven and earth. At times He also graciously allows gale force winds to blow, but always for my good. Through these storms, I learn that there is more to life than getting what I think I deserve. He has something better.

> In Thy presence is fulness of joy;
> In Thy right hand there are pleasures forever.
> (Psalm 16:11, NASB)

Resist Blaming Others for the Problems You Face

All of us contribute to one another's blessings as well as problems. But, blaming someone else is a dead-end street that will really hurt us in the long run. Even if someone else is responsible, focusing on that person's fault will not bring us the supernatural strength we need to weather the storm.

Quite frankly, most of the problems I face, especially interpersonal conflicts, have two sides of blame. Even when the other person is grossly at fault, God will not let me escape responsibility for my contribution to the debacle. The longer I resist the confession of my own sin, the longer I wait for God's refreshing. If I have done something wrong, my primary responsibility is to make it right. I need to let God deal with anyone else who is at fault.

From what we know of Daniel, he had every right to blame his countrymen for his situation. He not only refused to blame them, but toward the end of his life, he humbly identified himself with the sin of his people before God.

Remember That God Wants to Use Us in Grander Ways Than We've Ever Dreamed of Being Used

The path to greatness never avoids the rough road of life. Repeatedly God reminds us that He wants to make us more than we could ask or dream of and that His path is often rocky and difficult. In fact, sometimes it will feel as if we are dying. But it will help if we remember Paul's words:

> Therefore, we do not lose heart. Though outwardly we are wasting away, yet inwardly we are being renewed day by day. For our light and momentary troubles are achieving for us an eternal glory that far outweighs them all. So we fix our eyes not on what is seen, but on what is unseen. For what is seen is temporary, but what is unseen is eternal. (2 Corinthians 4:16-18)

As we lean into the gales of life, we need constantly to keep in mind that God's plans for every Christian are "plans to prosper you and not to harm you, plans to give you hope and a future" (Jeremiah 29:11). Satan wants to destroy us, but God wants to prosper us. We need to hang the cradle of our lives on the firm bough of God's love, grace, mercy, power, and wisdom.

In the summer of 1967, a beautiful high school senior dove from a platform into Chesapeake Bay. When she woke up hours later, she found herself strapped to a gurney, paralyzed from the neck down. That tragic interruption in her life, no less than Daniel's deportation, presented Joni Earickson with an opportunity for a relationship with God deeper than she had ever dreamed. Through this tragedy God took a self-centered teenager and catapulted her into national prominence and a place of influence she could never have imagined. Years after the accident she can say,

> Few of us have the luxury—it took forever to think of it as that—to come to ground zero with God. Before the accident, my questions had always been, "How will God fit into this situation? How will He affect my dating life? My career plans? The things I enjoy?" All those options were gone. It was me, just a helpless body, and God.
>
> I had no other identity but God, and gradually He became enough. I became overwhelmed with the phenomenon of the personal God, who created the universe, living in my life. He would make me attractive and worthwhile—I could not do it without Him.[6]

Today Joni Earickson-Tada is one of the most articulate spokes-persons I know of the goodness and sovereignty of God. Her ministry, Joni and Friends, impacts thousands of individuals, physically impaired and whole every year. Trust God. He knows what He's about. An unknown poet said that as well as it has ever been said by pen or tongue:

God KNOWS

When God wants to drill a man,
And thrill a man,
And skill a man;
When God wants to mold a man
To play the noblest part;
When He yearns with all His heart
To create so great and bold a man
That all the world shall be amazed,
Watch His methods, watch His ways!
How He ruthlessly perfects
Whom He royally elects!
How He hammers him and hurts him,
And with mighty blows converts him
Into trial shapes of clay which
Only God understands;
While his tortured heart is crying
And he lifts beseeching hands!
How He bends but never breaks
When his good He undertakes;
How He uses who He chooses,
And with every purpose fuses him;
By every act induces him
To try His splendor out—
God knows what He's about.[7]

THE BIG IDEA

No matter where we're headed, how fast we're traveling, or how urgent we think the trip is, we can count on being inter-rupted. But seemingly devastating interruptions always bring opportunities.

Use the following thoughts and questions to stimulate your thinking about adversity and opportunity.

"I have told you these things, so that in me you may have peace.
In this world you will have trouble.
But take heart! I have overcome the world."
JOHN 16:33

We continue to shout our praise
even when we're hemmed in with troubles,
because we know how troubles can develop passionate
patience in us, and how that patience in turn forges
the tempered steel of virtue,
keeping us alert for whatever God will do next.
In alert expectancy such as this,
we're never left feeling shortchanged.
Quite the contrary—we can't round up enough containers
to hold everything God generously pours into our lives
through the Holy Spirit!
ROMANS 5:3-5
EUGENE H. PETERSON, ***The Message***

A measure of a man's success is not what he achieves,
but what he overcomes.
BOOKER T. WASHINGTON

An average view of the Christian life
is that it means
deliverance from trouble.
It is deliverance in trouble,
which is very different.
OSWALD CHAMBERS
My Utmost for His Highest

Pain insists upon being attended to.
God whispers to us in our pleasures,
speaks in our conscience,
and shouts in our pain.
It is His megaphone to rouse a deaf world.
C. S. LEWIS
The Problem of Pain

The marvel is, in the Biblical view,
not that men die for their sins,
but that we remain alive in spite of them.
JOHN W. WENHAM
The Goodness of God

Begin with the world as it is today
and try to work back to God,
and everything will seem to show
that God has no connection with the world at all.
But begin with God and work down to the world,
and light, much light, is cast on the problem.
Because God is holy, His anger burns against sin;
because God is righteous, His judgments fall upon those
who rebel against Him; because God is faithful,
the solemn threatenings of His Word are fulfilled;
because God is omnipotent, none can successfully resist Him,
still less overthrow His counsel;
and because God is omniscient,
no problem can master Him and no difficulty baffle His wisdom.
It is just because God is who He is and what He is
that we are now beholding on earth what we do. . . .
We could not expect anything other
than is now spread before our eyes.
ARTHUR PINK
The Sovereignty of God

Notice God's unutterable waste of saints,
according to the judgment of the world.
God plants His saints in the most useless places.
We say—God intends me to be here because I am so useful.
Jesus never estimated His life along the lines of greatest use.
God puts His saints where they will glorify Him,
and we are no judges at all of where that is.
OSWALD CHAMBERS
My Utmost for His Highest

Difficult circumstances often create paradigm shifts,
whole new frames of reference by which people
see the world and themselves and others in it,
and what life is asking of them.
STEPHEN COVEY

The Chinese word for crisis is written by combining the symbol for danger and opportunity.

Adversity reveals genius; prosperity conceals it.
HORACE

Adversity causes some men to break;
others to break records.
WILLIAM A. WARD

❖

Mishaps are like knives,
that either serve us or cut us,
as we grasp them by the blade or the handle.
JAMES RUSSELL LOWELL

❖

The secret to success in life is for a man to be ready for his
opportunity when it comes.
BENJAMIN DISRAELI

The richest chords require some black keys.
ANONYMOUS

A Christian is like a tea bag;
it's not much good until it has gone through hot water.

Look at your adversities as adventures.

Keep your face to the sunshine
and you cannot see the shadow.
HELEN KELLER

CHAPTER TWO

Keeping Your Mind Out of the Gutter When You Live in a Sewer

DANIEL 1:6-21

There wasn't much memorable about the summer job I had in 1971—except for one thing. Without fail, every Friday at 12:15, right in the middle of lunch, the Port-a-Potty waste removal truck arrived at our construction site. Trust me. You've never seen a construction crew move so fast. We scattered in all directions to find air that was fit to breathe. We just knew that the driver took sadistic pleasure in showing up just in time to spoil our lunch. I guess a guy who drives that kind of "dump truck" would have to find something to take his mind off the smell. I wonder how much Dial soap and Aqua Velva it took to lose that awful aroma at the end of the day. You can't work with sewage and not pick up the odor.

Likewise, it's a rare person who can live and work in a moral sewer without being personally contaminated. Character pollution seems to be one of the perils of living in a contaminated culture—even for Christians. When George Gallop, Jr., surveyed and compared the behavior of Christians and nonChristians, he discovered some alarming trends. Most Americans who profess Christianity don't act significantly different in their daily lives than nonChristians. In his words, those who attend church "are just as likely as the unchurched to engage in unethical behavior."[1] Increasingly, the only difference between Christians and nonChristians is where they spend

Sunday morning. Even this distinction is blurred as a growing per-centage of Americans say they can sustain their faith without attend-ing church.

On the other hand, many Christians have opted out of mean-ingful contact with our decaying culture, isolating themselves instead of striving to be a fragrant aroma of Christ to the world. You know the type. All their friends are Christians. They fill every moment of spare time with fellowship and Bible study with other Christians. They look for a home surrounded by other Christians. They want to work only for a Christian employer or hire Christian employees exclusively. Their only contacts with the nonChristian world are brief encounters when they dart from one Christian activity to another. This kind of an attitude is deadly to the cause of Christ. Evangelist Leighton Ford comments on this paranoia:

> This "closed corporation mentality," a sort of Christian isola-tionism, has been a constant barrier to evangelism. Many Christians have been so afraid of being contaminated by worldliness that they have avoided any social contacts with unconverted persons. As a result, they have no natural bridge for evangelism; what witnessing they do is usually artificial and forced rather than the spontaneous outgrowth of genuine friendship.[2]

If we follow Christ's example, however, we have no choice but to engage our culture and penetrate society. In doing so we will be called to mix with unbelievers and fraternize with sinners—to be alongside, not aloof. Even a casual study of the gospels reveals that Jesus went out of His way to cultivate relationships with worldly, sinful people. Sure, they ruined His reputation with the religious right, but they didn't ruin His character. He walked the careful line between contact and contamination.

But this line is a difficult one to walk. More than a few Christians have been pulled into the current of the culture and have found themselves swept downstream before they were able to get an oar in the water. Let me tell you about Jon, who was a prime example.

I first met Jon while he was living in a 5 x 7 cell at the Ellis II Unit of the Texas Department of Corrections when I conducted an in-prison seminar for Prison Fellowship. He was a nice looking young man, and I wondered why he was in there. As I got to know Jon, I found out that his parents had been missionaries in Spain. He grew up with a Bible in his hand and a soccer ball at his feet. In Spain they take soccer seriously and so did Jon. In fact, he was good. Really good. So good that on graduating from college, he signed a contract to play professional soccer for the New York Cosmos.

Jon played with the Cosmos for five seasons. The life and glamour of a professional soccer player brought more freedom that Jon was prepared for. Drugs, wild parties, and loose women were more than he could handle. God was a distant memory as he sank deeper in a cesspool of sin. The evening of January 13, 1983, God reached in and pulled him out. John was arrested at a night club in Dallas for possession and delivery of cocaine. He was convicted and sentenced to twenty-five years in the Texas prison system.

Thankfully the story has a happy ending. While awaiting trial, Jon turned his heart back to the Lord, repented, and felt the wonderful freedom of forgiveness in Jesus Christ. When he arrived at Ellis II, Jon met Chaplain John Larson who helped him get his life back together and grow in his relationship with Christ. By the time I met Jon, the smell of the sewer was gone, replaced by the fragrant aroma of Jesus Christ. Jon was a delight to be around and took the job of ministering to his fellow inmates seriously.

Since his release, Jon founded Jon Kregel Ministries and has spoken to thousands of students across America warning them of the dangers of drugs. Everywhere he travels, Jon is amazed at the naiveté of young people and adults alike who think that Christian kids are safe from drug abuse. That's exactly the attitude that caused Jon's downfall. A person cannot successfully swim in a sinful cultural current without developing strong spiritual muscles.

Fortunately, Daniel had well-developed spiritual muscles when he was thrown into the Babylonian current. He encountered numerous challenges to his faith and faced opportunities daily to compromise his commitment: some subtle, some overt; some calculated to subvert his faith, some seemingly innocent. Although submerged in a patently pagan society, Daniel was able to spiritually prosper. Unlike many American Christians who have retreated into the cloistered walls of Christian fellowship, Daniel had no choice but to fully engage the culture of his day—a culture overtly hostile to godliness. Despite this fact, he emitted a fragrant aroma of godliness. In three particular tests designed to destroy his faith, Daniel refused to compromise.

THE TEST OF FORTITUDE

When the company of young Jewish hostages arrived from Jerusalem, they immediately faced their first challenge. All of a sudden they were Babylonians. Their old life as Hebrews was over. To indicate this new authority and lifestyle, their names were changed from Hebrew to Babylonian names. What appeared to be an innocent change, however, was a subtle attack on their identity as God's children. Look at the changes:

Daniel, which means "God is my judge," was changed to Belteshazzar, meaning "Bel's prince";

Hananiah, which means "Yahweh is gracious," was changed to Shadrach, meaning "Command of Aku";

Mishael, which means "Who is like God?" was changed to Meshach, meaning "Who is like Aku?"; and

Azariah, which means "Yahweh has helped," was changed to Abednego, meaning "Servant of Nebo."

Their Hebrew names, which connected them with their God, were replaced with names that extolled three gods of the Babylonian pantheon: Bel, Nebo, and Aku. According to their captors, the young men no longer belonged to the defeated God of the Hebrews. They belonged to the victorious Babylonian gods. Like water constantly dripping, every time they heard their new names called, the young Jews were reminded of their new identity. They were now Babylonian; they were expected to live by Babylonian customs, follow Babylonian law, accept Babylonian philosophy, and worship Babylonian gods. Big change!

How did they respond to this particular test? They endured it, which many times is the only thing a person can do when called a demeaning or devaluing name. Whether someone is devaluing your character, hurling racial slurs, or asserting tyrannical authority, the greatest challenge is not to stop the person, but rather to stop your mind from mutilating your own identity. Interestingly, we never find Daniel campaigning to restore his God-honoring name. He accepted the fact that in Babylon he would be called Belteshazzar. However, he never referred to himself by his Babylonian name anywhere in the book of Daniel. Although he lived in Babylon over seventy years, Daniel never thought of himself as a Babylonian. Until the end of his life, he refused to forget that he was Daniel, and God was his judge.

THE TEST OF TRUTH

Not only did Daniel and his friends have to endure the subtle brainwashing of Babylonian names, they were to be thoroughly indoctrinated in Babylonian thinking by studying under the most learned scholars of Babylon for three years. After that, they were to enter the king's service. Their education was calculated to change the way they saw the world and to make them think like Babylonians. It was also designed to replace their biblical perspective with a pagan world view.

This tactic is still used in modern education. When I enrolled in Southern Methodist University in the fall of 1968, every freshman was required to take a course entitled "The Nature of Man." Many thought this course was designed to subvert and change young students' biblical world view. Many of the professors felt it was their obligation to challenge the "shallow faith" of the mushy freshman minds in their classroom. Sad to say, the professors were highly successful. Many young minds were turned from the truth.

Incredibly, each morning on my way to this class, I walked over the university seal inlaid in the floor of Dallas Hall. Inscribed on the seal were Christ's words, the motto of the university: "The Truth Shall Make You Free." Those words referred not to the "truth" of subjective humanistic philosophy, but to the truth of Holy Scripture. However, almost every time I sat in that classroom, I encountered a curriculum designed to undermine my confidence in the Bible and God. I was taught that people who believe the Bible are ignorant, miracles are myths, and man is the master of his fate.

The students who dared challenge the intellectual genius of the professors were often ridiculed and verbally abused. Far from their homes and the support of their parents and churches, more than a few lost their faith as a result of this class. Those who survived the ordeal were young men and women who were securely founded in the Word of God and had a strong personal relationship with Jesus Christ.

Because I was not a Christian at this time, I watched the confrontations with a great deal of interest. An honest seeker of the truth, I was more impressed with the expressions of faith of my fellow classmates than the intellectual barrages of liberal professors. In fact, I was so intrigued with their faith, I listened to their reasoning and sided with them in the spring of 1969. God used this liberal curriculum that was intended to destroy faith to bring me to Christ.

We know from archaeology a great deal about the Babylonian curriculum. Daniel and his friends studied linguistics (six languages), astronomy and astrology, agriculture, architecture, math, natural science, and literature—the latter being the most direct attack on their faith and confidence in God. The Babylonians had their own accounts of important biblical events. The Enuma Elish replaced the account of Creation, the Edapamin was the Babylonian version of the fall of man, and the Gilgamesh Epoch was the story of the Flood. All of this literature not only extolled Babylonian deities, but portrayed a pagan view of life and ethics.

How did the young Jewish students respond to this attempted indoctrination? They applied themselves and mastered the curriculum. And they survived. But they were so grounded in the truth of Scripture, the falsehoods did not master them. As immersed in the culture as they were, Daniel and his friends never let the culture penetrate them. They never forgot who they were or Who they belonged to.

THE TEST OF FIDELITY

Although Daniel endured his name change and participated in the educational system, there were some things that his conscience simply would not allow him to tolerate, such as eating the food offered by the king. The problem was not the lavishness of the food or the strength of the drink, nor was it the eating habits of a picky teenager. The issue was fidelity with God. All the meat and wine in the king's household was first offered sacrificially to the Babylonian gods. According to God's law, for Daniel to partake of it would be to participate in idolatry. Since Daniel was an astute young man, he knew that Jewish idolatry was precisely the reason he was in Babylon. He would not blur the line between right and wrong made clear in the law. He knew it was wrong and decided to just say "No!"

But this matter of refusing the king's fare was a touchy situation, so it was important that Daniel handle it carefully, which he did. He handled it so well, in fact, that his strategy is worth studying.

Make Up Your Mind Ahead of Time

The first principle of his strategy is probably the most crucial. Before the situation presented itself, Daniel made up his mind that he would be obedient to God, no matter what the cost. Verse 8 of chapter 1 reads, "But Daniel *resolved* not to defile himself with the royal food and wine" (italics mine).

I've learned personally that making up my mind ahead of time is crucial to obedience. In the heat of the moment and the pressure of making a decision, it's all too easy for me to rationalize. Taking time to plan ahead when things are calm and I can think clearly through the issues usually insures that I will make the decision I want to make. Otherwise it's easy for me to cave in to the pressure of friends or circumstances. As for Daniel, the day he arrived in Babylon, his decision was already made. He would allow nothing to come between him and his God. Not even the preservation of his own life was worth sacrificing his relationship with God.

Analyze the Situation

Daniel exercised a great deal of wisdom in dealing with people by stopping to determine their basic intentions. Interestingly, Daniel and his friends could participate in the very things that were meant to destroy their Jewish faith—Babylonian names and education. But taking part in any idolatrous activity, like eating meat sacrificed to idols, put them in direct violation of the First Commandment and compromised their relationship with the one Person they could count on in Babylon. The Babylonians, however, were polytheistic and had no concept of the exclusive relationship God demands of His people. Adding a few new gods to the worship agenda was no big deal to a Babylonian.

The intention of the king's diet was not to undermine Daniel's faith, but to preserve his health. "But the official told Daniel, 'I am afraid of my lord the king, who has assigned your food and drink. Why should he see you looking worse than the other young men your age? The king would then have my head because of you'" (Daniel 1:10). Daniel took into account the motives of the official and planned his response accordingly.

Find a Way to Cooperate, If Possible
Daniel had a cooperative attitude. Two things stand out about his conversation with the official. Daniel was polite and respectful of authority. When asked to violate his conscience, he did not belligerently demand his rights or complain. Instead, he graciously asked permission to try another diet.

Suggest a Workable Compromise
Daniel offered a creative alternative to the problem. He recognized the dilemma: God strictly forbade idolatry, and the king held the official accountable for the good health of the young men. But what seemed to be an impasse was not a problem at all. Realizing these goals were not mutually exclusive, Daniel proposed a ten-day test of eating only vegetables (which were not offered to idols) to see if his health would be as good as those on the regular diet. This plan allowed both the official and four young men to remain obedient— the official to King Nebuchadnezzar and the Jews to their God.

Leave the Outcome in God's Hands
Daniel waited on God for the results. Since they were not vegetarians, Daniel had no way of knowing how this diet would affect their physical condition in man's eyes. He did know, however, that it would affect the way they looked in God's eyes. As it happened, at the end of ten short days Daniel and his friends appeared healthier than the rest. God had honored their faith and obedience with

such a change in appearance that the king's official permanently changed their diet.

GRADUATION

As a result of their commitment, we read, "To these four young men God gave knowledge and understanding of all kinds of literature and learning. And Daniel could understand visions and dreams of all kinds" (Daniel 1:17). God blessed the four young men not only with superior wisdom, but spiritual insight as well. The key that unlocked the door of spiritual insight was their obedience.

> At the end of the time set by the king to bring them in, the chief official presented them to Nebuchadnezzar. The king talked with them and found none equal to Daniel, Hananiah, Mishael, and Azariah; so they entered the king's service. In every matter of wisdom and understanding about which the king questioned them, he found them ten times better than all the magicians and enchanters in his whole kingdom. (1:18-20)

It's hard to read about Daniel and not marvel at the distance from hostage to honor graduate. He did not only survive but flourished because he knew his God and was committed to obeying His Word. Before Daniel enrolled in the graduate program in Babylon, he had received his undergraduate education in the Scriptures in Jerusalem. Therefore, he could say with David,

> Your commands make me wiser than my enemies,
>   for they are ever with me.
> I have more insight than all my teachers,
>   for I meditate on your statutes.
> I have more understanding than the elders,
>   for I obey your precepts. (Psalm 119:98-100)

SURVIVING THE SEWER

When we start talking about living in a cultural sewer, many of us want to disengage from the culture and build our own Christian paradise. But there's a problem with this plan: we want to be obedient, flourishing Christians.

Accept the Responsibility

We have a responsibility toward those that live in the "sewer." In Matthew 5:14-16, Christ outlined our obligation as concisely and beautifully as I have ever heard it explained:

> You are the light of the world. A city on a hill cannot be hidden. Neither do people light a lamp and put it under a bowl. Instead they put it in its stand, and it gives light to everyone in the house. In the same way, let your light so shine before men, that they may see your good deeds and praise your Father in heaven.

Isolation from the world is not only a direct violation of God's will, it is dangerous for our spiritual welfare. When we refuse to be what God called us to be, the light within us grows dim. In fact, when we isolate ourselves from the sinful world, we are actually succumbing to the selfish, self-preserving ways of the world. By hiding, we become self-absorbed and empty, the opposite of what God wants for us. He has called His children to let His light shine through them into the darkest places of sin.

The Apostle Paul challenges Christians to "become blameless and pure, children of God without fault in a crooked and depraved generation, in which you shine like stars in the universe, as you hold out the word of life" (Philippians 2:15-16). When we live like this, cooperating with His design for us, our life is satisfying, not empty.

But isolation is not only dangerous for our own spiritual welfare; it is disastrous for the world. Many Christians think of spiritual darkness only in the remote places of the world. What is often missed, however, is the darkness immediately around us. It seems easier to pray for a New Guinea tribesman to come to Christ than for our unbelieving neighbor next door. We need to recognize and engage the darkness closest to us—in our neighborhoods, our schools, our work place, and even our churches. If we don't let our light shine in the immediate darkness, our culture will be lost.

In his book *Lifestyle Evangelism*, Joe Aldrich recounts the following legend of Christ's conversation with Gabriel when Christ returned to Heaven.

"Master, you must have suffered terribly for men down there."

"I did," He said.

"And," continued Gabriel, "do they know about how you loved them and what you did for them?"

"Oh, no," said Jesus, "not yet. Right now only a handful of people in Palestine know."

Gabriel was perplexed. "Then what have you done," he asked, "to let everyone know about your love for them?"

Jesus said, "I've asked Peter, James, John, and a few more friends to tell other people about Me. Those who are told will in turn tell still other people about Me, and my story will be spread to the farthest reaches of the globe. Ultimately, all of mankind will have heard about My life and what I have done."

Gabriel frowned and looked rather skeptical. He knew well what poor stuff men were made of. "Yes," he said, "but what if Peter and James and John grow weary? What if the people who come after them forget? What if way down in the twentieth century, people just don't tell about you? Haven't you made any other plans?"

And Jesus answered, "I haven't made any other plans. I'm counting on them."[3]

Hate Darkness, Not the Victims of Darkness

Fortunately, there are many Christians who take their responsibility to engage the culture seriously. However, they often forget that those caught in darkness are not the enemy, but victims of the enemy, Satan. That's why Paul gives us specific instructions about the quality of our encounter with the world around us. He writes, "Be wise in the way you act toward outsiders; make the most of every opportunity. Let your conversation be always full of grace, seasoned with salt, so that you may know how to answer everyone" (Colossians 4:5-6).

It's important to understand that we can be firm in our faith and committed in our behavior, without being obnoxious in our conversation. A harsh attitude of condemnation toward those who live in the darkness has no place in biblical Christianity. A cursory reading of the gospels reveals that the only condemnation coming out of Christ's mouth targeted the religious leaders who claimed to live in the light while hoarding darkness in their hearts. They were men and women who knew the truth but practiced a lie. On the other hand, Christ's kindest and most gentle words were reserved for those who were captives of the darkness, those considered outcasts by the religious elite.

Accept the Hardships

Living in a world where we come face to face with sin and rub shoulders with individuals committed to their own selfish agendas tends to get our hands dirty. We'll be laughed at, disregarded, passed over, and attacked by men and Satan. We may even be criticized by other Christians who call us soft on sin and question our spiritual integrity because we have not separated ourselves from the sinful world.

Paul and the Christians of the first century considered it a privilege to suffer for Christ's sake. Paul said, "For it has been granted to you on behalf of Christ not only to believe on him, but also to suffer for him, since you are going through the same struggle you saw I had, and now hear that I still have" (Phillipians 1:29-30).

Set Your Limit

Draw the line ahead of time beyond which you will not go. Before Daniel took one step toward Babylon, he had settled some things in his mind. He had firm convictions of his own. He determined to remain loyal to God no matter what the cost, knowing there was nothing worth compromising his relationship with God. What he would eat and drink in Babylon was settled before the steak ever hit the plate—no matter what his stomach told him, no matter what others did. The answer was "No!"

It's too late to decide our ethical standards while we are filling out our income tax form. It's too late to determine our commitment to integrity in the midst of a lucrative business deal. It's too late to decide whether we will experiment with drugs or alcohol once we are at the party. It's too late to determine to maintain sexual purity once we're in the back seat of a car. It's too late to determine our viewing standards once we are in the hotel room or standing in front of the video rack. We must determine what we will do ahead of time.

Control Your Thought Life
Perhaps the most dangerous challenge we face is the daily barrage of mind messages designed by the world and its evil prince to slowly desensitize us to sin and chip away at our resolve. Engaging our culture can be hazardous to our spiritual health. Slowly the culture can penetrate our heart. Like the proverbial frog thrown into a kettle of boiling water, we would jump out immediately. But immersed into a pot of water that is being heated gradually, we wouldn't feel the danger until we're cooked.

Daniel was immersed in the Babylonian culture for over seventy years, but he never thought of himself as a Babylonian. He was always Daniel, never Belteshazzar.

Gather Your Allies
One of the main reasons for Daniel's fortitude was the support group he gathered around him. A group of honest peers should call us to action if we get too comfortable in the hot water of the world. Although we must be willing to stand alone if the situation arises, God never intended for us to live in isolation from others. It's hard to think of Daniel compromising his faith, but that might well have been the case if his three friends had not been around. Since they were there, we know they each encouraged the others' faith.

Anyone who has traversed a difficult road with a friend knows the value of mutual support. In Galatians 6:2 Paul commands us to "carry each other's burdens, and in this way you will fulfill the law of Christ." We need each other. Solomon wisely outlines the dangers of aloneness and the benefits of close allies:

Two are better than one,
    because they have a good return for their work:
If one falls down,
    his friend can help him up.
But pity the man who falls

and has no one to help him up!
Also, if two lie down together, they will keep warm.
But how can one keep warm alone?
Though one may be overpowered,
two can defend themselves.
A cord of three strands is not quickly broken.
(Ecclesiastes 4:9-11)

This kind of relationship cannot be experienced sitting in the eleven o'clock service on Sunday morning staring at the back of someone's head. It comes when Christians meet face to face and deal with the real issues in their daily lives. Together they massage the Word of God into the creases of their real world experiences. They cry together, laugh together, and pray together. In his excellent book, *Maximize Your Ministry*, Bob Slocumb states, "Ordinary Christians must have a regular place to identify and clarify what Christ calls them to do and be. ... We need the support of people to whom we can tell our stories and who will listen and care."[4]

For the past twenty years I have worked to establish small groups of men who encourage and stand with each other in the real world. I've seen men stand and stumble spiritually, and be supported and encouraged by their group. I've seen men make costly, difficult decisions—maintaining their integrity. I've seen men fail and then be picked up and restored by their comrades when the rest of the Christian community turned their backs. I've seen men make commitments to love their wives, and promise to hold each other accountable for their moral purity. I have seen them walk with each other through the treacherous passages of life. One man expressed the way he felt about his support group like this:

On December 9 of this past year I had to face what I've always considered to be one of the most difficult times of any person's life, the loss of my father. More than just my dad and mentor, he was my friend. I guess we have a tendency to consider our fathers immortal and when they're gone, there is a tremendous void in our lives.

It was also in December that I realized how important a

group of men that meets every Thursday morning is to me. Outside of my immediate family, I don't think I've experienced so much caring and support as I have from our group.

Not only were they there to support me during the weeks leading up to the loss of my father, but they were there to help me pick up the pieces. They gave me the opportunity to share my experience and emotions that I wouldn't feel comfortable doing with just anybody.

Even though there is not a day that goes by that I don't think about my dad, it's comforting to know that there's a family around for support when needed. Not only were these guys supportive of me then, they have been ever since. They made me realize that we all have so much in common whether it's worries and problems, or hopes and goals. I guess that's called living.

It's difficult for me to put into words what each person in our Thursday morning family means to me. I guess the best way for me to say it is,

"I love you guys!"

In an interview, George Gallup told me, "The small group is the core to any kind of laity movement, because in those groups people are empowered and inspired to put their faith into action and reach out to those outside and inside the church."

Never Compromise Your Relationship with God

The most valuable thing we have in life is our fellowship with God. We can't afford to do anything that will cloud that relationship. Not only is God the source of the strength we need to resist the world, He is the only source of spiritual insight as well. To turn from Him is to invite the fog when we need clear visibility the most.

Because Daniel and his friends were faithful with the insight they had been given, God gave them more insight. Oswald Chambers observed, "The golden rule for understanding spiritually is not intellect, but obedience."[5] If a person wants knowledge, then intellectual curiosity is an adequate escort. But if he wants understanding—to be able to see past scientific facts, lifeless words, and cold data, to the rhyme and reason of things and the meaning of the universe—

it is available only for those who walk in the light. British educator Walter Moberly observes,

> If you want a bomb, the chemist's department will teach you how to make it; if you want a cathedral, the department of architecture will teach you how to build it; if you want a healthy body, the department of physiology and medicine will teach you how to tend it. But when you ask whether and why you should want bombs, or cathedrals, or healthy bodies, the university is dumb and silent. It can help and give guidance in all subsidiary but not in the attainment of the one thing useful.[6]

All truth is God's truth, and understanding, whether focused on scientific or spiritual matters, is given by the divine Teacher, the Holy Spirit. God has not pledged to keep a sinful world happy, comfortable, or well-informed. He has promised spiritual insight only to those who walk with Him. When our concerns are only for what we want, God must shake His head at our prayers for guidance and direction. If He spoke to us He might say, "Why should I let you in on my plan—so you can tell me you don't like it?" Christ said to Nicodemus, "If I told you earthly things and you do not believe, how shall you believe if I tell you heavenly things?" (John 3:12, NASB).

If things are dark in our mind, one of two reasons has brought it about. God is either teaching us to trust Him for guidance along a path we do not know, or there is something we will not obey. When God speaks, we must listen and obey. To be sure, He will bring more light to us even if it is to see Him more clearly in the darkness of our circumstance. Even though we will not be able to see clearly at the moment, we can be sure that God knows the way.

As Christians committed to living in the cultural sewer, we need all the resources available to simply survive—much less save our society: spiritual insight from God; encouragement and support of committed friends; and all the grace and power we can contain from our Lord Jesus Christ. The place where these resources flow most freely is not behind cloistered walls where we think we're safe from sin. The place of greatest safety and security—the place you and I are most likely to survive—is following hard after Jesus Christ. Today, just as in His days on earth, we can find Him engaging the strongholds of greatest darkness.

THE BIG IDEA

Rather than hide from evil, we are called to engage our culture—no matter how perverse. Yet, there is a clear and present danger of being sucked into the immoral, godless vortex of the world system. The only way to survive is to be fully engaged simultaneously with God.

Use the following thoughts and questions to stimulate your thinking about being involved with the world.

"Whoever has my commandments and obeys them,
he is the one who loves me. He who loves me will be loved
by my Father, and I too will love him and show myself to him."
JOHN 14:21

I will lead the blind by ways they have not known,
along unfamiliar paths I will guide them.
ISAIAH 42:16

You cannot think a spiritual muddle clear,
you have to obey it clear. . . . The tiniest thing we allow
in our lives that is not under the control of the Holy Spirit
is quite sufficient to account for spiritual muddle,
and all the thinking we like to spend on it will never
make it clear. Spiritual muddle is only made plain
by obedience.
OSWALD CHAMBERS
My Utmost for His Highest

I said to the man who stood at the gate of the Year,
"Give me a light that I may tread safely into the unknown."
And he replied, "Go out into the darkness
and put your hand into the hand of God.
That shall be to you better than light
and safer than a known way."
MINNIE LOUISE HASKINS

Safety is a matter of presence not place. If Christ is present, no place is dangerous. Read Psalm 23. Is David safer retreating to the quiet streams or surrounded by his enemies? Where are you safest?

What are the greatest sources of potential pollution in your life?

Who around you is smelling the fragrant aroma of Christ coming from your life?

We do not know what God is after,
but we have to maintain our relationship with Him
whatever happens. We must never allow anything to injure
our relationship with God; if it does get injured,
we must take time and get it right.
The main thing about Christianity is not the work we do,
but the relationship we maintain
and the atmosphere produced by that relationship.
OSWALD CHAMBERS
My Utmost for His Highest

CHAPTER THREE

Holding Life Together
When Hell Breaks Loose
DANIEL 2:1-45

U pon hearing the news, I dropped what I was doing and drove immediately to John and Betty's home in southwest Fort Worth. I, along with about thirty other friends, formed a steady stream into their home. We were welcome, but uninvited. The women made their way into the kitchen to see what they could do. The men gathered in the living room and said little, except to offer sad-eyed greetings to new arrivals.

I had recently finished four years of seminary—the place where one supposedly learns the answers to the tough questions of life. I wanted desperately to say something that would make sense out of this senseless tragedy. But I was speechless. My mind froze on one question—a question that silently perplexed every person present. *Why, Lord?* Why again?

Only eighteen months earlier, the same group of people had rushed to this very home—shocked to hear that this couple's twenty-one-year-old son, Paul, died on the rain-slick streets of Fort Worth in an auto accident. The pain, which had been almost unbearable at first, had just begun to disappear. After all, they had two other wonderful children, Alan and Barb, and Paul was with his heavenly Father. This family's strong Scandinavian stock and their faith in God helped them go on with life.

But then, just when life was getting back to somewhere near normal, bam! Another blow.

The call came early in the morning. The Texas Department of Public Safety had found Alan's twisted car near a narrow east Texas road. Driving home from college, he had fallen asleep at the wheel, missed a sharp curve, and died instantly when his car hit a tree.

A second son lost, just one month away from his twenty-first birthday. "Wasn't it enough," I protested to God in my mind, "to lose one son?" This seemed like more than enough.

The older I get, the more dark threads I see woven into the fabric of human existence—especially in the lives of God's children. I am reluctantly learning that the world in its present condition is a battleground, not a playground. At times, in my confusion and frustration, I feel like giving God some advice about how He seemingly mistreats us. "Good grief, Lord," I complain. "Can't You see that You'd have more friends if You treated the ones You have a little better?"

It's a wonder to me that many of God's children who have suffered the deepest wounds, and have the most to whine about, are often those with the greatest degree of love and devotion to Him. When everyone else around them is falling apart, their faith holds life together. Like the calm in the eye of a hurricane, they experience a tranquility that comes from a steadfast assurance of God's presence and power in the midst of chaotic circumstances.

Daniel knew that kind of calm, and so did his three friends, Hananiah, Mishael, and Azariah—even in the face of crisis. You'd think that after Daniel was ripped away from his home and country, bombarded with temptations and tests, isolated from all but a few faithful friends, then subjected to relentless indoctrination, he, if anybody, deserved a vacation from pain. Well, he did get a short vacation—then hell broke loose again.

After Daniel survived the initial challenges of life in Babylon, he rose to the head of the class during his pagan education. Through all the pressure and pain, he remained faithful to God. Both God and men were so pleased with Daniel's performance, he and his three compatriots entered the king's service, surpassing all expectations. Life was finally making sense again to Daniel. There seemed to be a reason for his sacrifices. He was to be God's man in the court of King Nebuchadnezzar. His future looked very promising. Then the king had a bad dream.

The opening verse of Daniel 2 informs us, "In the second year of his reign, Nebuchadnezzar had dreams." (The manner in which the Babylonians counted the years of a king's reign indicates that these dreams happened about the time of Daniel's graduation, some three years after his arrival in Babylon.) King Nebuchadnezzar's dreams were not sweet dreams. They were nightmares, and they so upset him that "his mind was troubled and he could not sleep." Evidently, after one particular dream occurred repeatedly, the king assembled his entire cabinet of magicians, enchanters, sorcerers, and astrologers, and asked them for help. "I have had a dream that troubles me, and I want to know what it means."

"No problem," the Babylonian bureaucrats thought. After all, they had formulas for dreams and such. "Tell your servants the dream, and we will interpret it," they responded with confidence. Nebuchadnezzar, however, was not so gullible. He demanded, "This is what I have firmly decided: if you do not tell me what my dream was and interpret it, I will have you cut into pieces and your houses turned into piles of rubble. But if you tell me the dream and explain it, you will receive from me gifts and rewards and great honor. So tell me the dream and interpret it for me." No pressure.

Nebuchadnezzar didn't trust the crafty crew of advisors he had inherited from his father. Perhaps Nebuchadnezzar questioned their loyalty. More likely he was legitimately skeptical of their supposed supernatural ability to decipher messages from the gods. It was just too easy to make up some wild interpretation. Anyway, it would be impossible to challenge the validity. So Nebuchadnezzar demanded that they reveal to him the content of the dream in order to prove their ability to accurately interpret it.

After desperate negotiations and pleadings under the threat of death, Nebuchadnezzar's advisors could neither discern the dream nor persuade the king to tell them its content. For years they had hidden behind their sham of spiritual skills. Now Nebuchadnezzar called them to account, and found them wanting.

Don't misunderstand. These men were not buffoons. They were the most learned individuals of their day, the wisest of the wise. But when it comes to reading the mind of God, the best minds the world has to offer are useless. Finally, with their fraud exposed, they sheepishly admitted, "What the king asks is too difficult. No one can reveal it to the king except the gods, and they do not live among men." At this, the enraged king ordered the execution of every advisor, veteran and novice alike, including Daniel and his friends.

The picture would be almost comical if the proposed ending were not so tragic. The most powerful monarch in the world and the most intellectually astute sages of the day were all going to pieces—at least until they met a seventeen-year-old kid who happened to know the God who does dwell with men. He dwells not only in Jerusalem, but in every place man's foot can tread—including Babylon.

I've often wondered what I would have done in this situation. I'm embarrassed to confess this, but I think that if I had been Daniel, there's a good chance I would have fallen apart like everyone else. I would have been tempted to say, "Look God! You brought me to this sorry place, and took away my family and nation. You know the misery index has been pretty high down here. This is no picnic, to say the least. But did You hear me complain? No. I studied my tail off. I thought that maybe, just maybe, You might use me for a big job You needed done—You know, changing the world or something. But no. What do I get for obeying You? A visit from the death squad!"

In contrast, notice Daniel's response when faced with imminent death. He didn't cry unfair to either God or man, nor did he put God on the spot. Daniel kept his cool and was calm enough to accurately evaluate the situation, ask pertinent questions, and quickly suggest an alternative plan. Realizing that God was in control, Daniel decided to stick out his neck and try to be part of the solution. Seneca the pagan philosopher said, "Only Christians and idiots are not afraid to die." Daniel was no idiot. But he knew God held his life in His hands and had absolute confidence that God could reveal the king's dream—if He chose to do so.

After the king granted a stay of execution, Daniel gathered his friends, Hananiah, Mishael, and Azariah, to strategize their course of action: "He urged them to plead for mercy from the God of heaven concerning this mystery, so that he and his friends might not be executed with the rest of the wise men of Babylon" (verse 18). Notice how the four young men approached God. Not demanding: "Lord, You just can't let this happen! You must tell us the mystery." Not self-justifying: "Lord, we don't deserve to die. Give us a break, and let us in on the secret."

On the contrary, Daniel and his friends knew that God was not obligated to answer in any way. If He did choose to reveal the dream to them, it would be an act of His grace, not because of anything the young men did or didn't do. So they based their appeal on God's character, not theirs. They knew that He was a God of mercy.

As it happened, God did reveal the dream to Daniel. I must honestly admit that if God had revealed that dream to me, I would have been more than a little excited—uncontrollably elated might be more like it. I probably would have run at record speed and burst into the king's presence unannounced to tell him the news.

But what did Daniel do? What began as a screaming interruption in Daniel's life became a song of praise. He stopped to sing his song of worship to God, then he delivered the news to the king. Also, before Daniel explained the message from God, he expressed his concern for the welfare of the wise men and his concern that God, not himself, should receive the glory for this revelation.

What a guy, and what a lesson. Because Daniel wanted to give God honor before men, God gave Daniel honor before men.

Still, there are two burning questions in this passage.

WHY DID GOD ANSWER DANIEL'S PRAYER?

Why does God answer some prayers and not others? This question has haunted sincere Christians for centuries. The answers God has given to our prayers have often amazed my wife, Kathy, and me. We have been equally amazed at some He has not answered (at least in a way that we recognized). One such experience revolves around the birth of our third son, James.

Our first two boys, John and Joel, were born with a significant degree of trauma. Twenty years ago I took Kathy to the hospital to give birth to our first child. Unknown to the medical staff, John's umbilical cord was wrapped around his neck. As a nurse monitored his heartbeat during labor, she noticed it became dangerously slow. She knew something was wrong, and in a matter of minutes, Kathy was in the delivery room undergoing an emergency caesarean section. The doctor miraculously got John out in time to avoid death or brain damage.

Four years later, our second son, Joel, came into the world with his chest caving in with every labored breath. Soon we knew why. The doctors called it respiratory distress syndrome, which meant Joel's lungs did not manufacture the necessary lubricant needed to breathe properly. He lay in the infant intensive care unit at Harris hospital in Fort Worth for three days before we knew if he would live.

With that kind of track record in the delivery room, we were a little skeptical about a third run. But after six years, we got the urge to have another child. As soon as we knew Kathy was pregnant, we began to pray for James's health—specifically his lungs—and for a safe, adventure-free delivery. Thirty-six weeks into the pregnancy, I checked Kathy into the hospital as her doctor tried to stop early contractions. After seven days, not knowing how much stress the scar on Kathy's uterus would handle, the doctor made the decision to perform a C-section three weeks before the baby's due date. He assured us that although it was early, the chance of the baby having a lung problem was remote.

In the delivery room, as the doctor worked to get the baby out, I nervously watched and talked to Kathy. My excitement soon turned to alarm as the doctor turned and looked at me. I could see the deep furrow in his brow and the concern in his eyes peering above the blue surgical mask. "He's not ready," he said. I'll never forget the next several minutes as we waited for James to cry. He didn't. James had Joel's condition—only much worse.

We watched our friend and pediatrician, Joe Bates, standing over James and watching his little chest cave in every time he tried to take a breath. That night we transferred James from Tyler by ambulance to the neo-natal intensive care unit at Methodist Hospital in Dallas. Kathy and I had a tearful prayer, then I left with two friends to follow James to Dallas. During the two-hour trip, I kept asking the Lord, "Why? We prayed and pleaded with You that James wouldn't go through this."

The critical circumstances didn't allow me much time for self pity. Soon my prayer changed to pleading that God would heal

James. Over the next few days I was very aware of the sovereignty of God every time I prayed. For a week we waited to know whether James would make it. Then the good news came.

Nine years later it's still a puzzle to me: Why didn't God heed our prayer for James's health in delivery, but then so graciously preserve his life in answer to our second prayer? I can only believe that God's purposes were somehow better served in this way. I also find some answers from Daniel's experience.When I look at his prayer for enlightenment and deliverance, I see five reasons why God answered his prayer.

First, Daniel Asked

This may seem like a trite observation that should go without saying, but there's a problem I see in my own life, as well as in the lives of others. Often, our desires and requests go unspoken. We mistakenly assume that God "wouldn't do that," so we don't ask. In the New Testament James reminds us that one reason we "do not have" is because we "do not ask" (James 4:2). The minute we catch ourselves pouring cold water on a desire of our heart by saying, "God would never answer this prayer," we should stop to pray for that desire right there on the spot. Thoughts of unbelief come straight from the pit of hell, sent to keep us from asking the great things of God He might very well want to do for us.

Second, Daniel Was Available

Daniel was willing to take a risk, be part of the solution. Of course, you could argue that there wasn't much of a risk when the alternative was to be cut into little pieces. But anytime we make ourselves available to God, we put ourselves at risk. Every time we step out of the shadow of our cocoon we put not only our reputation, but God's, on the line. We trade the safety of the sidelines for the possibility of failure.

However, Daniel knew something every Christian should realize. There is far more danger in giving God a busy signal than answering His call. There is more to lose protecting yourself on the sidelines than making yourself available to God on the playing field. Temporary safety is too high a price to pay for loss of fellowship with the Source of Life.

Third, Daniel Was Humble

Daniel was willing to let God have His way and give Him all the credit. Humility is the common thread among men and women whom God has used greatly. They are not impressed with their own gifts, training, background, achievements, personality, or insights. It is the greatness and wisdom of God that captures their interest.

One of the smartest men I ever met was my Hebrew professor in seminary. With degrees from Harvard and Cambridge, Dr. Bruce Waltke was by anyone's definition brilliant. I met him in the hall one day after he had preached a stirring sermon in chapel. Every member of the student body walked from chapel amazed by Dr. Waltke's exegetical ability. When I thanked him for his message, he immediately responded with an exuberant expression of the greatness of God. I was awed by Dr. Waltke's gift. He was awed by his God. Great men who know God are conspicuously unconscious of their greatness because of the great Company they keep.

Fourth, Daniel Was Obedient

There is a direct relationship between Daniel's commitment to be obedient to God in the details of his life and God's willingness to use him as a channel of His revelation. Daniel's gift of wisdom came as a result of his refusal to defile himself in Babylonian idolatry. Christ explains in John 14:21, "Whoever has my commands and obeys them, he is the one who loves me. He who loves me will be loved by my Father, and I too will love him and show myself to him."

Fifth, God Sovereignly Chose to Answer

Daniel explained the purpose of God in verse 30: "But as for me, this mystery has not been revealed to me for any wisdom residing in me more than in any other living man, but for the purpose of making the interpretation known to the king, and that you might understand the thoughts of your mind" (NASB). Daniel understood that although he had done his part, as important as that was, it was no guarantee that God would answer the way Daniel preferred. He knew that ultimately the situation rested in the hands of a sovereign God. Far from quenching Daniel's resolve, God's sovereignty stimulated his response. It also gives us a clue to answer a second question.

HOW DID DANIEL REMAIN SO CALM IN THE CRISIS?

Pain, especially traumatic pain, has a way of compelling us to focus on ourselves. When we hurt, whether emotionally or physically, nothing much else matters. Our awareness of the world around us shrinks in direct proportion to the intensity of our discomfort. Perhaps you, like me, have sometimes cried out in anguish, "God, where are You?" There have been times when I've felt toward God like C. S. Lewis did when he lost his wife. He wrote:

> Meanwhile, where is God? This is one of the most disquieting symptoms. When you are happy, so happy that you have no sense of needing Him, if you turn to Him then with praise, you will be welcomed with open arms. But go to Him when your need is desperate, when all other help is vain and what do you find? A door slammed in your face, and a sound of bolting and double bolting on the inside. After that—silence. You may as well turn away.[1]

When we feel as if God has shut the door and cannot hear our cries, it's easy for our faith to take wing and for us to panic. So how do we hold onto God even when it seems as if He has let go of us? Where does the faith come from to keep knocking when the lights are out and it looks as if no One is home? What is the source of a faith that doesn't take flight in crisis, that doesn't buckle under pressure? The answer is clear in Daniel's case: He knew his God. Verses 19-23 catalog the characteristics Daniel knew his God possessed.

Daniel Knew His God Was There

God was present with Daniel—not left behind in the Temple in Jerusalem. His God was not some local deity with limited jurisdiction. Daniel knew His wisdom and power were just as strong in "enemy territory" as they were in the city of God, and just as available in his workplace as they were in the place of worship. Wherever Daniel laid his head, he had absolute confidence that his welfare was in the hands of his ever-present God. You can't get any safer than that.

Daniel Knew His God Was Sovereign

Daniel also rested in the knowledge that his God was absolutely sovereign—even over the most powerful monarch in the world. Nebuchadnezzar himself was on the throne and in authority at God's bidding, and God could "take him out" at any time.

Daniel Knew His God Was the Source of Wisdom

Daniel also believed that God and God alone was the source of all wisdom and knowledge, and that He loves to reveal Himself to those who seek Him with a whole heart. Daniel knew that no one could conceal anything from God's awareness, including a dream hidden in the recesses of the mind of a king. In short, Daniel had every reason to be confident, not because of the circumstances, but because of the person he knew God to be. Therefore, Daniel could be totally realistic about the threat of the king's impending justice, and remain calm and optimistic about the outcome at the same time.

KEEPING LIFE NAILED DOWN

Quite frankly, it is difficult to be realistic about life and remain positive at the same time. Idealism inevitably leads to disillusionment. Realism without God leads to despair. Several lessons emerge from Daniel's life that can help us maintain equilibrium and keep life nailed down when all hell breaks loose.

Accept the Fact That Life Is Out of Our Control

Every Tuesday noon for six years I met with a group of men. We prayed for each other and studied God's Word. As we discussed the book of Philippians, Lee, a seasoned attorney, responded with a profound insight. He said, "The things that matter the most to us in life are the things we control the very least." This was not an idle observation. It came from a man who had battled cancer for two years.

If we haven't learned that life is out of control yet, all we need to do is wait. God will allow us to experience this fact—first hand—in order that we might know Him better. One sage said it well: "Life is meant to bring us a succession of experiences to show us our need of Christ." Whether our faith holds up or folds up will largely depend on whether the object of our faith is capable of controlling what we can't. The object of Daniel's faith was the omnipresent—always present, omnipotent—all powerful, and omniscient—all-knowing God.

A strong faith in God is not something we inherit. Neither is it something mystical that falls on some people while eluding the rest of us. Faith is something developed, cultivated, and learned by each individual. It begins with knowledge—sound knowledge—of the object of faith. *TO KNOW YOU*

Develop Your Knowledge of God

A reporter once asked Albert Einstein's wife if she understood the theory of relativity. She replied, "No, but I know Albert, and he can be trusted." Can you and I say the same thing about God? "No, I don't understand what God is doing in my life right now. But I know God, and He can be trusted." Although I'm not there yet, God is giving me opportunities every day to learn more of Him.

The great tendency of most Christians is to use God to solve our problems. God wants us to use our problems to find Him. Otherwise we tend to use God rather than worship Him.

The first goal of the Christian is knowing God. Getting acquainted with Him is far more important than anything else that goes on in life. God Himself makes this very clear:

> Let not the wise man boast of his wisdom
> or the strong man boast of his strength
> or the rich man boast of his riches,
> but let him who boasts boast about this:
> that he understands and knows me,
> that I am the Lord, who exercises kindness,
> justice and righteousness on the earth,
> for in these I delight. (Jeremiah 9:23-24)

There is something absolutely compelling about really knowing God. Perhaps that is why so many of us let temporal problems weigh upon us so heavily. We don't really know God, and the god we do know is not large enough to handle the problems we face. The

God is bigger than any problem I have. any!!

lowercase "g" in god in the previous sentence is not a typo. When we think inferior thoughts of God, we are considering an image constructed in our minds, an image that has no reality in fact.

Most men and women know God by hearsay and not personal experience. That "god" of our imagination is never capable of dealing with life. No wonder we panic when calamity comes. If we worship the invention of our minds or anyone else's, we will feel hopelessly on our own when life gets out of hand. And that is all too often. A. W. Tozer makes a jolting statement in his classic *Knowledge of the Holy*:

> What comes into our minds when we think about God is the most important thing about us.
>
> The history of mankind will probably show that no people has ever risen above its religion, and man's spiritual history will positively demonstrate that no religion has ever been greater than its idea of God. Worship is pure or base as the worshiper entertains high or low thoughts of God.
>
> For this reason the gravest question before the Church is always God Himself, and the most portentous fact about any man is not what he at any given time may say or do, but what he in his deep heart conceives God to be like. We tend by some secret law of the soul to move toward our mental image of God.[2]

We cannot afford to worship the God we want, then keep Him on the shelf until we have a problem and need to summon Him. We must worship the God who is—the God who has revealed Himself in the pages of Scripture and in the lives of history.

So how do we come to know the true God? Though we can never contain God in our minds, there are two ways we can pursue knowledge of Him. The foundation step is learning what God has revealed about Himself in the Bible. He desires for us to know Him, and every time we open the Bible, we can ask God to show us what He is like.

As we study the historic sections of the Bible, we learn how God acted in the past, what He concerns Himself with, and what characteristics He demonstrates.

In the prophetic sections God personally instructs us about Himself. In addition, we can read what godly men wrote about their knowledge of God, as we do in Daniel 2:20-23. These are all God's authoritative revelations of Himself. We can also learn about God from other sources: books, songs, friends, and especially nature. But we must always check our thoughts for accuracy against the revelation God has given of Himself in Scripture.

In the Gospels we see God's clearest revelation of Himself in Jesus Christ. John tells us, "No one has ever seen God, but God the One and Only, who is at the Father's side, has made him known" (John 1:18). Christ told His disciples, "Anyone who has seen me has seen the Father" (John 14:9). In Hebrews 1:3 we read, "The Son is the radiance of God's glory and the exact representation of his being."

In the New Testament letters we find God's deepest longings for His children. The Bible gives us more than a lifetime of learning and opportunities to know God.

As we begin this great adventure we can be sure that Satan will thwart our attempts. C. S. Lewis captured this evil intent of the demonic world in *The Screwtape Letters*. Describing to his apprentice tempter the image of God that most men have in their minds, Screwtape writes,

> They [human beings] have never known that ghastly luminosity, that stabbing and searing glare which makes the background of permanent pain to our lives. If you look into your patient's mind when he is praying, you will not find that. If you examine the object to which he is attending, you will find that it is a composite object containing many quite ridiculous ingredients. . . . But whatever the nature of the composite object, you must keep him praying to it—to the thing that he has made, not to the Person who has made him.[3]

If Satan succeeds in keeping our minds confused about God, he will control our lives and succeed in corrupting our faith.

Thinking correct thoughts about God is foundational, but it is only the beginning step of faith. Many Christians have deluded themselves into thinking they know God because they hold to orthodox doctrine. The sad fact is that it is possible to know about God and not know Him personally. Knowledge will remain lodged in our heads, never penetrating our hearts, unless we translate our knowledge about God into faith by acting on what we know.

Take the Risk of Faith

The cost of faith is always a risk. No risk, no faith. It's that simple. Knowledge about God translates into faith in God only when we take a risk in the crucible of life. Satan's strategy is to paralyze us in fear. The more we give in to fear and shrink back, the harder it becomes to move forward in faith. John Wesley, founder of the Methodist Church, said that fear is faith in the enemy. Every time I give in to fear, I strengthen my faith in my own weakness. In a very real sense my faith is looking for somewhere to light, somewhere to invest itself. It will establish itself in whichever direction I choose to act.

The only way we can develop the confidence that what we believe about God is true is to try Him out. That's why God allows the world to feel the pain of estrangement from Him. That is why husbands and wives hurt each other. That's why our children disappoint us, That's why health and finances fail, why the roof leaks and the car breaks down and we meet conflicts at work and even at church.

God is shouting to us, "The world cannot help you, but I can." Try Me out. Keep knocking, not because you can see a light on, but because you know that I am home. 'Never will I leave you; never will I forsake you.' Keep working not because you feel strong, but because I am 'working in you to will and to act according to [my] good pleasure.' Keep demonstrating love to your mate, even when you feel empty and rejected, because I am 'able to do immeasurably more than all [you] ask or imagine, according to [my] power that is at work within [you]'" (Hebrews 13:5, Philippians 2:13, Ephesians 3:20).

Every time we step out on what we believe to be true about God, the more natural that kind of response becomes. Every time we exercise faith, our faith becomes stronger. As we step out, we meet the God of reality in our circumstances and find Him to be everything we hope Him to be. Theory never becomes reality in our lives without practice.

The summer before Kathy and I married, I worked at a construction project on the Texas coast. Most of the summer I spent hanging from my heels joining fiberglass pipe thirty to sixty feet above the ground.

I'll never forget the first day the foreman took me for a climb to join my crew. I met Sid and Mike about forty feet up in the air. They were sitting on a 2' x 12' board, precariously resting on two pieces of angle iron tack-welded onto the steel beam of the super structure. When Mike called me to come on out beside him, I did some quick calculations.

First I glanced at Sid. He was a college football player—probably weighing in at about 230 pounds. Mike was a little lighter, but carried a significant beer gut, so I estimated about 190. That's roughly 420 pounds. Add my 180 pounds and I figured we were looking at about a 600 pound load. If the lumber didn't break, I was sure that the angle iron would bend.

Being a construction novice, I questioned the wisdom of Mike's invitation. They both laughed and told me to get my butt out there. I quickly weighed the thought of being unemployed for the summer against my fear, and decided to see if they knew what they were talking about. I slowly inched my way out—literally crawling. When I finally made it to my place, Mike and Sid laughed as our feet dangled from our perch. To my amazement, we didn't fall. These guys knew what they were talking about after all.

By the end of the summer I was hanging by my toes from the top of the plant. I was a man of "faith." There is nothing magical or mystical about it. Whether it's faith in a scaffold, a friend, a physician, an attorney, or God, it all develops the same way:

Learning ⟶ testing ⟶ experiencing ⟶ believing

Faith is a function of our knowledge of God and our willingness to act on what we know Him to be. The more we act on correct knowledge, the stronger our faith becomes.

If that's true, we can never afford to forget that the answer to our problems is a Person. That's where our faith must rest. The more we come to know that Person, the more He brings life into perspective. God wants to show each of us how adequate He is to meet our every need. As we begin to grasp His capability, the problems we meet shrink in importance. A. W. Tozer observed well, "The man who comes to a right belief about God is relieved of ten thousand temporal problems for he sees at once that these have to do with matters which at most cannot concern him very long."[4]

Entrust Yourself to Your Faithful Creator

As he began his praise of God, Daniel acknowledged God's sovereignty over all men and nature: "He changes times and seasons; he sets up kings and deposes them" (2:21). In his epistle, it is not simply for prosaic variety that the Apostle Peter calls God Creator: "So then, those who suffer according to God's will should commit themselves to their faithful Creator and continue to do good" (1 Peter 4:19). Grasping the size of the God who created, preserves, and rules all creation has been a constant source of strength to God's people who find themselves in the temporary clutches of evil men and circumstances. In Isaiah 40, God asks,

> To whom will you compare me?
>> Or who is my equal? says the Holy One.
> Lift your eyes and look to the heavens:
>> Who created all these?
> He who brings out the starry hosts one by one,
>> and calls them each by name.
> Because of his great power and mighty strength,
>> not one of them is missing.
> Why do you say, O Jacob,
>> and complain, O Israel,
> "My way is hidden from the LORD;
>> my cause is disregarded by my God"?
> Do you not know?
>> Have you not heard?
> The LORD is the everlasting God,
>> the Creator of the ends of the earth.
> He will not grow tired or weary,
>> and his understanding no one can fathom.
> He gives strength to the weary
>> and increases the power of the weak.
> Even youths grow tired and weary,
>> and young men stumble and fall;

but those who hope in the LORD
 will renew their strength.
They will soar on wings like eagles;
 they will run and not grow weary,
 they will walk and not faint. (40:25-31)

It's incredible to ponder the size of the universe. To simply look at the night sky and consider the impressive power it took to arrange it all has been a faith-boosting exercise ever since Adam first gazed into the heavens. But consider what we know today. When we look into the night sky, we know that we're not seeing just stars and planets. Some of those points of light are entire galaxies. Our own galaxy, the Milky Way, is an average-size, 140-billion-star system shaped like a spinning pin wheel. It is a mere 100,000 light years in diameter and 1,000 light years thick. It's mind boggling to think that if we could travel at the speed of light, roughly 186,000 miles per second, we could travel from one side of our galaxy to the other in 100,000 years. If that isn't incredible enough, scientists estimate that there are about a billion or so more of these star systems lighting the universe, and they are an average of ten million light years apart.

If this is true, nothing in our lives presents a significant challenge to the power, wisdom, or knowledge of our Creator. The story is told of a woman who asked G. Campbell Morgan, "Do you think we ought to pray about even the little things in life?" Dr. Morgan, in his typical British manner, replied, "Madam, can you think of anything in your life that is big to God?"

Because God is who He is, men have run to Him as their refuge in times of distress. He is the One who keeps life nailed down when all hell breaks loose. He is the One who gives me hope when things look hopeless. He is the One who encourages me when fear and doubt close in around me. Those that survive the storms of life are the ones who have run to their faithful Creator for refuge. One of the most beautiful songs in the Bible has to be Psalm 46.

God is our refuge and strength,
 an ever present help in trouble.
Therefore we will not fear, though the earth give way

and the mountains fall into the heart of the sea,
though its waters roar and foam
and the mountains quake with their surging. (verses 1-3)

Now that's what I call secure. But note, God is not only a haven; He is a rejuvenation center. He gives us strength and help to face the earth-shattering occurrences of life.

Develop Close Relationships with Other Christians
Our faithful Creator is the ultimate refuge. But there are times when He uses a more tangible place of safety—sort of a hope and strength franchise on earth. That franchise is given to the Church. During the difficulties of the first century, Christians were urged to "consider how we may spur one another on toward love and good deeds. Let us not give up meeting together, as some are in the habit of doing, but let us encourage one another—and all the more as you see the Day approaching" (Hebrews 10:24-25).

This is not a reference to a church service where you sit in a pew, stare at the back of someone's head, and watch the performance. It happens in a group of people who take the ministry of encouragement seriously. That ministry has at least four parts.

The ministry of encouragement includes comfort. Comfort reminds a person that he or she is safe even in the midst of excruciating pain. When we remind each other of God's love and commitment, we give each other hope. Because God is who He is, we have a future.

The ministry of encouragement includes exhortation. Exhortation is an appeal to someone to do the right thing: to stand, resist, endure, hang tough, make the hard choice, and choose God's best. When we remind each other of who God is, who He has made us to be, and how He wants us to live, we stand in God's place lending strength to the resolve of a brother who may be weak.

The ministry of encouragement includes appreciation. Appreciation values a person's work. When we remind a person of the contribution he has made in someone's life, we breathe hope into the heart that may be discouraged. We stand in God's place reminding that person that God wants to use him for great and mighty things.

The ministry of encouragement includes affirmation.
Through affirmation, we value a person for who he or she is. While
desiring improvement, we accept a person without demanding
change. When we affirm someone's value by our words or actions,
we stand in God's place reminding that person of God's uncondi-
tional love and commitment.

Everyone needs to be a part of a group like that—an earthly
refuge. When you read the accounts of Daniel's life, it is obvious that
he and his three friends had this kind of relationship. Through the
hardships of life in Babylon, they had grown not only in their faith,
but also in their relationship with one another. They were committed
to stand together, giving each other the support anyone might need.

One of the ways they demonstrated this commitment was
through prayer. In group prayer, the refuge of earth and the Refuge
of heaven combine in thunderous power. Christ Himself promised
in Matthew 18:19-20, "Again, I tell you that if two of you on earth
agree about anything you ask for, it will be done for you by my Father
in heaven. For where two or three come together in my name, there
am I with them." All of us need all of the praying we can get whether
we are in a crisis or not.

I can't imagine what it would be like to go through life without
someone else to pray with. Not only do Kathy and I pray together, but
I have a group of men that will pray with me about anything I bring
to them. There have been times when I didn't have the faith to ask
for what I really needed, but someone in the group did. There have
been times when I have held the faith for others.

That kind of commitment and closeness didn't develop overnight
with either my wife or my friends. It grew from a commitment to
one another built on the conviction that we need each other desperately in both the painful and prosperous times of life. It was built
on the belief that God has given us each other for this kind of encouragement. I see God so much more clearly now, having seen Him
through the eyes of others.

Sing Your Song
In my opinion we never see God more clearly than through the lens
of pain. When the comfort the material world has to offer grows thin
and transparent, we can begin to see the "substance" of God,

unclouded by earthly distractions. When that happens, there is something in our heart that jumps for joy. We learn a new song of praise to God. Just as God gave Daniel a new song of praise, He wants to give us a song as well. What begins in pain can end in joyful praise. I don't know what any of us will face in the future, but I do know there is a sovereign Creator we can trust who says, "Come, taste and see that I am good." David described his experience in Psalm 40:

> I waited patiently for the Lord;
>> he turned to me and heard my cry.
> He lifted me out of the slimy pit,
>> out of the mud and mire;
> he set my feet on a rock
>> and gave me a firm place to stand.
> He put a new song in my mouth,
>> a hymn of praise to our God.
> Many will see and fear
>> and put their trust in the Lord. (Psalm 40:1-5)

Daniel sang his song in private (Daniel 2:20-23) with his friends, as an immediate response of praise and thanksgiving to God. Then he also sang his song for the king. When the music played by our character matches the message of our song, we have beautiful harmony. Men and women will be attracted to us—and ultimately to our God because the song He gives us is always about Him.

THE BIG IDEA

Faith is not some mystical ability given to a select few. It is a function of our knowledge of God and our willingness to risk based on that knowledge. We can strengthen our faith by growing in knowledge of God and being willing to act on who and what we know Him to be.

Use the following thoughts and ideas to stimulate your thinking about faith.

❖

*Now faith is being sure of what we hope for
and certain of what we do not see.*
HEBREWS 11:1

*Without faith it is impossible to please God,
because anyone who comes to him must believe that he exists
and that he rewards those who earnestly seek him.*

HEBREWS 11:6

Read psalm 31.

*Be strong and take heart,
all you who hope in the LORD.*
PSALM 31:24

Bear one another's burdens and thus fulfill the law of Christ.
GALATIANS 6:2, NASB

*Real faith as the Bible conceives of it,
is responsiveness to God,
who has made himself known to us in Jesus Christ.
And unbelief is unresponsiveness,
the hardening of our wills in a refusal to respond
as we ought to that which we know is true.*
HANNAH HURNARD
Hinds' Feet on High Places

*Almost everything said of God is unworthy,
for the very reason that it is capable of being said.*
POPE GREGORY THE GREAT
Magna Moralia

Read *The Knowledge of the Holy* and *The Pursuit of God* by A. W. Tozer.

In the National Cathedral in Washington, D.C., is a stained glass portrayal of George Washington praying at Valley Forge. Beneath the scene are the words, "Preserve me, O God, for I take refuge in Thee." Read Psalm 16.

The man who has God for his treasure has all things in One.
Many ordinary treasures may be denied him,
or if he is allowed to have them, the enjoyment of them
will be so tempered that they will never be necessary
to his happiness. Or if he must see them go,
one after one, he will scarcely feel a sense of loss,
for having the Source of all things he has in One all satisfaction,
all pleasure, all delight. Whatever he may lose he has actually
lost nothing, for he now has it all in One,
and he has it purely, legitimately and forever.
A. W. TOZER
The Pursuit of God

Let nothing disturb you, let nothing frighten you:
everything passes away except God;
God alone is sufficient.
SAINT THERESA

Every time you venture out in the life of faith,
you will find something in your common-sense circumstance
that flatly contradicts your faith. Common sense is not faith,
and faith is not common sense. . . . Can you trust Jesus Christ
where your common sense cannot trust Him?
OSWALD CHAMBERS
My Utmost for His Highest

Before me, even as behind,
God is, and all is well.
JOHN GREENLEAF WHITTIER

Fear knocked at the door.
Faith answered.
No one was there.
OLD SAYING

Ten minutes spent in Christ's society every day,
aye two minutes, will make the whole day different.
HENRY DRUMMOND

Don't be afraid to take a big step if one is indicated.
You can't cross a chasm in two small jumps.
DAVID LLOYD GEORGE

A little faith will bring your soul to heaven;
a great faith will bring heaven to your soul.
CHARLES SPURGEON

Faith in God is indispensable to statesmanship.
ABRAHAM LINCOLN

The summing up of our Lord's teaching
is that the relationship which He demands
is an impossible one unless He has done a supernatural work
in us. Jesus Christ demands that there
be not the slightest trace of resentment
even suppressed in the heart of a disciple

when he meets with tyranny and injustice.
No enthusiasm will ever stand the strain that Jesus Christ
will put upon His worker. Only one thing will,
and that is a personal relationship to Himself which has gone
through the mill of His spring-cleaning until there is only one
purpose left—I am here for God to send me where He will.
Every other thing may get fogged,
but this relationship to Jesus Christ must never be.
OSWALD CHAMBERS
My Utmost for His Highest

CHAPTER FOUR

The Rock in the Swamp

DANIEL 3:1-30

The 1993 hit movie *Indecent Proposal* may have caused as many Americans to question their moral ethics as any church service has in the last few years. The movie proposed a moral dilemma: Would you, or would you permit your mate to, have sex with someone else—for the right price? In the movie, $1 million did the trick.

What if we upped the ante to $10 million in real life? According to George Gallup's findings in *The Day America Told the Truth*, Americans are ready to trade some dear things for that kind of money. Twenty-five percent said they would abandon their families, 25 percent would abandon their church, 23 percent would become prostitutes for a week, and 7 percent would kill a stranger. Alarmingly, the figures remained consistent even when the potential payoff was reduced to five, then four, and finally three million. All of us must ask ourselves what we would do in a situation when we have something to gain by violating our conscience. In the past, being tempted to participate in something shady was less of a dilemma. Now it seems that compromise has almost become a daily way of life for many Americans. Today society is adrift. Relativistic thinking has corroded the moral anchors that once brought stability and showed men and women how to live. News analyst Eric Sevareid described our situation like this: "Millions of Americans are desperately search-ing for a moral rock upon which to stand in what feels like a swamp of values." That rock used to be the Judeo-Christian faith, which brought both definition and vitality to the social dimension of America.

Sad but true, while so many people are looking for answers, the church is stuttering. Large numbers of Christians have disengaged from the culture, leaving huge gaps in society with no Christian influ-ence, no light to quench the darkness. And when Christians are present, they are more often than not morally camouflaged.

To our shame, we tend to use the same inappropriate language, tell the same off-color jokes, watch the same morally debased movies and television programs, treat our coworkers with the same lack of dignity, love our families when it's convenient, and make decisions based on the same ethic of greed. We tend to drive with the same ferociousness toward the same ends as nonChristians— power, position, and possessions. Increasingly, the only difference between a Christian and his or her nonChristian neighbor, busi-ness associate, colleague or friend is where they spend Sunday. Even this distinctive is fading as more and more believers decide that with their busy schedules they can do without one more meet-ing a week.

If we are like most American Christians, we compromise more than we want to admit. According to George Gallup, even though 94 percent of us believe in God and 84 percent believe that Jesus is God's Son, fewer than ten percent of us can be called committed Christians. In his research, Gallup found that people who attend church regularly are virtually as likely as those who don't to engage in unethical behavior.[1] Bob Slocum, businessman and author of *Maximize Your Ministry*, discovered why this may be true. After teaching a Sunday morning class that addressed the issues of ethics and right and wrong, a bright young businessman approached Slocum with the following observations:

> He thought that in talking about good and evil I was three levels above where most people are living.
>
> He said that when people must make a business or per-sonal decision, the first question they ask is, "Do I or don't I want to do it?"—not "Is it good or evil?" If they get to the next

level, they ask whether it is legal or illegal. At the third level, they may ask whether it is right or wrong as judged by friends and peers. Only at the fourth and highest level would the question arise of good or evil as judged by God. And the young man didn't think most people ever get to that level.[2]

Although my hope is better than that for you and me—that we would stand firm for what we believe—most of us are apt to cave in or compromise rather than pay the price for doing what is right. But the problem we tend to forget is that there is also a price for compromise.

Iraq might not be the first place we would look for an example of integrity, considering Sadam Husein's ruthless regime in Baghdad. But I'm sure that there are many Christians in Iraq today who are standing firm for the truth—whatever it may cost them. Their situation may, in fact, be just as perilous as the one surrounding the godly young men who faced the despotic dictums of Nebuchadnezzar some 2500 years ago in ancient Babylon.

Well established in their careers as Babylonian officials, Daniel's three friends, Shadrach, Meshach, and Abednego, who at the time were in their mid-thirties, were offered a simple alternative. Bow or burn. Caught in the web of global politics, they were called to choose between their commitment to God and their allegiance to Nebuchadnezzar. With no other options—short of compromising their faith—they chose to be faithful to God and suffer the consequences.

I sincerely hope that we never see the day in North America when choosing whether to obey one's conscience or obey God will result in a life-threatening consequence. This possibility, however, is not as farfetched as it was thirty years ago. Even as I write this book, there is a clearly observable strategy among some of the national media aimed at discrediting evangelical Christians and painting our "medieval" adherence to moral absolutes as hostile to the First Amendment. However, no matter how bad (or good) it gets, there will always be a price to pay for making a choice between right and wrong. The account of Daniel's three friends provides a clear paradigm of integrity for those of us who want to stand for what is right. The situation unfolds in chapter 3.

Nebuchadnezzar is involved in a building project. Scholars of ancient history estimate the year to be 586 BC. That year is significant for two reasons. First, it marked the fall and absolute destruction of Jerusalem as well as the end of Nebuchadnezzar's conquests of other nations. With his enemies defeated and permanently subdued, the king of Babylon now turned his attention to leaving his mark on the landscape of the Middle East.

Second, the year 586 BC signified the beginning of grand building projects that would reconstruct the city of Babylon into the grandest city of its day. Among the most famous of these landmarks are the gates of Ishtar and the Hanging Gardens of Babylon, one of the Seven Wonders of the World. Besides these architectural masterpieces, Nebuchadnezzar also refortified the city of Babylon and built untold buildings for himself and his subjects to enjoy.

Evidently, the first of these huge projects was a self-memorial of sorts just outside Babylon, some six miles from the city gate on a flat field known as the plain of Dura. Today, there still remains on this site a brick pedestal forty-five feet wide and twenty feet high that may well have served as the base for Nebuchadnezzar's "Image of Gold." The gleaming image must have been awe-inspiring. It was some twenty feet higher than the "Colossus at Rhodes," and it was composed of, or at least covered in, gold. The nature of the image is not clear from the text. Most likely, the image is of Nebuchadnezzar himself, the pedestal composing a substantial part of the height.

Though the Bible does not explicitly state the purpose, there was clearly a personal reason for the construction of the image. Among other things, this image was Nebuchadnezzar's clear "declaration of independence" from God. In the unforgettable dream some sixteen years before, recorded in Daniel 2, God spoke to Nebuchadnezzar, outlining his place in history. Instead of modeling the image after the vision, using silver, bronze, iron, and clay, which symbolized the succession of kingdoms to follow his, Nebuchadnezzar made the entire image of gold, symbolic of himself in the dream.

Though young men usually feel invincible and immortal, Nebuchadnezzar had more reasons than most to do so. He was, without dispute, the most powerful monarch the world has ever known. No one else, before or since, has ruled over more people and property with such absolute power as Nebuchadnezzar. Had he been a poet rather than a builder, he might have penned the

Babylonian equivalent of William Henley's "Invictus."

> Out of the night that covers me,
> Black as the pit from pole to pole,
> I thank whatever gods may be,
> For my unconquerable soul. . . .
>
> It matters not how straight the gate
> How charged with punishments the scroll,
> I am the master of my fate,
> I am the captain of my soul.

To a man like Nebuchadnezzar, there was certainly no way some Hebrew god was going to call the shots. Dream or no dream, Nebuchadnezzar was the master of his fate. After all, he had defeated God's people three times—twice since the dream, and on Hebrew turf as well.

The golden image also served an important political purpose. Upon its completion, Nebuchadnezzar called every important official from every province to Babylon for the dedication. This was more than a political junket to see the king's handiwork, however. As a result of nineteen years of conquest, Babylon became a patchwork of Near Eastern nations that were now provinces knitted together into one empire under Nebuchadnezzar's might. The gathering before the image was calculated to unite the empire, and to show the king's awesome authority, power, and willingness to crush (or toast) any disloyalty. So, when the officials gathered, they were commanded to fall down and worship the image of gold when they heard the music begin. It was, in a sense, a pledge of allegiance to Nebuchadnezzar and also to the Babylonian gods.

The scene must have been something to behold. From his reviewing platform, the king watched this nervous multitude made up of thousands of officials from every nation and language arrayed in their finest attire, stretched out over the plain of Dura. At the sound of the music, everyone fell down in worship before the image. With a blazing furnace in the background, no one wanted to be the last one to fall and worship and have his loyalty questioned. As thousands of the most powerful men of the earth bowed low to worship Nebuchadnezzar and his gods, three men stood tall and worshipped the true King of kings, remaining absolutely loyal to Him.

Like children looking around during the prayer to see who else has their eyes open, sure enough, a few people peeked and saw Shadrach, Meshach, and Abednego standing in the crowd. "At this time some of the astrologers came forward and denounced the Jews." The accusers were the astrologers or Chaldeans, pure-blooded Babylonians who served as the king's chief advisors. An interesting idiom describes their motive. The Aramaic for "denounced" literally means "ate the pieces of." These men were jealous—an emotion that has gotten men and women into trouble since the beginning of time.

Jealousy was at the root of the murder of Abel, selling Joseph into slavery, Saul's persecution of David, and the crucifixion of Jesus. Today it is the root of many a fight between feuding Christians. It is jaundice of the soul. Proverbs calls it "rottenness to the bones." Galled by these foreigners' high position and apparently flippant attitude at this occasion, the astrologers went straight to the king. The jealous Babylonians wasted no time in making three accusations against the Hebrews:

1. They were disloyal to Nebuchadnezzar.
2. They didn't serve Babylonian gods.
3. They didn't worship the image.

As usual, jealousy resulted in a slippery grip on reality, causing the astrologers to think the worst of the three men. Shadrach, Meschach, and Abednego certainly wouldn't worship the image or serve the Babylonian deities, but they were never disloyal to Nebuchadnezzar—until he tried to pull rank on God and commanded them to worship the image.

Nebuchadnezzar's immediate response was not altogether unexpected. He was furious! From his pagan paradigm that allowed for the worship of a multitude of deities, this act could mean nothing but treason. As he had time to think about the stiff-kneed rebels before him, Nebuchadnezzar's attitude seemed to shift to astonishment. He asked them, "Is it true . . . that you don't serve my gods or worship the image of gold I have set up?"

Nebuchadnezzar obviously did not want to put these men to death. Comparing the charges with the loyalty they had exhibited over the years, Nebuchadnezzar could not believe they would disobey him now. He offered them a conciliatory second chance. But it was a second chance with a warning to the three Hebrews. It was also a challenge to God: "If you are ready to fall down and worship the image I made, very good. But if you do not worship it, you will be thrown immediately into a blazing furnace. Then what god will be able to rescue you from my hand?" One reason the book of Daniel is in the Bible is to answer this very question. There is a God who rescues!

It's interesting to follow Nebuchadnezzar's growing understanding of God. He certainly knew that God was intelligent—able to reveal secrets. He learned that sixteen years before. But what the king didn't know was that the God of Shadrach, Meshach, and Abednego was a God of power, who loves to exert His might on behalf of His children. This is an attribute the king was about to experience firsthand.

THREE MEN AND A CRISIS

Shadrach, Meschach, and Abednego had to ask themselves some questions, in much the same way we must every day. What do we do in a situation that calls us to violate our conscience? How should we respond when there is a clear attack on our faith? How far can we go when asked to participate in evil? These three men provide us with an excellent example to follow.

They Admitted Their Guilt
Shadrach, Meschach, and Abednego simply would not bow the knee to an image or any pagan deities. This was a black-and-white issue— no gray zones to discuss. They had clearly violated the king's command, and no amount of smooth talking changed anyone's mind about the matter.

But surely there was another answer—some way to rationalize compliance. Unfortunately, Nebuchadnezzar's intent was clearly a challenge to their faith. To rationalize their submission to this earthly king in this instance would have brought them into direct conflict with the true King of kings. Certainly they could have offered several

Rationalization: What good am I to God dead? I want to continue to serve Him here in this strategic position.
Problem: A person who compromises dilutes his or her integrity.

Rationalization: The government made me do it. I was just following orders.
Problem: No one can make me violate God's law. It is my choice, therefore my responsibility.

Rationalization: This will happen just one time. I'm not making a lifestyle of idol worship.
Problem: Sin is sin no matter how infrequent. And the first step is all too often the beginning of a longer journey than we think.

Rationalization: God is gracious. He will forgive me this once.
Problem: Presumption always strains a relationship. The fact is that presumptuous sin hinders me from experiencing the Father's love and power in my life.

Rationalization: I don't deserve to die. If God can't take care of me, I have to take care of myself.
Problem: We are all alive because of God's grace, not because we deserve it or are smart enough to protect ourselves.

Rationalization: We're a thousand miles from home, in a strange land, with strange customs. We don't want to offend our hosts. Besides, who will know?
Problem: God will know and be offended by sin. The question is, who would you rather offend?

rational alternatives, but as we analyze each option, we discover they would have cost more in the long run.

Not only do all of these rationalizations directly violate God's law, they call into question God's ability to work in the situation. Perhaps that's the reason we rationalize in the first place—we lack the assurance that David describes in Psalm 23: "The LORD is my shepherd, I shall not want."

They Refused to Defend Themselves
Shadrach, Meschach, and Abednego knew that this conflict was not about them. It was between two claimants for sovereignty over their lives. By getting out of the way, they made this issue very clear, which resulted in Nebuchadnezzar's challenge to God.

They Affirmed Their Faith in God's Ability to Deliver
The reckless abandon these three men had with Nebuchadnezzar is astounding. But it was built squarely on their confidence in God. Notice the specific way they responded:

If we are thrown into the blazing furnace, the God we serve is able to save us from it, and he will rescue us from your hand, O king. But even if he does not, we want you to know, O king, that we will not serve your gods or worship the image of gold you have set up. (Daniel 3:17-18)

Some might call this a lack of faith, but we must note carefully where their faith lay. The object of their faith was clearly God Himself and not what He would do for them (deliverance). But don't misunderstand. They were not questioning His power. After all, God had delivered them from imminent execution in Daniel 2. These three faithful Hebrews were not questioning God's ability. They were simply unsure of His specific purpose in this situation.

There are only two things that limit God's power: His character and His purpose. He will never use His power capriciously in violation of His holiness, goodness, justice, or any of His other attributes. And every time He moves, there is purpose behind His power. Sometimes God chooses to deliver us from temptations, trials, and adversity. Sometimes He delivers us through them. In this instance, Shadrach, Meschach, and Abednego knew God was perfectly capable of deliverance, but they had no specific promise that He would exercise His might in that way.

It is dangerous for anyone to try to read the future through the envelope. God never promised to deliver us from every ill circumstance, nor is He obligated to act the same way every time. But one thing is sure: God's power is always available to His children to give us the strength to face the difficult circumstances.

They Affirmed Their Complete Submission to God's Will

Whether God delivered Shadrach, Meschach, and Abednego from their painful sentence of death or not, they were committed to Him. What a contrast to so many of us who are willing to follow God until He leads us along the dark paths of life. Too many of us want a "heavenly grandfather" as C. S. Lewis put it, who says at the end of the day, "A good time was had by all." But not these men. God was their Master, and it was enough for them to know that He had a purpose. Even though He had not made Shadrach, Meschach, and Abednego privy to His plans ahead of time, they were willing to follow Him. In fact, they were willing to die rather than compromise their allegiance to the Kingdom of God.

They Refused to Obey the King

There was no name-calling, no antagonism—not even any bitterness. Shadrach, Meschach, and Abednego simply made a firm statement of allegiance to the God they believed ruled over Nebuchadnezzar. And they believed that it was now God's responsibility to call Nebuchadnezzar into account for the authority delegated to him as the king of Babylon.

Given the situation and Nebuchadnezzar's grandiose self-estimation, his response is not surprising. He was furious at Shadrach, Meschach, and Abednego's refusal to accept his mercy, and ordered their immediate execution before the assembled masses. Just to make sure no one interfered, the king ordered the furnace heated seven times hotter than usual before the men were thrown in. No way was he going to chance a cosmic intervention. Obviously Nebuchadnezzar didn't understand that whether the temperature was 100 degrees or 2500 degrees Fahrenheit, it made little difference to the Creator and Preserver of the laws of physics.

As the king peered into the furnace, thinking he would see charcoal, his worse fears as a rebel and greatest hopes as a man merged. There was indeed a God who was able to rescue them from his hand! And, that Deliverer was standing with His faithful followers in the midst of the fire. "Look!" Nebuchadnezzar said. "I see four men walking around in the fire, unbound and unharmed, and the fourth looks like a son of the gods" (Daniel 3:25).

You have to hand it to Nebuchadnezzar. Confronted with his own impotence, He readily acknowledged the awesome miracle he had seen. "Then Nebuchadnezzar said, 'Praise be to the God of Shadrach, Meshach and Abednego, who has sent his angel and rescued his servants!'" (verse 28). Not only that—Nebuchadnezzar commended their disobedience and promoted them, saying, "They trusted in him [God] and defied the king's command and were willing to give up their lives rather than serve or worship any god except their own God." Because of the integrity of these three men, Nebuchadnezzar, along with every leader in the empire, was able to see the miraculous power of God. In fact, a decree went out to the entire kingdom calling men to honor the God of Shadrach, Meshach and Abednego.

FACING THE FIRE

Though we may not face a literal fire, every Christian will meet situations where we must choose who we will follow. If we want to follow God and honor Him like Shadrach, Meschach, and Abednego, we would do well to follow their example.

Prepare Yourself Before the Test

As I write this chapter, football players all over the country are finishing their preseason preparation. Coaches everywhere—high school, college, and professional—recognize that preparation is absolutely essential. When I was in high school, we started "two-a-days" in mid-August to prepare for the football season, which started in September. If you've ever been unlucky enough to be in east Texas in August, you know it's the time when everyone dreams of a summer home in Colorado. Temperatures easily soar past 100 degrees, with humidity to match. It's miserable.

Quite frankly, I don't know how anyone lived here before air conditioning. I'll never forget those afternoons in full pads out in the sun. Everyone prayed for school to start—if you can believe that—so we could be delivered from the hands of the sadistic madman we had for a coach.

When the season finally arrived, it was apparent what he had accomplished. We were in better shape than any of the teams we faced. We consistently outplayed teams with more talent and size because we were prepared physically. When I lined up across from my opponent, I knew I had the advantage.

With this in mind, we would do well to ask ourselves how we prepare for temptations to compromise our faith. It's important that we understand that we never make decisions in a vacuum. Every decision we make is value-driven. You tell me the values you carry into temptation, and I can predict your behavior. If we hold worldly values, we will consistently compromise the faith in God we claim we have.

Our value system doesn't form overnight. As Bob Slocum pointed out in *Maximize Your Ministry*, values are a matter of "accumulation." The more we listen to the world's "music"—focusing on the values of the world—the more worldly thoughts we accumulate. The more we listen to God's "music"—focusing on God and what is important to Him—the more godly thoughts we accumulate. Over time we create a tendency of the soul, a predisposition toward or away from God, which Slocum calls polarity.[3]

The world is playing "music" constantly, emphasizing power, prestige, and possessions—calling us to pursue these prizes. Fortunately, Shadrach, Meshach and Abednego were listening to a different band. They spent hours listening to God's music, filling their minds with His thoughts—emphasizing character, servanthood, and God's glory.

In any circumstance we enter, we have a polarity—a predisposition based on the values we have developed depending on whose music we've been listening to. Make no mistake about it. When there is an important decision to make, two bands will be playing. So we must each ask ourselves, Whose music am I listening to? If the answer is to "worldly music," chances are we'll compromise. But if we're listening to "godly music," we'll probably choose integrity. Count on it.

IMPORTANT TO THE WORLD	IMPORTANT TO GOD
Personal Prestige	God's Glory
Power	Servanthood
Possessions	God's Approval
Recognition	Relationships
Pleasing Self	Pleasing God
Personal Happiness	Obedience
Personal Preservation	Faith
What I Make Myself	What God Made Me
The focus is on the gift.	The focus is on the Giver.
Living by a worldly value system produces emptiness and results in compromise.	Living by a biblical value system produces fullness and results in integrity.

Count the Cost

Both compromise and integrity always have a price. Inherent in every decision are things to gain and things to lose, depending on the way we choose. Take our three Hebrew friends. Choosing integrity as they did could have easily cost them their lives. On the other hand, choosing to compromise would have cost them something far dearer.

Whenever God's children make choices based on a worldly value system, the most precious area of loss is in regard to their relationship with God. Although I am absolutely convinced that nothing we do can separate us from God's love, every time we compromise, we damage the intimacy with our Father that channels His love to us. His attitude toward us never changes, but our attitude toward Him does—with ruinous results. David wrote in Psalm 15:1-2 (NASB), "O LORD, who may abide in Thy tent? . . . He who walks with integrity, and works righteousness, and speaks truth in his heart." Even though we remain God's children, when we compromise, we choose to live outside the tent of God's blessing.

Compromise also costs us our self-respect and others' respect as well. Far from gaining approval, poor choices usually diminish our reputation. Solomon said, "Better is the poor who walks in integrity, than he who is crooked though he be rich" (Proverbs 28:6, NASB).

Compromise with the world always dishonors God. No matter what your motive, the price of compromise is always loss of a positive influence for God. Whatever we may gain cannot outweigh this tremendous damage. On the other hand, Paul says, "Urge bondslaves to be subject to their own masters in everything . . . that they may adorn the doctrine of God" (Titus 2:9-10, NASB). When we choose to remain obedient to God, we glorify Him. Choose compromise and we detract rather than attract.

Determine the Intention

When someone is attempting to lure you into something you know is wrong, ask him why. Don't assume the worst about a person. Remember how Daniel avoided a major conflict when he first arrived in Babylon by discerning that the main concern of the official was Daniel's health. Once you understand the situation, you can offer an alternative course of action that allows you to maintain your integrity and accomplish the desire of your superior.

When someone demands that you violate your commitment to God, realize this person's conflict is not with you, but with God. The best thing that you can do in that circumstance is just what Shadrach, Meschach, and Abednego did; get out of the way and let God deal with the upstart. State your position frankly and refuse to discuss the matter further.

One of Satan's best tactics is to keep us talking and wear down our resolve. An old Russian fable makes the point quite well. It seems a hunter came to a clearing. There stood a bear! When the hunter raised his weapon, the bear shouted, "Wait! What do you want?"

The hunter replied, "A fur coat."

"That's reasonable," answered the bear. "I want a full stomach. Let's sit down and talk about it."

So they sat down. After a while the bear walked away alone—he had his full stomach and the hunter had his fur coat.

I'm sad to say there have been many times when I have stopped to discuss a matter and been eaten alive by temptation. I should have just said, "No!"

Put Your Welfare in God's Hands

One of the greatest decisions every one of us makes is who will take care of us. Repeatedly God challenges His children to entrust themselves to His care. Any alternative will invariably lead us away from obedience.

If I assume ultimate responsibility for my welfare, without fail I will be offered a way to save my skin that will violate God's law. If I doubt God's protection, I will cut and run every time.

I recently walked with a friend through the ordeal of a trial in federal court. Through a series of circumstances, the government charged him with a serious crime of which I believe he was innocent. His explanation of the events, however, scared his attorneys. They told him that his story might well be what happened, but that the jury wouldn't believe him. My friend wrestled with this possibility for weeks and finally determined to tell it exactly as it happened, whatever the consequences.

Sure enough, the attorneys where right. The jury didn't believe him. Even through this outcome, my friend knows that he was safer entrusting himself to God than taking matters into his own hands. Whatever eventually happens, God is going to use this man's integrity as he did Shadrach, Meshach, and Abednego's.

Find Some People to Stand Together

God does not intend for us to stand alone. We need each other. This is especially true in the area of ethical decisions. Several years ago, George's business was going through a severe reversal. On a trip to the west coast, he ran across an incredible opportunity to reverse a severe cash flow crisis. Unfortunately, it involved the distribution of soft-core pornographic videos. After a night of wrestling over the matter, he called his friend who offered the opportunity and said no.

The next Thursday at his small group, he told us the story. He said, "You all know I needed the money, but not bad enough to do something wrong. My relationship with God is too important to me." And then he added, "I wouldn't have made this decision two years ago before I joined this group."

We all need each other to help us make right choices, or as Paul said it, "bear one another's burdens" (Galatians 6:2, NASB). I need other people with whom I can discuss the dilemmas of my life, and who will encourage me to do what is right. I need others to stand with me shoulder to shoulder when I have to make a tough decision. And I need individuals who will lift me up when doing what is right costs me dearly. I need people to remind me of whom I know God to be when I lose my spiritual ball in the weeds. Integrity may mean standing alone, but it is incredibly easier with confederates standing together.

After reviewing an extensive study of men in combat, Colonel S.L.A. Marshal concluded,

> I hold it to be one of the simplest truths of war that the thing which enables an infantry soldier to keep going with his weapons is the near presence or the presumed presence of a comrade. . . . It is that way with any fighting man. He is sustained by his fellows primarily and by his weapons secondarily. Having to make a choice in the face of the enemy, he would rather be unarmed and with comrades around him than altogether alone, though possessing the most perfect of quick-firing weapon."[4]

WHICH SYSTEM WILL YOU CHOOSE TO LIVE BY?

The controlling factor behind your choices is your knowledge of God. Oswald Chambers writes, "Every time you venture out in the life of faith, you will find something in your common-sense circumstances that flatly contradicts your faith. Common sense is not faith, and faith is not common sense; they stand in the relation of the natural and the spiritual. Can you trust Jesus Christ where your common sense cannot trust Him?"[5] Is your knowledge of God strong enough to do battle with the doubts that will bombard your mind when you decide to step out from the rank and file and live distinctively for Christ?

Last year a friend of mine made a trip to Europe to meet with an important client and monitor the equipment he had purchased. The inspection was rather arduous, so at his client's invitation, my friend spent two days at a beach resort before returning to the U.S. He wanted to spend a quiet two days clearing his mind just staring at the ocean. Unfortunately Satan had other plans.

The first morning began as a delight for my friend. He had the beach to himself until a beautiful young woman claimed the lounge next to him and began a pleasant conversation. After a few moments when the discussion lulled, she nonchalantly removed her top and laid back to absorb the sun. My friend quickly looked away, laid back on his lounge, and closed his eyes. It was too late; the picture was indelibly etched on his mind. He told me, "I couldn't win. I opened my eyes and did battle with the magnet pulling them toward the girl. I closed my eyes and I couldn't get her form out of my mind." After an hour of pitched battle, my friend got up, said goodbye, and went to his room for a cold shower.

That evening his phone rang. The young woman had inquired, found his name, and wanted to have dinner together. He thanked her but told her he planned to have dinner in his room.

"Bill," he told me, "I don't know how, but I said no. I don't know what was on her mind, but I know what was on mine."

I asked him why he made that decision, and he told me that the temptation was incredible—no one would have ever known. Then he said, "I wish I could say I didn't want to commit adultery—I did. But I knew it wasn't right. I asked God to help me keep from doing it. Somehow a day later I was on the plane. I dodged the bullet." Then he paused and said, "I don't know what I would have done if she had come to my room."

This is not just another traveling salesman story. Whether it is facing the flames or doing battle with the heat of illegitimate passion, men and women who live in the real world are faced with incredible ethical decisions like this every day. Just to put this story in perspective, this man was not coming home to a happy family. His wife had, over the past two years, been less than affectionate.

Rationalization told him no one would know. Rationalization told him this was an opportunity to get the affection he deserved. But faith told him it wasn't right. In his heart he knew the price was too high to pay for one night of pleasure.

As I listened to him relate his story, I couldn't imagine the power it took to turn away from the opportunity to compromise his moral values. Fortunately we have an incredibly powerful God who is committed to deliver us from the evil one's schemes. As weak as he felt, God met him at his point of need when my friend cried out to Him. God will do the same for each of us.

THE BIG IDEA

Integrity and compromise always come with a price. Every decision we make is value-driven. If we adopt the world's value system, it will lead inevitably to compromise. If we adopt biblical values, it will lead inevitably to integrity. Which values we adopt will be determined by how much we value God. And how much we value God is in direct proportion to our knowledge of what He has done for us.

Use the following thoughts and ideas to stimulate your thinking about integrity.

No temptation has seized you except what is common to man.
And God is faithful; he will not let you
be tempted beyond what you can bear.
But when you are tempted, he will also provide a way out
so that you can stand up under it.
1 CORINTHIANS 10:13

The integrity of the upright guides them,
but the unfaithful are destroyed by their duplicity.
PROVERBS 11:3

The sorrows of those will increase
who run after other gods.
I will not pour out their libations of blood
or take up their names on my lips.
PSALM 16:4

For I have chosen him [Abraham],
so that he will direct his children and his household
after him to keep the way of the LORD
by doing what is right and just,
so that the LORD will bring about for Abraham
what he has promised him.
GENESIS 18:19

Therefore, I urge you, brothers, in view of God's mercy,
to offer your bodies as living sacrifices, holy and pleasing
to God—this is your spiritual act of worship.
Do not conform any longer to the pattern of this world,
but be transformed by the renewing of your mind.
ROMANS 12:1-2

A friend loves at all times,
and a brother is born for adversity.
PROVERBS 17:17, KJV

What is the greatest challenge to your integrity?

Who will stand with you when the heat is on?

To choose to suffer means that there is something wrong;
to choose God's will even if it means suffering

*is a very different thing. No healthy saint ever chooses
suffering; he chooses God's will, as Jesus did,
whether it means suffering or not. No saint dare interfere
with the discipline of suffering in another saint.*
OSWALD CHAMBERS
My Utmost for His Highest

*Don't say things.
What you are stands over you the while,
and thunders so that I cannot hear what you say
to the contrary.*
RALPH WALDO EMERSON

*In order to be a leader, one must have followers,
and to have followers one must have confidence.
Hence the supreme quality for a leader is unquestioned
integrity. Without it no real success is possible,
no matter whether it is a section gang, on a football field,
in an army, or in an office. If one's associates find him guilty
of phoniness, if they find that the individual
lacks forthright integrity, he will fail.
His teachings and actions must square with each other.
The first great need therefore is integrity.*
DWIGHT EISENHOWER

*You cannot play with the animal in you
without becoming wholly animal;
play with falsehood without forfeiting your right to the truth;
play with cruelty without losing
your sensitivity of mind. He who wants to keep
his garden tidy doesn't reserve a plot for weeds.*
DAG HAMMERSKJÖLDT
Sketches

If I have to do the wrong thing to stay on the team,
I am on the wrong team.
Author Unknown

When principles that run against your deepest convictions
begin to win the day, then battle is your calling,
and peace has become sin;
you must at the price of dearest peace,
lay your convictions bare before friend and enemy,
with all the fire of your faith.
Abraham Kuyper

To go against one's conscience is neither safe nor right.
Here I stand. I cannot do otherwise.
Martin Luther

CHAPTER FIVE

The Slippery Slope of Success

DANIEL 4:1-37

Texas has certainly seen both sides of the economic track in the last few years. Jokingly, some good friends and I founded the fictitious Texas Association of Formerly Wealthy Persons. We thought a good laugh would help ease the pain of the transition from BMW to VW. We limited membership to individuals who could attest that at least three of the following statements were true:

- ◆ Had at least two serious conversations with your spouse about getting a job.
- ◆ Removed the telephone from your personal vehicle.
- ◆ Snooped through your spouse's checkbook to determine "what's happening to all that money?"
- ◆ Missed more than three interest payments on a lifestyle loan.
- ◆ Dropped membership in one or more private clubs.
- ◆ Sold a Rolex watch for cash.
- ◆ Switched the family dog from canned to dry dog food.
- ◆ Sold an imported European car and bought a Ford or Chevy.
- ◆ Invested in an oil well.
- ◆ Paid no attention to the new tax laws.

Membership included a one-year subscription to the TAFWP newsletter, chock-full of helpful information such as:

♦ "How to Live Without Domestic Help"
♦ "Tips on Talking Your Son Out of Going to Harvard"
♦ "Survival Tips for Sleeping in an Economy Motel"
♦ "Save Money on Floaters by Selling Her Jewelry"
♦ "How to Solve Cash Flow Problems with a Charge Card"
♦ "Reasonable Explanations for Selling a Mercedes"
♦ "Fundamentals of a Lawn Mower"
♦ "How to Avoid Calling a Plumber: Reset Buttons Made Easy"
♦ "Coping with Rejection: When the Men's Store Stops Calling"
♦ "What to Do When Your Pool Gets Dirty"
♦ "How to Dip Your Dog"
♦ "Good Reasons to Tell Your Friends Why They Saw You at a Pawn Shop"

God interrupts our lives in two dramatic ways: in adversity and in prosperity. In each case He is speaking. But more often than not, we listen more attentively in adversity than in prosperity. At least I do. When things are really going my way, it's easy to let little things slip. I'm not as careful about spending time listening to God speak to me from His Word, because the path ahead seems safe. I don't feel the compelling need to pray and stay in close communication with God because I feel satisfied with how things are going. As I trust more in myself and my circumstances, my relationship with God begins to chill.

Thomas Carlyle warned us, "Adversity is sometimes hard on a man; but for every one man that can stand prosperity, there are a hundred men that will stand adversity." There is something about success that tends to promote prideful self-sufficiency, rather than making us humbly grateful to God. Prosperity and spirituality have rarely gone together in human history.

To make us truly wealthy, a very patient God at times depletes earthly wealth and thins our success. He ruthlessly and persistently pursues us to give us His very best. If we will not honor Him in our prosperity, He graciously erodes our standing in the world until all we have to lean on is Him.

Losing it all can have a shattering effect on people. It can also bring us face to face with our utter dependence on God. Both of these were true of King Nebuchadnezzar. Immediately when we come to chapter 4 of Daniel's book, we know something significant has happened in the life of the king. The entire chapter is the exact record of an official edict sent throughout the whole Babylonian kingdom.

King Nebuchadnezzar,
    To the peoples, nations and men of every language, who
live in all the world:

    May you prosper greatly!

    It is my pleasure to tell you about the miraculous signs
and wonders that the Most High God has performed for me.

How great are his signs,
    how mighty his wonders!
His kingdom is an eternal kingdom;
    his dominion endures from generation to generation.
    (verses 1-3)

Nebuchadnezzar himself wrote these opening lines, as well as the story to follow to inform his kingdom of his complete submission to the one true God. His pilgrimage of faith included the tests of adversity and prosperity.

THE CRISIS OF SUCCESS

Toward the end of his reign, between 586 and 562 BC, with his enemies subdued and his grand building projects completed, the king tells us, "I, Nebuchadnezzar, was at home in my palace, contented and prosperous." Unfortunately, even in the case of the wealthiest man in the ancient Near East, contentment with worldly prosperity was short-lived. Our gracious God would not allow Nebuchadnezzar, or any of His children for that matter, to be content with the meager wealth of the world. He made us for a richer existence, and deep inside our being we know it. Whether God personally interrupts us, as He did Nebuchadnezzar, or our spirit simply grows lean feeding on the empty diet the world provides, we soon learn that this world can't satisfy us.

For the third time God stepped in Nebuchadnezzar's path and interrupted his life. This time, Nebuchadnezzar had a dream of a huge, sumptuous tree that provided food and shelter for every creature in the forest. Then by decree of God, the tree was cut down and stripped bare. The dream was a frightening vision of impending judgment, and Nebuchadnezzar knew it. With the hot breath of the Almighty on his neck, the king made one last attempt at independence from Daniel's God. But alas, the king's advisors could not interpret the dream and its vision.

Interestingly, it wasn't until after his other advisors failed him that Nebuchadnezzar finally conferred with Daniel. The king expressed his confidence in his chief advisor and proceeded to tell Daniel everything. Although Nebuchadnezzar disagreed with Daniel over religion, the king nonetheless respected him highly and trusted his integrity and competence.

On hearing the vision, Daniel was "greatly perplexed for a time." It was not confusion that tied his mind in knots; it was concern. Daniel was "alarmed." After close to forty years of serving the king, as different as they were, these two men obviously cared for each other. The king told Daniel, "Do not let the dream or its meaning alarm you." Daniel lamented, "My Lord, if only the dream applied to your enemies and its meaning to your adversaries."

It is amazing to me that Daniel bore no ill will toward the man who was responsible for the interruption of his personal life and destruction of his homeland. Instead, he felt tremendous remorse about the calamity that was about to fall on Nebuchadnezzar. I'm afraid I would not have felt as gracious.

After getting a handle on his emotions, Daniel proceeded to tell the king the bad news: God would strip Nebuchadnezzar of his sovereignty and he would live as a beast until he recognized the absolute authority the Most High had over the kingdoms of men. Until Nebuchadnezzar recognized that his kingship was a gift of God, and bowed the knee to God alone, the king would remain without authority to control himself or his kingdom.

As any friend would do, Daniel appealed to the king: "Therefore, O king, be pleased to accept my advice: Renounce your sins by doing what is right, and your wickedness by being kind to the oppressed. It may be that then your prosperity will continue." The word Daniel used means "separate, make a division" between yourself and sin. He pleaded with Nebuchadnezzar to make a clean break from those things that displeased God and to choose a lifestyle that pleased Him. Note three things about Daniel's appeal.

> **APPEALING TO THOSE IN AUTHORITY**
> ◆ Win the respect of the authority.
> ◆ Develop a deep concern for his or her welfare.
> ◆ Speak graciously.
> ◆ Outline the behavior to avoid.
> ◆ Outline the behavior to embrace.
> ◆ Outline the consequences of each.
> ◆ Be willing to stand by him or her whatever happens.

First, Daniel was compassionate. Like any good friend, he did not want his friend to suffer. Understandably, Daniel wanted to short-circuit, if possible, the necessity for judgment. If Nebuchadnezzar made a clean break from the things that displeased God, maybe this would eliminate the need for God's judgment. None of us like to see those we love suffer. Daniel was no different.

Second, Daniel's confrontation took tremendous courage. The king had the authority to end Daniel's life with a whim. It's doubtful any other man ever spoke this directly to Nebuchadnezzar and lived to tell about it. Courage is often driven by conviction—in this case it was also fueled by compassion. Daniel was so concerned, he put aside his own self-interests and moved to the aid of his friend. That's what love does.

Third, the appeal had a context. Lengthy conversations about sin, good and evil, and pleasing God must have transpired between Nebuchadnezzar and Daniel long before this crisis. Otherwise, Daniel's advice would have been meaningless to the king. Nebuchadnezzar knew the demands of a Holy God. Unfortunately, knowing is not obeying.

Nebuchadnezzar had come a long way from the brash days of his youth when he took Judah's finest young men into captivity. In chapter 1 of Daniel, Nebuchadnezzar treated the Almighty with disdain and the disrespect of a subjugated enemy. He removed the utensils from the house of God and took them to the temple of his gods in Babylon. In chapter 2, confronted with his first nightmare, Nebuchadnezzar's fear turned to amazement as God revealed the dream to Daniel. In chapter 3, Nebuchadnezzar's arrogance toward God turned to respect as He delivered Shadrach, Meshach, and Abednego from certain death. But in chapter 4, we still find a prideful, if somewhat respectful and curious, attitude residing in Nebuchadnezzar. By the end of this chapter, however, pride melted into submission, trust, and worship.

Interestingly, at no time during his pilgrimage did Nebuchadnezzar seek God. God sought him. Surely the ruthless, relentless pursuit of sinners is one of the most incredible characteristics of our God. He would not give up on this arrogant man. God would go to any length to bless Nebuchadnezzar, including crush him if necessary.

Perhaps the king straightened up for a while, but soon when God did not act, Nebuchadnezzar's arrogance returned. It's curious how we often take the patience of God as an indication of His indifference toward our sin. In Psalm 50:21, God says, "These things you have done and I kept silent; you thought I was altogether like you." However, God's purpose in postponing immediate judgment is well explained in the Bible. Peter reminds us, "The Lord is not slow in keeping his promise, as some understand slowness. He is patient with you, not wanting anyone to perish, but everyone to come to repentance" (2 Peter 3:9).

God gives us plenty of time to confirm our choice of judgment. In a sense He asks us over and over, "Are you sure? Are you sure this is what you want?" In Nebuchadnezzar's case, God gave him a year to repent: "Twelve months later, as the king was walking on the roof of the royal palace of Babylon, he said, 'Is not this the great Babylon *I* have built as the royal residence, by my mighty power and for the glory of *my* majesty?'" (italics mine).

Stretching out before his eyes were architectural masterpieces of the ancient world: an enormous palace, an exquisite procession way with 120 flanking lions, the famous Ishtar gate, the temples, and the world-famous Hanging Gardens of Babylon. Nebuchadnezzar had not only created a beautiful city, he had built an impregnable fortress with double defensive walls covering seventeen miles. A moat, artificial lake, and canals protected and supplied the city with water. It was impressive, and Nebuchadnezzar was hellbent on doing as he pleased—dream or no dream. He was the most powerful man in the world.

The arrogant words were still on Nebuchadnezzar's lips when a voice came from Heaven pronouncing his sentence:

> This is what is decreed for you, King Nebuchadnezzar. Your royal authority has been taken from you. You will be driven away from people and will live with the wild animals; you will eat grass like cattle. Seven times [years] will pass by for you until you acknowledge that the Most High is sovereign over the kingdoms of men and gives them to anyone he wishes. Immediately, what had been said about Nebuchadnezzar was fulfilled. (4:31-33)

With a swiftness that staggers the imagination, the mighty monarch became a raving maniac, racing from the palace, casting off his clothes as he ran. For seven unimaginable years Nebuchadnezzar lived and behaved like a beast on the palace grounds. The king's malady is not unknown to psychology today. It is a disorder called zoanthropy, in which the victim thinks and behaves like an animal.

Nebuchadnezzar's state was no arbitrary condition, however. The essence of God's justice is always to allow us to feel the true implications of our choices. God had given Nebuchadnezzar the choice to live as a true human being, dwelling under the lordship of God's sovereign rule. By choosing to ignore his Maker, the king had reduced himself to the level of an unthinking animal. G. K. Chesterton described Nebuchadnezzar and all men when he wrote,

> We talk of wild animals, but man is the only wild animal. It is man that has broken out. All other animals are tame animals, following the rugged respectability of the tribe or type. Man is wild because he alone, on this speck of rock called earth, stands up to God, shakes his fist, and says, "I do what I want to do because I want to do it, and God had better leave me alone."[1]

God let Nebuchadnezzar taste the consequence of his choice. C. S. Lewis calls this way of judgment God's "kind hardness" or a "severe mercy." God is committed to interrupting the destructive behavior of those He loves, even if it means hurting them temporarily.

When Nebuchadnezzar awoke from this beastly nightmare, it's interesting to note that he held no bitterness over his condition or the lost years of his life. On the contrary, he was absolutely grateful for this merciful interruption of his arrogance: "At the end of that time [seven years], I, Nebuchadnezzar, raised my eyes toward heaven and my sanity was restored. Then I praised the Most High; I honored and glorified him who lives forever."

With his mental faculties freshly restored, Nebuchadnezzar worshipped God as his first act of sanity. Reason reaches its highest potential when it leads us to worship our Creator. God made us thinking, rational beings so we could know Him and relate to Him. How kind is God's hardness when He drives us to reach our full potential as His creatures. Notice that Nebuchadnezzar's words are no longer "me" and "my," but "He" and "His."

> His dominion is an eternal dominion;
> > his kingdom endures from generation to generation.
> All the peoples of the earth
> > are regarded as nothing.
> He does as he pleases
> > with the powers of heaven
> > and the peoples of the earth.
> No one can hold back his hand
> > or say to him: "What have you done?"

From Nebuchadnezzar's account we discover that God not only restored the king's sanity, but also restored his sovereignty. In any other situation, a usurper would have been sitting on Nebuchadnezzar's throne the day after the king's "attack." At any sign of weakness, ancient Near Eastern kings could expect a rival to challenge them for the throne.

However, in this case, any potential successor to Nebuchadnezzar had to deal with a formidable friend of the king, namely Daniel. It is because of Daniel's faithfulness that Nebuchadnezzar could say, "At the same time that my sanity was restored, my honor and splendor were returned to me for the glory of my kingdom. My advisors and nobles sought me out, and I was restored to my throne and became even greater than before."

It is because of the integrity and influence of a faithful friend like Daniel that we also read, "Now I, Nebuchadnezzar, praise and exalt and glorify the King of heaven, because everything he does is right and all his ways are just. And those who walk in pride he is able to humble."

You and I will see Nebuchadnezzar in Heaven because he had a committed friend who feared God more than the king's rejection and retribution. We will all bow before the Lord Jesus and worship together, shoulder to shoulder with Nebuchadnezzar, the mighty king of Babylon, and his chief advisor, Daniel. We will stand there not because of the greatness of our deeds, or the purity of our lives, but because we cast ourselves on the great mercy of God.

PASSING THE TEST OF PROSPERITY

In his epic novel, *Ben Hur*, Lew Wallace wrote, "No person is ever on trial so much as at the moment of excessive good fortune." No doubt about it: prosperity is a much harder test to pass than adversity. The following letter appeared in a career advice column in the *Dallas Morning News*:

> I have read your column for some time and now have a question that may surprise you. I'm 43, a successful professional still on my way up and unhappy. With my long hectic work hours, I sometimes feel that I'm running between the raindrops. My personal life has been a series of exploding relationships, including one divorce. I feel I'm successful but not driving on the scenic route. Do many of your readers express a similar problem?[2]

Any way you slice it, success is a gift of God. However, it's not much of a surprise to most of us who have reached our fortieth year on this planet that success is not only hard to enjoy, it can be downright hazardous to our health at times. One retiring executive echoes the sentiments of far too many when he writes, "I let my job eat out the center of my life, leaving me only the crusts." Physically, reaching for the gold ring can destroy our health. Relationally, it seems much easier for greed and selfishness to take hold and drive us apart from those we love. Most damaging of all, however, is the effect that success and prosperity can have on our relationship with God. If He should bless you with success, what can you do to make sure you pass the test? We can learn several things from Daniel and Nebuchadnezzar.

Acknowledge the Source of Prosperity

In Nebuchadnezzar's dream God made the source of the king's prosperity very clear. God called on Nebuchadnezzar to "acknowledge that the Most High is sovereign over the kingdoms of men and gives them to anyone he wishes." This idea runs counter to American culture. If you asked a hundred successful people the source of their prosperity, you would hear answers like hard work, superior wisdom, business savvy, or some other personal characteristic. You might encounter other persons who were "intelligent" enough to be born into wealth and consider prosperity a right. You might even run into a Christian who believes success is a result of his or her obedience to God's laws or rules of business—and anyone who follows them can be prosperous too. All of these reasons, however, place the source of prosperity squarely on man's shoulders. This belief that "I am the source of my own prosperity" is so culturally strong in North America that it has become a paradigm. Michael Korda, author of *Success*, describes America's success paradigm fairly well when he writes,

> Though hard work is certainly an ingredient of success, it is not the only ingredient. If you are going to work at all, and most of us have to, you might as well become rich, famous and successful in the process. The people who succeed do not as a rule work all that harder than the people who fail . . . they have simply mastered the rules of success. . . .
>
> It's simple to analyze your success potential:
> ◆ Are you ambitious?
> ◆ Are you willing to work hard when you have to?
> ◆ Are you willing to put your own interests first?
> ◆ Are you willing to take risks?

♦ Do you sincerely want to be rich?

♦ Have you got the guts to accept change?[3]

Nebuchadnezzar would have given a resounding yes to all of these questions. He followed the rules of success. And he needed a paradigm shift just as most of us do.

Even common sense tells us that we need a significant paradigm shift in the area of success and prosperity. Living in Texas over the past several years would educate anyone that there are factors simply out of our control. Several of my friends, for example, went to bed one night proud of what they had achieved and accumulated in the oil industry. The next morning they woke up to the fact that a few Arab sheiks had more control over the size of my friends' bank accounts than they did. Market conditions, economics, government, health, coworkers, and even the weather affect our ability to accumulate and conserve wealth. All of these thing are out of our control.

So what is the bottom line? If there are things out of our control, we cannot insure our success.

Quite frankly, Americans had a much more spiritual attitude about material wealth when most of us lived on the farm. Men and women who made their living from the soil knew that much of their success was absolutely beyond their control. Good soil conditions, the right combination of sun and rain, along with a lot of back-breaking work and help from their neighbors, was required for success. After completing their work, most of our ancestors fell on their knees and asked their Senior Partner to sovereignly send the sun and rain in correct proportions.

Clearly, God is the source of wealth and prosperity. And from our study we know He deals severely in mercy with those who claim credit for His work. A thorough examination of Scripture also reveals we need a significant paradigm shift if we are going to pass the test of prosperity. Read the following verses:

> When you have eaten and are satisfied, praise the LORD your God for the good land he has given you. Be careful that you do not forget the LORD your God, failing to observe his commands, his laws and his decrees that I am giving you this day. Otherwise, when you eat and are satisfied, when you

build fine houses and settle down, and when your herds and flocks grow large and your silver and gold increase and all you have is multiplied, then your heart will become proud and you will forget the Lord your God, who brought you out of Egypt, out of the land of slavery. He led you through the vast and dreadful desert, that thirsty and waterless land, with its venomous snakes and scorpions. He brought you water out of hard rock. He gave you manna to eat in the desert, something your fathers had never known, to humble and to test you so that in the end it might go well with you. You may say to yourself, "My power and the strength of my hands have produced this wealth for me." But remember the Lord your God, for it is he who gives you the ability to produce wealth, and so confirms his covenant, which he swore to your forefathers, as it is today. (Deuteronomy 8:10-18)

The Lord sends poverty and wealth; he humbles and he exalts. (1 Samuel 2:7)

Why do the wicked live on, growing old and increasing in power? They see their children established around them, their offspring before their eyes. Their homes are safe and free from fear; the rod of God is not upon them. (Job 21:7-9)

I said to the Lord, "You are my Lord;
    apart from you I have no good thing." . . .
Lord, you have assigned me my portion and my cup;
    you have made my lot secure.
The boundary lines have fallen for me in pleasant places;
    surely I have a delightful inheritance. . . .
You have made known to me the path of life;
    you will fill me with joy in your presence,
    with eternal pleasures at your right hand.
      (Psalm 16:2,5-6,11)

Unless the LORD builds the house,
    its builders labor in vain.
Unless the LORD watches over the city,
    the watchmen stand guard in vain.
In vain you rise early and stay up late,
    toiling for food to eat—
    for he grants sleep to those he loves. (Psalm 127:1-2)

When times are good, be happy;
    but when times are bad, consider:
God has made the one
    as well as the other.
Therefore, a man cannot discover
    anything about his future. (Ecclesiastes 7:14)

My God will meet all your needs according to his glorious riches in Christ Jesus. (Philippians 4:19)

Constant friction between men of corrupt mind, who have been robbed of the truth and who think that godliness is a means to financial gain. (1 Timothy 6:5)

It's clear that God is the absolute source of prosperity. He alone determines the boundaries of our lifestyle. While God will not allow us to claim total credit for gaining success, we can, however, cause the loss of success by our lack of faithfulness. On the other hand, don't make the mistake of thinking that the loss of wealth is necessarily a result of unfaithfulness. Take Job for example. God said Job was absolutely righteous, yet he lost everything. In other words, hard work, obedience, and sacrifice don't insure success, but the absence of these may very well precipitate the loss or lack of success.

Anyone might ask then, "If this is true, why should I work hard and play by God's rules if it isn't going to get me anywhere?" The answer is simple. Work hard and play by God's rules because it pleases Him, and because the life of obedience is the life He desires for us. We obey God because of who He is, not primarily for what He will do for us.

If any reason crowds out this prime motivation, we are inviting God's merciful interruption of our lives. God will not be used. We cannot manipulate Him into blessing us. He does what He chooses, and no one can hold back His hand of blessing or adversity. He is absolutely committed to our becoming what He created us to be (which also happens to be the place of greatest fulfillment), and will not allow us to venture far down the road of manipulative obedience. As soon as we hear ourselves saying, "This isn't fair. I played by all the rules!" we know we are operating under a worldly paradigm.

All of this is not to say that our desire for a return on our labor is wrong. Some misguided Christians have joined collectivists in condemning the profit motive in business. However, God Himself made us with a desire to be rewarded for labor. It is an inherent desire of man. Solomon tells us,

> Then I realized that it is good and proper for a man to eat and drink, and to find satisfaction in his toilsome labor under the sun during the few days of life God has given him—for this is his lot. Moreover, when God gives any man wealth and possessions, and enables him to enjoy them, to accept his lot and be happy in his work—this is a gift of God. (Ecclesiastes 5:18-19)

Our ultimate reward, however, comes from God and is not primarily an earthly one. The greatest reward I can ever receive is to stand before Christ and hear Him say, "Well done, good and faithful servant! You have been faithful with a few things; I will put you in charge of many things. Come and share your master's happiness" (Matthew 25:21). This is my destiny as a Christian, my greatest reward. My desire for earthly return for my labor must always remain subject to this ultimate reward. And when life doesn't reward me the way I like, I have the satisfaction of knowing that God's reward can be mine in full measure.

Use Prosperity Properly

If prosperity is a gift of God, it comes with an obligation to use it according to God's will. The sixth chapter of 1 Timothy gives us some helpful insights into a biblical paradigm of success. Listen to Paul's instructions to the prosperous:

> Command those who are rich in this present world not to be arrogant nor to put their hope in wealth, which is so uncertain, but to put their hope in God, who richly provides us with everything for our enjoyment. Command them to do good, to be rich in good deeds, and to be generous and willing to share. In this way they will lay up treasure for themselves as a firm foundation for the coming age, so that they may take hold of the life that is truly life. (1 Timothy 6:17-19)

Some very clear elements of the biblical paradigm of wealth emerge. First, arrogance has no place in the life God has blessed with prosperity. We have no right to use prosperity as a measuring stick of our worth. If it is a gift, then we didn't earn it, don't deserve it, and can't acquire it on our own. So what can we brag about?

Prosperity doesn't say a thing about our worth as people. Far from making us proud, prosperity should make us extremely humble and engender a gracious attitude toward others. To use the clothes we wear, the cars we drive, the things we accumulate, and the houses we buy as measuring sticks—as indications of our superiority—is an absolute abomination to God. It is a slap in the face of our generous heavenly Father. Arrogance says to Him in no uncertain terms, "I did this on my own. I don't need You."

Second, we can't depend on prosperity as a source of security. Pearl Bailey is credited with saying, "Money isn't everything, but it sure does quiet my nerves." Granted, it might temporarily soothe our insecurity, but by its very nature, it is "so uncertain" as Paul says. Those of us living in the 1990s know this to be true. Something so uncertain can't keep the hounds of insecurity at bay for very long. Our only certain source of security is Jesus Christ. I like how *The Living Bible* translates Psalm 23: "Because the Lord is my Shepherd, I have everything I need." God knows exactly what I need, He has every resource available to Him, and He is absolutely committed to my welfare. Now that's security. Why would I want to entrust my safety to anyone or anything else?

Paul's third instruction about prosperity is to enjoy it. God's unchanging intention is that we take pleasure from the gifts He has given us. We shouldn't feel arrogant about prosperity, but neither should we feel guilty about enjoying the good gifts of God. In my experience, only the person who hopes in Christ and understands that prosperity is a gift can really enjoy what God has given. When we rest our security on our wealth, we will always become entangled in preserving it—something we simply can't guarantee. When God says it's over, no man's grip is firm enough to hold on. Most people who strive after wealth eventually find that it controls them rather than their controlling it. When we know that Christ and what He provides is enough, then we can enjoy what God gives.

Fourth, we are to put our wealth to work. The attitude that prevents the enjoyment of God's blessings from slipping into selfish indulgence is compassion toward the needs in the world around us. Paul tells us to be "rich in good deeds, and to be generous and willing to share." In other words, we are not to use wealth as a security blanket, or a score card, but rather as a tool. How big is this tool supposed to be? According to Paul, the extent of my compassionate use of wealth is to be commensurate with the extent of my prosperity. In other words, if I am rich, I am to be rich in good works.

Paul was no stranger to prosperity. He knew that there is a tendency for people to do less, not more, when their prosperity increases. The same holds true today. According to *The Wall Street Journal*, 1 percent of the nation's households own one-third of the nation's private wealth, 60 percent of the corporate stock, 30 percent of interest-bearing assets, and nearly 10 percent of its real estate.[4] Interestingly, the Bible never has a problem with the concentration of wealth in one group. God does, however, have a problem with the fact that this group statistically uses such a small portion of its wealth in any form of charitable causes. Interestingly, in 1991 American households with incomes of less than $10,000 gave an average of 5.5 percent to charity, while those making more than $100,000 gave only 2.9 percent.[5] I don't think that I would commend the latter group for being "rich in good deeds."

Don't misunderstand. God doesn't need our gifts. The godly use of wealth is as much for our benefit as for the needs of the world. If we are not a channel for God's resources, then even His best gifts will become stagnant and pollute our soul. Paul describes God's desires for the cycle of wealth in 2 Corinthians 9:6-11:

Remember this: Whoever sows sparingly will also reap sparingly, and whoever sows generously will also reap generously. Each man should give what he has decided in his heart to give, not reluctantly or under compulsion, for God loves a cheerful giver. And God is able to make all grace abound to you, so that in all things at all times, having all that you need, you will abound in every good work. As it is written:

"He has scattered abroad his gifts to the poor;
his righteousness endures forever."

Now he who supplies seed to the sower and bread for food will also supply and increase your store of seed and will enlarge the harvest of your righteousness. You will be made rich in every way so that you can be generous on every occasion, and through us your generosity will result in thanksgiving to God.

In order for us to "take hold of true life" we will have to turn loose of wealth and let it flow out, as well as in. When we do, God promises always to continue to give us all that we need to accomplish what He desires for us to do.

I ran across a poem by an unknown writer that expresses my frustration with my own attitude so well.

One by one He took them from me
    All the things I honored most;
'Til I was empty-handed;
    Every glittering toy was lost.
And I walked earth's highways, grieving,
    In my rags and poverty.
Until I heard His voice inviting,
    "Lift those empty hands toward Me!"
Then I turned my hands toward heaven,
    And He filled them with a store
Of His own transcendent riches,

'Til they could contain no more.
And at last I comprehended
    With my stupid mind, and dull,
That God cannot pour His riches
    Into hands already full.[6]

If God is the source of prosperity, then its purpose is

- ◆ to bring a sense of accomplishment (Ecclesiastes 5:18-19);
- ◆ to enjoy God's goodness (Proverbs 10:22);
- ◆ to meet the needs of my family (1 Timothy 5:8);
- ◆ to further the teaching of God's Word (1 Timothy 5:17-18);
- ◆ to help others in need and serve my fellow man
  (1 Corinthians 16:1-2);
- ◆ to bring glory to God (2 Corinthians 9:12-15).

The purpose of prosperity is not

- ◆ to satisfy my greeds (1 Timothy 6:17-18);
- ◆ to satisfy my pride (James 1:10);
- ◆ to bring me ease (Luke 12:15-21).

Understand Prosperity's Dangers

The fact that prosperity is so dangerous has made some Christians mistakenly run the other way, making poverty a virtue. However, vows of poverty are just as worldly as greedy ambitions; both focus on the externals rather than the heart. Every Christian needs to understand that if God has given or does give you prosperity in the future, it is a test as well as a blessing. Each of us needs to be aware of the personal dangers and watch for any sign of their infestation in our heart. Here are just a few:

- ◆ Pride (Hosea 13:6)
- ◆ Superiority (Psalm 49:16-20)
- ◆ Self-deception (Psalm 50:21)
- ◆ Injustice (Nehemiah 5, Job 12:5, 1 John 3:17)
- ◆ Grief (Psalm 16:4, Proverbs 23:4-5, 1 Timothy 6:9-10)
- ◆ Anxiety and worry (Ecclesiastes 5:10-12)
- ◆ Poverty of the soul (Luke 9:24)

Make Yourself Accountable to Others

One of the greatest mistakes any Christian can make is to isolate himself and his actions from the scrutiny of others. Accountability is important. But it has also been used unmercifully to assault Christians who dance to a different drumbeat than we do. I have been a victim more than once of brothers who wanted to judge my motives by their personal prejudices.

But the fact remains that I need others to help me see the blind spots in my life. It is difficult for me to spot the creeping pride, the intrusive superiority, the initial withering of the soul that can so easily occur as my eyes shift in almost unnoticeable increments from Jesus to wealth. I need brothers and sisters in Christ who lovingly but firmly remind me that I am made for better stuff than that. So do you.

Be careful not to gather only like-minded individuals around you, thereby thinking you have achieved accountability. I read an interesting article in *The Wall Street Journal* describing why smart people fail. One of the key contributing factors is that highly intelligent people gather other highly intelligent men and women around them who hold the same assumptions. With no one to challenge their faulty thinking, smart people inevitably find themselves at the precipice of failure, incredulous about what has happened.

It doesn't take a trained sociologist to figure out that men and women, almost by default, divide themselves along socio-economic lines. The result is that we tend to talk to ourselves, reinforce our prejudices, and miss our common problems. Our thinking becomes ingrown, perhaps highly intelligent or highly spiritual, but nonetheless ingrown and provincial. Prosperous people tend to foster each other's greed. Less fortunate tend to cut each other too much slack in the areas of self-pity, bitterness, and lack of hope. If we are going to escape the dangers of prosperity, we have to break these barriers.

Unfortunately, most of us break barriers and learn lessons the hard way, like Nebuchadnezzar. There is no teacher of reality like experience, and fortunately God gives this to us generously. Just like Nebuchadnezzar, we can profit from our pain and learn from our mistakes.

The crew of the Double Eagle II certainly understood this. In

August 1978, the first successful six-day trans-Atlantic balloon cross-
ing became a reality when Double Eagle II touched ground in a bar-
ley field in the small village of Miserey, France. Success, however,
did not come easily. Thirteen unsuccessful attempts were made
before this historic trip was completed. Maxie Anderson, one of the
members of the successful crew, evaluated their reason for success:
"I don't think that you can fly the Atlantic without experience, and
that's one reason it hadn't been done before. Success in any venture is just the intelligent application of failure."[7]

Someone said that failure and success are the two greatest
impostors. I would agree. Most of us tend to think that failure means
it's over and success means you have arrived. Nothing could be further from the truth. Even though Nebuchadnezzar failed the test of
prosperity initially, that failure became the back door to enduring
spiritual prosperity. Each of us can learn through our own failures
as well. Who knows what great things God might do through us,
once we have learned to pass the test of prosperity.

THE BIG IDEA

Prosperity and success are gifts, not rights. I am to exercise
stewardship, not ownership, over the things God has given to
me. Otherwise, what I own will possess me.

Use the following thoughts and ideas to stimulate your thinking
about responding to prosperity.

"Where your treasure is, there your heart will be also."
MATTHEW 6:21

"Therefore I tell you, do not worry about your life,
what you will eat or drink; or about your body, what you willl
wear. Is not life more important than food,
and the body more important than clothes?"
MATTHEW 6:25

Do not wear yourself out to get rich;
have the wisdom to show restraint.
Cast but a glance at riches, and they are gone, for they will
surely sprout wings and fly off to the sky like an eagle.
PROVERBS 23:4-5

"Seek first his kingdom and his righteousness,
and all these things will be given to you as well."
MATTHEW 6:33

"What good is it for a man to gain the whole world,
yet forfeit his soul?"
MARK 8:36

If you can keep your head when all about you
Are losing theirs and blaming it on you;
If you can trust yourself when all men doubt you,
But make allowance for their doubting too;
If you can wait and not be tired by waiting,
or being lied about, don't deal in lies;
Or being hated, don't give way to hating,
And yet don't look too good, nor talk too wise;
If you can dream—and not make dreams your master;
If you can think—and not make thoughts your aim;
If you can meet with triumph and disaster,
And treat those two impostors just the same; . . .
If you can talk with crowds and keep your virtue,
Or walk with kings—nor lose the common touch;
If neither foes nor loving friends can hurt you;
If all men count with you, but none too much;
If you can fill the unforgiving minute
With sixty seconds' worth of distance run—
Yours is the Earth and everything that's in it,
And—what is more—you'll be a man, my son!
RUDYARD KIPLING
"If"

*Don't rejoice in successful service,
but rejoice because you are richly related to Christ.*
OSWALD CHAMBERS
My Utmost for His Highest

*There are two tragedies in life. One is to lose your heart's
desire, and the other is to gain it.*
GEORGE BERNARD SHAW

*Few rich men own their own property.
The property owns them.*
ROBERT G. INGERSOLL

*With the great part of rich people, the chief employment
of riches consists in the parade of riches.*
ADAM SMITH
The Wealth of Nations

*Prosperity knits a man to the world.
He feels that he is "finding his place in it,"
while really it is finding its place in him.*
C. S. LEWIS
Screwtape Letters

*You can tell the character of every man
when you see how he receives praise.*
LUCIUS ANNAEUS SENECA

❖

Nothing is easier than self-deceit.
DEMOSTHENES

❖

My best friend is the one who brings out the best in me.
HENRY FORD

God has not called me to be successful;
he has called me to be faithful.
MOTHER TERESA

God cannot give us happiness and peace apart from himself,
because it is not there.
C. S. LEWIS

You never know what is enough
unless you know what is more than enough.
WILLIAM BLAKE

Failure is only the opportunity to begin again more intelligently.
HENRY FORD

To live with small means; to seek elegance rather than luxury,
and refinement rather than fashion; to be worthy,
not respectable, and wealthy, not rich; to study hard,
think quietly, talk gently, act frankly; to listen to the stars
and birds, to babes and sages, with open heart;
to bear on cheerfully, do all bravely, awaiting occasions,
worry never; in a word to, like the spiritual, unbidden
and unconscious, grow up in the common.
WILLIAM ELLERY CHANNING

CHAPTER SIX

The Truth About Consequences
DANIEL 5:1-30

C alvin Coolidge, the twenty-fifth President of the United States, was a man of few words. People called him "Silent Cal." His motto was, "If you don't say anything, you can't be called upon to repeat it." He was so tightlipped that one newspaper man reported, "When he opened his mouth, a moth flew out." One Sunday morning when world news was a little flat, reporters accosted Coolidge as he emerged from church. The dialogue went like this:

"How was church, Mr. President?"

"Fine."

"What did the preacher preach about?"

"Sin."

Trying to prime this reluctant pump, the reporter asked in desperation, "What did he say about it?"

To this question Coolidge uncharacteristically gave a rather lengthy reply. "He was against it."

I am sad to say that this has been one of the more profound public statements made about sin in this century. Theologians and preachers have preferred to say as little as they can about God's holiness, man's sinfulness, and God's wrath toward sin—His judgment. These topics have become associated in our day with fanatics and prophets of doom. If you are like most Americans, you will probably have a hard time remembering the last time you had a conversation about God's holiness, heard a sermon on God's wrath, or read a book that dealt frankly with judgment. It seems as though religious leaders have spent more time trying to make God as palatable to twentieth century taste as possible, rather than introducing the God of the Bible.

But the Bible has no inhibitions. In fact, it labors the point. To the consternation of God's "press agents," there are more references to God's anger and wrath in the Scriptures than to His love and mercy. "Now wait a minute," you may be thinking. "That's the Old Testament. The God of the New Testament is a God of love." He certainly is—just the same as He was in the Old Testament. And He has the same attitude toward sin in both testaments, too. He's against it!

Many people do not realize that the majority of our information about hell comes from the teaching of Christ Himself. From His words, we learn what an agonizing place those who don't escape the effects of sin will call home in eternity. The whole undercurrent of the New Testament flows with the certainty of coming universal judgment while stressing how sinful men and women can get right with God beforehand.

Perhaps the reason the idea of an angry God perplexes so many is that we read His emotions through our own. We make a colossal error if we equate God's attitude and actions toward sin to human anger and revenge. They are vastly different, and it's important that we come to grips with what God reveals to us about Himself in this area. Because He is holy, God is different—very different—from men.

For example, unlike us, God's anger toward sin is never arbitrary. He never "lets off steam." Unfortunately there are times when I come home from a bad day and let my anger and frustration slosh out on my family. God's judgments, on the other hand, are never irrational, and He never loses control. God's feeling about sin is a settled attitude toward evil wherever He finds it. His anger toward that which is destroying His creation and those He loves is both predictable and understandable.

God's action toward sinners is always purposeful. I rarely stop to think about how my anger will affect someone else. But God precisely calculates His response to turn us from a path of destruction back to Him. He wants us to know we are offtrack and heading for disastrous results if we don't change.

Think of it like this. We would severely reprimand a mother or father who let a child play in the street without punishment. That child needs to be warned of impending danger. We would call any parent who didn't take swift action irresponsible. The parent might protest by saying, "He really wanted to play in the street and would be really upset if I called him in. I only wanted to make him happy." If that happened, we would question both the parent's sanity as well as the quality of his or her love for the child.

In the same way, if what the Bible says is true about the eternal destiny of those who continue in sin, the cruelest thing God could do is commit Himself to the happiness of people who persistently choose to rebel against His goodness.

God's judgment is always just. God is committed to administer justice to those who break His law. He is never cruel. He never goes beyond what strict justice requires. Unlike us, He never overreacts. In other words, He never gives us more than what we deserve. That's what makes God's judgment so frightening.

Our problem, however, is that often we evaluate ourselves by those around us. We can always find someone whose actions make us look pretty good. Unfortunately, we also look pretty bad compared to others. God's standards are not some arbitrary comparison of human performance. He evaluates us based on who He created us to be compared to what we are. Compared to that standard of righteousness, we all fall short of God's glory.

Neither is God evaluating us based on the minimal evidence gleaned from observing our outer behavior. He looks at your heart and my heart and the motives behind those things you and I would hold up as our righteousness. Anyone who has contemplated the moral perfection of God and the moral mess within ourselves knows we are in trouble apart from God's mercy.

God's judgment is something men and women choose for themselves. No one remains under God's judgment unless they choose to do so. Strange as it seems, some do just that. Essentially, God's judgment gives us what we choose in all its implications. When we sin, in essence we say to God, "I reject You as my sovereign ruler. I do not want to live under Your domain." In response, God leaves us to our own self-made hell, withdrawing the pleasures and joy of His reign. Though we may raise our fist and demand that He bless us, we have no right to sin and expect Him to fork over the goodies. He will give us exactly what we ask for in sin, even when it is not what we really want.

Although many times we don't recognize it, what we desire is to find satisfaction for our soul, and as His creatures, we can find lasting fulfillment only in God. The consistently focused desire in all of God's judgments is that we experience and recognize the emptiness we have chosen and return to the fullness of a right relationship with Him. His arms are ever open and ready to receive us the moment we change our mind and turn back to Him. John's gracious words make this clear:

> "God so loved the world that he gave his one and only Son, that whoever believes in him shall not perish but have eternal life. For God did not send his Son into the world to condemn the world, but to save the world through him. Whoever believes in him is not condemned, but whoever does not believe stands condemned already because he has not believed in the name of God's one and only Son." (John 3:16-18)

This merciful severity of God is exactly why we have the book of Daniel. The citizens of Judah thumbed their nose at God and expected Him to maintain their prosperous lifestyle. Instead, after numerous warnings, God graciously interrupted their destructive behavior with an invasion by Nebuchadnezzar. As a result, Daniel and eventually most of Judah's citizens who didn't die by the sword ended up in exile in Babylon.

But God was not interrupting only Judah's life. Over Nebuchadnezzar's forty-three-year reign God repeatedly interrupted this proud king's self-aggrandizing schemes. Finally, this powerful despot recognized his need of a relationship with Daniel's God and bowed the knee to the King of kings. There he found a peace and rest he had found nowhere else with all his ability to buy happiness.

God incredibly blessed Nebuchadnezzar and the entire empire through Daniel and the other faithful Jews deported to Babylon. Under Nebuchadnezzar's rule and Daniel's influence, Babylon truly reached its golden age, spiritually and culturally. However, in 562 BC Nebuchadnezzar died. Over the following six years, the gold quickly tarnished under three successive evil kings. Finally, in 556 BC, Nebuchadnezzar's son-in-law Nabonidus seized the throne and held it for seventeen years. In 553 BC, only nine years after Nebuchadnezzar's death, Nabonidus made his son Belshazzar co-regent and ruler over the province of Babylon while Nabonidus retired to Tema in Arabia.

Belshazzar knew of all that God had done for his grandfather, Nebuchadnezzar. Unfortunately, Belshazzar chose not to learn from Nebuchadnezzar's life. He not only rejected his grandfather's God, he rejected his chief advisor as well. By the time we come to the fifth chapter of Daniel, a quarter of a century has passed since Nebuchadnezzar confessed his allegiance to God, and Daniel is nowhere in sight. Since he is no longer an active part of the king's court, God spared Daniel's righteous eyes the decadence that returned to the palace—the kind of decadence that filled the palace as the sun set the evening of October 12, 539 BC. Neither Babylon nor its king would witness another morning. God was about to judge a nation and its unrighteous king.

As the western sky turned red and a cool evening breeze drifted over the ancient city of Babylon, servants frantically made their final preparations for the grandest feast of Belshazzar's reign. The wine stewards checked their casks. They would serve the best wine first. Then when taste buds were dull, they would uncork a lesser quality. An army of cooks perspired in hot kitchens putting the finishing touches on thousands of dishes. In the royal apartments, a thousand of the king's nobles put on their finest robes and jewelry. At most state dinners, women were absent. But this time the harem was a buzz as chamber servants combed, perfumed, and dressed the king's wives and concubines for an evening of degrading display and drunken sexuality.

Incredibly, outside the walls, the army of the Medes and Persians prepared for siege. Cyrus had already crushed Nabonidus's army, and only the city of Babylon lay outside his control. One would think that with your city under siege, you might think twice about throwing a celebration. But inside Babylon's supposed impregnable defenses, the people felt safe. After all, they were behind a moat, a rampart, 100 bronze gates, and walls wide enough to drive four chariots abreast. Probably to bolster the confidence of those inside the besieged city, Belshazzar threw the party of his life.

As the wine casks emptied—so went good sense. Belshazzar's perverted mind, caught in a self-aggrandizing moment, culminated his arrogance. He gave orders to bring in the sacred pitchers and goblets brought back by Nebuchadnezzar from God's Temple in Jerusalem. There were other vessels from other temples in his treasury, but God's vessels were special. Very special—and very sacred. They belonged to the most powerful God in the ancient world—the God who had revealed Himself to and claimed the allegiance of Belshazzar's grandfather.

Belshazzar's line of thinking was clear. If the Babylonian gods had defeated the Hebrew God, then surely they were safe against the puny Persian deities. Belshazzar assured his nobles of this, and offered toast after toast to his gods until everyone was drunk. Since sexual immorality was part of the worship of the chief Babylonian deity, Bel, it is probable that as abundant wine lubricated lust, Belshazzar's nobles threw restraint aside and indulged themselves fully, degrading the women present at the feast.

Like his grandfather before him, Belshazzar's pride kept him from hearing and seeing spiritual reality. Had he heeded the stories of God's pursuit of his grandfather, he would never have challenged God as he did. Unlike his grandfather, however, given the opportunity to respond to God, Belshazzar refused. He did not understand that the privilege of revelation always brings the responsibility of response, and God's patience was finally at an end. Belshazzar chose to live in disregard of what he knew God had revealed of Himself to Nebuchadnezzar. He chose to live outside God's protection. He chose judgment.

Robert Louis Stevenson said, "Everyone sooner or later sits down to a banquet of consequences." Belshazzar may have thought he knew the menu, but he didn't realize that God was serving dessert. As wine brought the temporary illusion of peace, safety, and invincibility, shouting and intoxicated laughter echoed through the banquet hall.

Suddenly all grew deathly quiet. Picture the scene. Hush settled over hundreds of inebriated men and women as table by table of those still clinging to consciousness gasped in horror at the supernatural phenomenon occurring before their eyes. Were they seeing things? No, everyone saw it—everyone except those at the king's table, who sat in a niche facing out over the huge banquet hall. Soon the head table was aware that the only noise in the room was coming from them. They looked out in amazement at the dropped jaws and wide eyes. "What? What's going on?" Then the king turned, looked behind him, and saw it.

Rising from his pillow to stand in unbelief, Belshazzar saw a hand—not floating in space—scratching huge letters into the plaster relief of Belshazzar's accomplishments on the wall behind him. The room was still—only the horrifying scratching noise echoed through the room as the hand finished its message. Then as mysteriously as it came, the hand was gone, leaving only a mysterious message from God and the knocking knees of the king of Babylon. As he stared at the words, his legs gave way. Courage ran like hot wax from his body, and the powerful king collapsed to the floor.

When he had recovered sufficiently, the king called in all his advisors. This elite group had failed to connect on two previous occasions under Nebuchadnezzar, and were up to the plate for their third swing at deciphering God's message. Now with the very words in front of them, this baffled bunch of baggy-eyed bureaucrats went down swinging—three strikes and they were out. As brilliant as they were, they could not decipher the message. The privilege of understanding God's mind belongs to those who know Him. Fortunately, there was someone near who knew God well—Daniel.

Apparently the mood swing in the banquet hall was detected down the halls of the palace as laughter turned to wailing. The queen-mother heard and came to the king. Sizing up the situation, she took control and gave her son some firm advice. In so many words she said, "Pull yourself together and call Daniel. He did it before as chief of your "father's" advisors (Aramaic has no word for grandfather), and he can do it again." She should know. She was Nitocris, Nebuchadnezzar's daughter. Interestingly, she called Daniel by his Hebrew, not his Babylonian, name, which indicates that she knew Daniel personally and probably his God as well.

Mothers seem never to give up. However, there is a time when God says enough. An old hymn reminds us, "Once to every man and nation comes a time when he must choose." That time had come and passed for Belshazzar and Babylon. They had chosen all right—chosen judgment, and God's appointed executioner stood outside the city gates. Babylon, however, would fall not only as a result of the enemy from without, but because of the enemy from within.

THE ENEMY FROM WITHIN

After what must have seemed like an eternity, Daniel, the stately octogenarian, marched into the banquet hall, a stark contrast to the cowering king. When given a chance to speak, there was anger in Daniel's voice. He refused the rewards and rejected the phony words of honor offered by the king. The contrast between Daniel's attitudes in chapters four and five is enormous. Gone was the respect, the personal concern, and the grief that Daniel felt for Nebuchadnezzar as he faced divine judgment in his day. It was replaced by disgust, indifference, and resolve. Why? Nebuchadnezzar was arrogant, but his was an arrogance of ignorance. Belshazzar's arrogance stood in the full midday light of God's revelation.

Before explaining God's message of pronounced judgment, Daniel leveled four acerbic charges against King Belshazzar.

Belshazzar Rejected the Truth

After rehearsing Nebuchadnezzar's pilgrimage to faith, Daniel turned to the king and said, "But you his son, O Belshazzar, have not humbled yourself, though you knew all this." Belshazzar knew the story well. He had known his grandfather, and in all likelihood, was well aware of Nebuchadnezzar's insanity, repentance, conversion, and restoration. He knew that God was the Revealer of hidden things, the Deliverer of those who were faithful to Him, the eternally sovereign Ruler of the world who does what He pleases with the peoples of the earth. Belshazzar knew all of this and yet refused to follow his grandfather's faith. He failed to profit from Nebuchadnezzar's mistakes and refused to take to heart the solemn warnings God had given. He willfully chose to turn his back on the truth.

Belshazzar Arrogantly Challenged God

Daniel's voice boomed the second charge: "You have set yourself up against the Lord of heaven. You had the goblets from his temple

brought to you and you and your nobles, your wives and your concubines drank wine from them." Most men are content just to ignore
God. Unfortunately, Belshazzar didn't stop there. He defied God to
exercise authority over his life, saying in essence, "Stop me if you
can." God rarely drops that kind of challenge.

Belshazzar Worshiped False Gods

With a slow, deliberate gaze at the images of gold, silver, bronze,
iron, wood, and stone scattered around the hall, Daniel marveled
at the idiocy of worshiping them. Given the choice between the one
true God and gods who could neither hear nor speak, these people
chose the latter. Why would someone make that choice? The answer
is clear. We don't have to submit to what we create; it serves us. If
we were honest, most of us would have to admit that we want that
kind of god.

Belshazzar Wasted His Life

Daniel uttered the last incredible charge: "You did not honor the
God who holds in his hand your life and all your ways" (5:23).
Belshazzar had wasted his life and missed the purpose of his being.
Rather than seeking God's glory, he had lived totally for himself.
Now what glory he had would be snuffed out with a swiftness he
could not imagine.

Belshazzar is not the only leader in history who has tried to
muscle in on God's glory. Take Louis XIV of France, for example.
Of all the courts of Europe, Louis XIV had the most magnificent.
He called himself "Louis the Great." Before he died in 1715, he gave
elaborate instructions to be carried out at his funeral. To com-
memorate his greatness, it would be the most spectacular funeral
ever given a European monarch. On his orders, a single candle
burned on his gold coffin, illuminating the darkness to dramatize his
greatness. As the service began, thousands waited in hushed silence.
Bishop Massilon approached the coffin, snuffed out the flame, and
declared in a voice that echoed through the silent cavernous cathedral, "Only God is great!"

Silence answered Daniel's charges, and he turned and read the
four-word inscription: "MENE, MENE, TEKEL, UPARSIN." The message
was composed of three Aramaic words: *mene*, meaning "to number";

tekel, meaning "to weigh"; and *peres* (the singular form of *uparsin*, "to divide." Daniel interpreted each one.

♦ Mene: "God has numbered the days of your reign and brought it to an end."
♦ Tekel: "You have been weighed on the scales and found wanting."
♦ Peres: "Your kingdom is divided and given to the Medes and Persians."

We might paraphrase the message on the wall like this: "Your number is up. You're a moral lightweight. You've squandered your privileges. The party's over." Literally, it was over. Ironic as it may seem, the last official act of the government of Babylon was to reward Daniel, the man who proclaimed its demise. There was no repentance, no wailing, just resignation. In a few hours Belshazzar would be dead. Babylon the Great was assigned its page in history.

THE ENEMY FROM WITHOUT

While the party raged on into the evening, the Persian camp came to life, making final preparations for a party of their own for Belshazzar. According to the historian Heroditus, Cyrus divided his army into three groups. One group gathered in the north where the Euphrates River entered the city. The second group gathered in the south where the river exited the city. A third group marched upstream where they diverted the river into a swamp, making it fordable downstream at the city. The Persian army waded the river and entered Babylon without a fight.

The most powerful empire of the ancient world fell that night without a fight, unable to defend itself against the judgment of God. Not to diminish the Persian force without, Babylon's real enemy was within. Unlike his grandfather, Belshazzar refused to respond to God's revelation, wasted his life, and suffered the irreversible consequences. The same can happen to any man or culture that turns away from the truth.

As I read this chapter at this time in our nation's history, I can't help but wonder all the more how close we are to God's judgment on America. At some point we may go too far, setting in motion events as impossible as delaying the sunset on that fateful day 2500 years ago in Babylon.

IS THE SUN SETTING ON NORTH AMERICA?

Ominous shadows are falling across our great land, and many social critics are predicting a new "dark age" as Western civilization falters under the attack of a new breed of barbarian. The Goths and Vandals of our present age are not the crazed, drunken invaders from without, but polished, persuasive, pleasant men and women from within who have rejected the truth. Scandal follows our leaders like a bad dream. Everywhere men and women trade convictions for cash, sacrifice integrity on the altar of success, and allow unbridled greed to eclipse character.

The darkness invades every area of life: politics, education, law, medicine, the arts. Even our most trusted institutions seem to be vulnerable. Many look at the church with cynicism, rendered impotent by hypocrisy from within. Sadly, there are enough church leaders who are as greedy and debauched as anyone in the culture, giving pause to even the faithful. The bedrock of society, the family, seems to be coming apart at the seams, and relationships are riddled by selfishness.

It doesn't take a Ph.D. in sociology to figure out that our culture is facing a threat of colossal proportions that could mean the end of the U.S. as we know it. It is not the danger of global warming, nuclear holocaust, or economic collapse. It is not the instability of the Middle East or the uncertainty of the Balkans. None of our former enemies maintain significant strength to cause a threat. As in the case of Babylon, it is a threat from within that threatens to undo two hundred years of history. Chuck Colson warns us with these words in *Against the Night*:

> The crisis that threatens us, the force that could topple our monuments and destroy our very foundation, is within ourselves. The crisis is in the character of our culture, where the values that restrain inner vices and develop inner virtues are eroding. Unprincipled men and women, disdainful of

their moral heritage and skeptical of Truth itself, are destroying our civilization by weakening the very pillars upon which it rests.[1]

The spiritual disease that plagued ancient Babylon is roaring unchecked through our society. Without a doubt, short of ancient Israel, no nation in human history has received the blessings God has poured on the United States of America. Nowhere has God's Word been so freely and widely proclaimed. No country has been so blessed materially by divine providence. Likewise, no culture outside ancient Israel has so turned from its Benefactor and rejected the truth in such a wholesale fashion. Oh yes, this is still a religious nation. We just don't listen to God anymore. As George Gallup describes us, "Religion is up, morality down." A large number of us still attend church regularly; we just don't let religion interfere with the rest of life.

The courts have banned spiritual truth from our educational system. Ideas of right and wrong have almost collapsed. Relativism has seized the minds of many of our educators, media leaders, physicians, and clergy. When you call someone's behavior "sinful," you may be violating someone's "civil rights." Right has been called wrong and has found its way into print.

For three centuries our cultural conceptions of right and wrong rested firmly on the teaching of the Bible. Holding to biblical ideas of right and wrong today, however, will get you scorned, laughed at, pitied, and sometimes attacked. In an article appearing in the February 1, 1993, edition of *The Washington Post*, Christians who phoned the Capitol to protest Clinton's lifting of the ban on homosexuals in the military were referred to as "poor, uneducated and easy to command." Consider also the slanderous association made on ABC's "20/20":

In the 1920s, the Ku Klux Klan urged the nation to adopt family values and return to the old-time religion. Similarly, Adolph Hitler launched a family-values regimen. Hitler's [methodology] centered on his ideas of motherhood. Fanatics in the Ku Klux Klan, the Nazi Party, the Hezbooah, or any other intolerant organization refer to themselves as religious warriors. As warriors, fanatics censor the thoughts of others and love to burn books. In the modern United States, new proponents of family values continue this tradition of fear and intolerance.[2]

If we stand up for the moral issues the Bible says are black and white, we can expect abuse in the 1990s.

These challenges on traditional values are not just friendly disagreements. They are challenges to the vitality of our nation. The quicksand of relativistic thinking cannot provide the basis for the individual responsibility needed to sustain freedom in a democracy. Self-government relies on discipline, and discipline on personal virtue. Secularism simply cannot nourish the character needed to produce self-governing individuals.

In the vacuum left by the banishment of spiritual truth, a new selfish individualism has taken the seat of ascendancy. Not only do we as a culture no longer ask what responsibilities we have toward others, we focus on what others owe us. We are "entitled" to whatever makes us happy. Losing our focus on the only One who can bring us pleasure, we have become fixated on pleasing ourselves.

Called by nothing higher than our selfish interests, we watch self-discipline erode. Left with nothing higher than our own self-interest to pull us higher than self, decadence is the natural next step. Social critic Russell Kirk has defined decadence as the loss of an aim or object in life. He writes, "Men and women become decadent when they forget or deny the objects of life, and so fritter away their years in trifles or debauchery."[3] Sound like Babylon? How about North America? Like Belshazzar and his nobles, we drown our fear about "the enemy without" by indulging in temporary pleasures that bring us a little relief from the haunting reality of an empty life. We don't want to know the truth. We want to hide in the dark.

If you think that this is scary, just read on. Three days into his new administration, President Bill Clinton took pen in hand and issued four executive orders lifting a degree of restraint in our growing disregard for life. They are as follows: (1) the ban on using "fetal tissue" for medical research was lifted; (2) the ban on abortion counseling in federally funded clinics was rescinded; (3) the importation process of the controversial abortion-inducing drug RU 486 was begun; (4) funding was provided for abortions in military hospitals overseas. Although he intended to, under duress, he did not sign the executive order that day lifting the ban on homosexuals in the military.[4] The frightening thought is that Bill Clinton probably knows what the Bible says about these things. Like Belshazzar, he seems to be disregarding what he knows to be true.

Writing nineteen hundred years ago, Chrysostom described us well: "Like men with sore eyes, they find the light painful, while the darkness, which permits them to see nothing, is restful and agreeable." Christ said it like this:

> "This is the verdict: Light has come into the world, but men loved darkness instead of light because their deeds were evil. Everyone who does evil hates the light, and will not come into the light for fear that his deeds will be exposed. But whoever lives by the truth comes into the light, so that it may be seen plainly that what he has done has been done through God." (John 3:19-21)

Don't misunderstand me. I believe the United States is still the greatest nation in the world. But the gulf between what we are and what we should be is alarming. The fact is that no nation or people that rejects God and His Word will escape His judgment. If we continue to walk in the darkness and presume on God's patience, we can expect the same fate as Babylon. It may not come overnight, but greatness and prosperity will slip from our grasp like water through open fingers. While we focus on pleasing ourselves, someone will steal our country and our freedom, and we will have no one to blame but ourselves.

HOW TO AVOID A WASTED LIFE

Like it or not, God holds each of us responsible for all that we do. Paul said it like this: "Do not be deceived: God cannot be mocked. A man reaps what he sows" (Galatians 6:7). Notice that this warning is given to individuals, not societies, though it is certainly applicable to the latter. If we are able to turn back the barbarians and the light begins to shine again in our land, it will be because men and women like you and me reflect the light one person at a time not with bullhorns and slogans, but with a personal righteousness that others cannot deny. Joe Stowell was right when he wrote,

> It is time to start reclaiming the most powerful weapon we have against the darkness. A weapon that seems to have suffered as we have picketed and politicked as though revival comes through governmental power. This weapon is the weapon of individual proclamation of light. . . . It is ignited not through public policy statements but rather in and through individual lives that are nonnegotiably committed to thinking and living from a biblical point of view.[5]

Otherwise, we will fare no better than Belshazzar and waste our life pursuing personal pleasure at the expense of God's glory. How can we avoid that kind of waste?

Listen Carefully to God

Never before in the history of the world has the Word of God been so freely accessible to God's people. As I look at my bookshelf, I count seven versions of the Bible. When I walk into a Christian bookstore, there are virtually thousands of books that proclaim God's Word. With this abundant privilege comes a tremendous responsibility—the responsibility of listening carefully and obeying.

When I read about Daniel and Belshazzar in Daniel 5, I think of the contrast in Psalm 1.

> Blessed is the man
>   who does not walk in the counsel of the wicked
> or stand in the way of sinners
>   or sit in the seat of mockers.
> But his delight is in the law of the LORD,
>   and on his law he meditates day and night.
> He is like a tree planted by streams of water,
>   which yields its fruit in season
> and whose leaf does not wither.
>   Whatever he does prospers.
> Not so the wicked!

> They are like chaff
> that the wind blows away. (verses 1:1-4)

This psalm begs the question, To whom are we listening? To the world with its inverted sense of morality? To the hedonist with his nearsighted focus? To the pragmatist who says, "If it works it must be right"? To the skeptic who says, "Prove it"? Or to Jesus Christ who said, "Thy Word is truth"?

What is God trying to say to you and me? Are we listening? Every one of us needs the constant communication that God makes available to us through His Word. As Psalm 1 says, we need to meditate on God's Word—read it and think about its meaning and application to our lives. We live in a day when images and messages that need evaluation by the truth constantly bombard us. When the message of our culture and the Word of God call us in different directions, we have to choose. We can't ride the fence or segment our lives into spiritual and secular so we can pretend to obey God in one area, while living by another value system in another.

What I do with God's Word will determine whether I am a lightweight like Belshazzar, easily toppled by the winds of change and adversity, or a strong, stable individual like Daniel, firmly planted in the truth; the kind of person who receives God's blessing, or the individual who falls into judgment; the kind of individual who impacts my culture or the person who is squeezed into the culture's mold.

Don't Move the Goal Line

Imagine a football game in which the goal line was constantly being moved. You would have eleven frustrated defensive players not knowing what line they were defending and eleven offensive players not knowing what point they had to reach to score. A sport like that would lose popularity fast, but in the realm of morality that is exactly what is going on in our country. Every time we turn around, we have a new list of what is sinful and what is not.

That certain things are sinful was not determined by some divinely capricious act calculated to make us miserable and keep us from the pleasures of life. In fact, God created every pleasure we can experience in this world. Satan created nothing—he can only pervert what God created. For example, our problem is not that we love sex or the beautiful form of God's creatures, but that we demand to enjoy this outside the marriage bond. Food is another example. The reason the taste of chocolate is so exquisite is because it is a gift of God. But some indulge in excess, and the enjoyment of food becomes the sin of gluttony. Money is not the root of all kinds of evil; the love of both money and the things that money can do are the problem. Satan takes these and the millions of pleasures God has given us in this world and trains us that we need these things above all else. Anytime the pleasures of God replace Him, it is sin.

Essentially, sin is that which is contrary to God's nature. That which is good by nature is congruent with His being. Far from wanting to deprive us of joy, God warns His creatures about those things that are destructive to those He created in His image.

As a Christian, I have no need to move God's standards. I realize that God wants the very best for me. If something is out of bounds, I can accept the limit, knowing that God wants only the very best for me. When I transgress these bounds, I have no need to justify my behavior, cover it, or change the rules to make myself acceptable. I have Jesus Christ, the atoning sacrifice for my sin, who stands as my Advocate before the Father and proclaims my purity. I can freely confess and admit when I am wrong and claim the promise of 1 John 1:9—"If we confess our sins, he is faithful and just and will forgive us our sins and purify us from all unrighteousness." When we begin to redefine what sin is, not only do we confuse others, but we miss the forgiveness and reconciliation available in Christ.

Live in Humility
Daniel's first accusation against Belshazzar was arrogance; knowing all he did, he still refused to humble himself. Giving God the place in our lives that He actually occupies in the universe is the first order of business for all of God's creatures. That He has given us a choice is at once a great mystery and precisely why we can have a person-to-person relationship with Him. As a person, I can choose to live life on my own or under His lordship.

Consider the tremendous humility of God who seeks sinners, who waits patiently for us to repent, and who repeatedly forgives our arrogance when we turn to Him. He has no prideful attitude, because He has nothing to lose. Our obedience to Him adds nothing to Him—and disobedience takes nothing away. But it makes all the difference in the world to you and me. The cost of nondiscipleship, as Dallas Willard describes it, is incredibly high:

> Abiding peace, a life penetrated throughout by love, faith that sees everything in the light of God's overriding governance for good, hopefulness that stands firm in the most discouraging of circumstances, power to do what is right and withstand the forces of evil. In short, it costs exactly that abundance of life Jesus said he came to bring (John 10:10).[6]

The wonderful thing about submitting ourselves to Christ is that not only do we avoid God's judgment, but we experience all of His richness in the abundant life of Jesus.

Never Give Up

I'm sure Daniel must have often wondered what God was doing during the years he watched Babylon's rapid return to paganism. Our job, of course, is not to change the world, but to be faithful to God, to pray for our communities (Jeremiah 29:7), to confront sin graciously when necessary, and call men and women to repentance (Daniel 4:27).

If Daniel's life reminds us of anything, it is that even the godliest of lives cannot guarantee the salvation of a culture from judgment. But good men and women can influence societies for good, and individual lives can be changed. Chuck Colson makes our aim crystal clear: "Our goal is to be faithful to the holy God who calls us to be the church, whether we actually make a difference in our world or whether it falls to pieces around us and dissolves into a stew of secularism."[7] We never know, however, when a sovereign God might use us as He did Daniel. Therefore, we need to be ready. In his years of retirement from public life, Daniel did not grow lazy or slack. He kept himself ready because he was faithful. When God returned Daniel to public life, he was as sharp as ever.

In the September 6 meditation in *My Utmost for His Highest*, Oswald Chambers reminds us that the life of Christ in us is like a river (John 7:38).

A river is victoriously persistent, it overcomes all barriers. For a while it goes steadily on its course, then it comes to an obstacle and for a while it is balked, but it soon makes a pathway round the obstacle. Or a river will drop out of sight for miles, and presently emerge again broader and grander than ever.[8]

Chambers goes on to remind us that although we might see God using others, there are times, because of some obstacle, that we can't see that we are any use at all. In times like these, when we seem to lack influence, we need to keep our focus on the Source of life, not the obstacle. Chambers reminds us, "The obstacle is a matter of indifference to the river which will flow steadily through you if you remember to keep right at the Source."

I don't know about you, but the obstacle is not a matter of indifference to me. I usually push, scream, and plead until I am discouraged and despair that God will ever do anything with me again. I am sad to admit that there are times when the influence I have for Christ is more important to me than my relationship with Him. How ironic. Not only am I actually living for myself rather than Christ, but I am slowing the flow of the only Force in my life that can move the obstacle, the powerful river of the life of Christ flowing through me.

During the times when we wonder what God is doing, we need to bear down on our relationship with Jesus, not the removal of the obstacle. We can allow nothing to come between Christ and us. If we keep our channel to the Source open and unconstricted, we can be sure rivers of living water will flow into us and then spring up to eternal life in others.

THE BIG IDEA

Privilege brings responsibility. When men and cultures continue to refuse God's mercy and His revelation, they can expect judgment. The life of a godly man or woman is the most powerful force on earth to turn men and women as well as nations back to God.

Use the following thoughts and ideas to stimulate your thinking about pride and its results.

A man who remains stiff-necked after many rebukes
will suddenly be destroyed—without remedy.
PROVERBS 29:1

Seek the LORD while he may be found;
call on him while he is near.
Let the wicked forsake his way and the evil man his thoughts.
Let him turn to the LORD, and he will have mercy on him,
and to our God, for he will freely pardon.
ISAIAH 55:6-7

"Then they will know that I am the LORD,
when I have made the land a desolate waste because of all
the detestable things they have done."
EZEKIEL 33:29

If any man builds on this foundation using gold,
silver, costly stones, wood, hay or straw,
his work will be shown for what it is,
because the Day will bring it to light. It will be revealed by fire,
and the fire will test the quality of each man's work.
1 CORINTHIANS 3:12-13

I have fought the good fight, I have finished the race,
I have kept the faith. Now there is in store for me the crown
of righteousness, which the Lord, the righteous Judge,
will award to me on that day—and not only to me,
but also to all who have longed for his appearing.
2 TIMOTHY 4:7-8

A good many people fret themselves over the rather improbable
speculation that the earth may be blown asunder
by nuclear weapons. The grimmer and more immediate
prospect is that men and women may be reduced
to a sub-human state through limitless indulgence
in their own vices—with ruinous consequences to society.
RUSSELL KIRK

We have reached a point in history when
the unchecked pursuit of truth,
without regard to its social consequences,
will bring to a swift end the pursuit of truth . . . by wiping out
the very civilization that has favored it.
That would indeed be the judgment of God.
LEWIS MUMFORD

Man can only be free through mastery of himself.
SAMUEL E. MORRISON

Liberty means responsibility. That's why most men dread it.
GEORGE BERNARD SHAW

The Christian ideal has not been tried and found wanting. It
has been found difficult and left untried.
G. K. CHESTERTON
What's Wrong with the World

In the end, more than they wanted freedom,
they wanted security and a comfortable life.
When the Athenians finally wanted not to give to the state,
but for the state to give to them; when the freedom they wished
for most was freedom from responsibility,
then Athens ceased to be free.
EDITH HAMILTON

Societies are tragically vulnerable
when the men and women who compose them lack character.
A nation or a culture cannot endure for long
unless it is undergirded by common values such as valor,
public-spiritedness, respect for others and for the law; it cannot
stand unless it is populated by people who will act on motives
superior to their own immediate interest. Keeping the law,
respecting human life and property, loving one's family, fighting
to defend national goals, helping the unfortunate, paying
taxes—all these depend on the individual virtues of courage,
loyalty, charity, compassion, civility, and duty.
CHUCK COLSON

As a thinking being, the modern Christian
has succumbed to secularization.
He accepts religion—its morality, its worship,
its spiritual culture; but he rejects the religious view of life,
the view which sets all earthly issues
within the context of the eternal.
HARRY BLAMIRES
The Christian Mind

The future is something which everyone reaches
at a rate of sixty minutes an hour,
whatever he does, whoever he is.
C. S. LEWIS

Living in the Lions' Den Without Being Eaten

DANIEL 5:31–6:28

A few years ago Harvey McKay wrote a best-selling book entitled *Swim with the Sharks Without Being Eaten*. Whether the metaphor is sharks or lions, you and I will encounter people who consider their appetites and desires substantially more important than our welfare. In fact, the higher we climb the ladder of influence, the more sharks and lions we'll meet. Count on it. Given the opportunity, unprincipled men and women will eat us alive. They can do this, however, only if we condescend to live on their level and play by their rules.

Personally, I have always thought of myself as a fairly likable person. I have heard not a few people say, "If they can't get along with Bill Peel, they have a problem." In my mid-thirties, I read passages in the Psalms about David and his enemies, and wondered to myself what it would be like to have someone hate my guts. Little did I know that by becoming senior pastor of a church, I would have plenty of opportunities to learn what this feels like.

Now in my mid-forties, I know what it is like to have an enemy. I know what it is like for someone to try to eat me alive, attempt to destroy my reputation, and attack my integrity. I have felt the white-hot heat of face-to-face conflict with someone who questioned my relationship with God, and demeaned my ability to serve Christ.

Encounters like this tend to make a person wonder whether the monks didn't have a pretty good idea; find a remote cave and shut yourself off from the world.

But there are two problems with the isolation approach. First, God has called us to engage the world fully, not retreat from it. In fact, as a Christian, I am much more dangerous to the lions than they are to me. I have the ability to face unprincipled men and women and win the conflict without succumbing to the temptation to fight by their rules of combat.

Second, as long as we are on this earth, we can count on Satan to stir up strife, even among Christian brothers and sisters. We will never reach a point in life—spiritually, vocationally, or socially—where we can expect smooth sailing. As long as we walk this planet, the potential of an attack is always present. This is especially true if we attempt to live for Christ, rather than slide for home.

At eighty-plus-years old, Daniel had no notion of sliding for home or coasting to Heaven—taking the easy road around potential lions. As Israel's seventy-year captivity came to a close, he knew this was no time to shrink from his responsibility to serve God and his fellowman. Even though it would have been easy for him to play it safe, Daniel again accepted a prominent place in public service when the new Persian government took over.

Whenever I read the sixth chapter of Daniel, I think of Frank Carter. Frank was a hard-working gas station owner for most of his life. At sixty-five he figured he was ready for a new challenge, sold his business, and did volunteer work for several ministries he loved. He was seventy-five and going strong when I first met him, busier than he had ever been in his life. He told me that he was going to have to retire from retirement so he could get some rest. I knew he was kidding. To him, those were the best years of his life. Whenever I asked Frank how he was doing, he had a standard reply. With a big grin that stretched across his lean face, he said, "If it got any better I couldn't stand it." He reminds me of a poem I heard called "How to Live."

> Don't be bashful.
>> Bite in.
> Pick it up with your fingers and
>> let the juice that may

> run down your chin.
> Life is ready and ripe.
> NOW
> Whenever you are.[1]

There was no way Frank would waste the best years of his life sliding for home. Neither would Daniel.

Verse 31 of Daniel 5 marks an historic transition. On October 12, 539 BC Belshazzar reigned as king of Babylon. On October 13, Darius the Mede took over the kingdom at the age of sixty-two. Bible scholars have disagreed whether Darius was a titular name for Cyrus (the supreme ruler of the Medo-Persian empire), or his chief general. It seems to me that the latter makes sense, Darius being appointed king of the province of Babylon, within the kingdom of Persia. As such, he was responsible to Cyrus, king of all Persia, for the affairs of Babylon.

In this capacity, Darius immediately began to reorganize the government of his province. He started by appointing 120 satraps who ruled over various parts of the kingdom. Over these individuals, Darius appointed three administrators. He charged them specifically with holding the satraps accountable "so the king might not suffer loss." One of these three satraps was Daniel.

Think about it a moment: new boss; new staff; new responsibilities; new procedures; new culture; add an eighty-plus-year-old government official brought out of retirement. Would you really expect to read in verse 3, "Now Daniel so distinguished himself among the administrators and satraps by his exceptional qualities that the king planned to set him over the whole kingdom." Note the three things we learn here about Daniel.

First, he was competent. The words *distinguished himself* translated literally from the Aramaic mean "to show one's self prominent." Daniel did excellent work. In fact, he did it decidedly better than anyone else. Over the years, God had moved him into a position that fully engaged his God-given core competencies. Rather than drain him, his work enthused and invigorated him emotionally and physically, because he was able to do what God had created him to do. As a result, no one could keep up with Daniel even in his eighties. No wonder Darius planned to place the entire kingdom under Daniel's able administration.

Second, Daniel was a man of character. "Exceptional qualities" characterized Daniel. He was a godly, Christlike man. Qualities like love, joy, peace, patience, goodness, kindness, faithfulness, gentleness, and self-control described his life. As the Apostle Paul wrote, "Against such there is no law" (Galatians 5:22). People of every time and place have respected these qualities. Unfortunately, many individuals fear that these characteristics make them very vulnerable in the dog-eat-dog environment of the workplace. This would be true if Jesus Christ was not present as the Lord of the workplace. Daniel faced every bit as hostile an environment as any of us faces today, and he found God faithful to protect him.

Third, Daniel had an incredible capacity. Not only was Daniel able to handle one-third of the entire province of Babylon, Darius was about to set Daniel over the entire kingdom. This was no small assignment since Babylon covered a land mass roughly half the size of the United States—in a day before fax machines!

Daniel's competence, character, and capacity for work opened doors to greater opportunities for influence—and soon led him into direct conflict with his peers. Unfortunately, not everyone wants to celebrate the success of another peson. More often than not, I hear negative comments coupled with the report of someone's success. "Did you hear that Joe's oil well came in at over a thousand barrels a day?" "Yeah, I heard but I don't believe it. He exaggerates about every well he ever drilled." Or, "Did you hear about Sally's promotion?" "Yeah, I heard. I wonder whose ego she polished to get it." Or "Did you see Jack's new car?" "Yeah, I wonder which of the kids he sold to buy it." Underlying each of these comments is a jealousy that runs deep in the human heart.

THE CONSPIRACY

It was no different 2500 years ago. As soon as Daniel's peers heard of the king's plan to promote him, they determined to sabotage his success. With probability on their side, they reasoned that any government official who had been around as long as Daniel must have a few skeletons in the closet somewhere. The Bible tells us what they found:

At this, the administrators and satraps tried to find grounds for charges against Daniel in his conduct of government affairs, but they were unable to do so. They could find no corruption in him, because he was trustworthy and neither corrupt nor negligent. Finally these men said, "We will never find any basis for charges against this man Daniel unless it has something to do with the law of his God." (6:4-5)

Today when good men won't run for office because of ubiquitous investigative reporters looking for dirt, it seems incredible that Daniel's enemies came up with absolutely nothing. They monitored his bank accounts, audited his books, checked the document shredder (cuneiform crusher in his day). He was not misusing the palace post office, writing hot checks, sexually harassing his female (or male) office staff, or involved in the Euphrates River Development Scandal. There were no bribes, no coverups, no scandals. The only evidence they found confirmed the wisdom of Darius' decision to promote Daniel.

◆ They found him to be *faithful*. He was "trustworthy."
◆ They found him to be *pure*. There was no "corruption."
◆ They found him to be *diligent*. There was no "negligence."

While Nebuchadnezzar and Belshazzar failed the test of prosperity, Daniel passed with flying colors. At the pinnacle of his career, publicly and privately, he was the same man—a man of impeccable integrity. What a contrast to Daniel's accusers. Trustworthy? Hardly. Free of corruption? These twisted men were out for their own advancement. Diligent? Do you think they did this on their time? Cunning? Now we're on target. Unable to find a problem anywhere, they created one.

Drawing a double blank in Daniel's public and private affairs, his enemies knew they would have to somehow trump him regarding his faith. The trap they set for Daniel was an incredible compliment to his integrity. The whole plot rested on Daniel's stubborn commitment to his God. Apart from his integrity, their plan would have been a washout.

The conspirators began to put their plot together. Appealing to

Darius's pride, the administrators and satraps tricked him into creating a law they knew Daniel would violate because of his commitment to God. In a show of solidarity, the conspirators sought an audience with the new king and presented their request:

> O King Darius, live forever! The royal administrators, prefects, satraps, advisers and governors have all agreed that the king should issue an edict and enforce the decree that anyone who prays to any god or man during the next thirty days, except to you, O king, shall be thrown into the lions' den. Now, O king, issue the decree and put it in writing so that it cannot be altered—in accordance with the laws of the Medes and Persians, which cannot be repealed. (6:6-8)

With the transition to the Persian government, this seemed to be a good idea—a pledge of allegiance, so to speak, to their new country. Obviously it was also an ego trip for Darius. Taking the bait, Darius signed the order making it law before he thought things through.

You might think that this wouldn't present a problem for the king. If he changed his mind, he could change the law. Unfortunately the conspirators did their homework well. Under Babylon the rule was rex lex: the king is law. In Persia, it was lex rex: the law is king. Though the king made the law, he also became subject to it. The moment he signed the decree, Darius put in motion forces that were beyond his legal control. He was caught by a plan calculated to cost Daniel his faith or his life. Either way, the conspirators believed they had Daniel neutralized.

DANIEL'S CONSISTENCY

What happened next shouldn't surprise me, but it does. Daniel's raw integrity seems almost outrageous in our culture, which is so used to hypocrisy and scandal in high places.

> Now when Daniel learned that the decree had been published, he went home to his upstairs room where the windows opened toward Jerusalem. Three times a day he got

down on his knees and prayed, giving thanks to his God,
just as he had done before. (6:10)

My first reaction as I read of the plot was, "This is not a problem. We can find a way around this." After all, who can stop a person from praying silently to himself? Daniel, however, kept everything in the open. He consistently walked through his daily prayer
routine as if the decree did not exist. As I see it, he had three choices:
(1) cease to pray; (2) close the window and pray in secret; or (3) pray
as usual.

Each choice had a tremendous price tag. Ceasing to pray would
have cost him his fellowhship with God—the one Person who could
deliver him. Praying in secret or silence would have cost him his
ability to influence those around him. Whatever his motives, everyone else would have thought he had sacrificed his relationship with
God in order to save his hide. The third option, praying as usual,
would cost him his life if the conspirators had their way. Taking the
lesser of three sacrifices, he chose to put his life on the line rather
than sacrifice either God's glory or God's fellowship on the altar of
security. Daniel prayed "just as he had done before."

The scene is almost comical—a large number of the king's officials following at a safe distance as Daniel returned to his home.
Other pedestrians must have stopped and stared as these men,
dressed in their robes of state, tried to move inconspicuously through
the streets of Babylon. Their excitement grew as they watched from
hiding when Daniel came to the window—and then knelt toward
Jerusalem and prayed openly. They had him! Or so they thought!
They forgot that he was praying to and asking for help from the God
who delivers.

Not surprisingly, the conspirators wasted no time in returning
to the king with their evidence. These lightweight, unprincipled men
are enough to make anyone ill. Notice how they presented the situation to the king as if they had nothing to do with it:

"Did you not publish a decree that during the next thirty
days anyone who prays to any god or man except to you, O
king, would be thrown into the lions' den?"
The king answered, "The decree stands—in accordance

with the laws of the Medes and Persians, which cannot be repealed."

Then they said to the king, "Daniel, who is one of the exiles from Judah, pays no attention to you, O king, or to the decree you put in writing. He still prays three times a day." (6:12-13)

What do you think was Darius's reply? Anger? Rage? "When the king heard this, he was greatly distressed; he was determined to rescue Daniel and made every effort until sundown to save him." Isn't his response surprising in the context of the angry, arrogant kings we encountered previously? What would have precipitated this unusual response?

The king's part in this certainly distressed him. Most of us live to regret decisions made in haste. But there is something more compelling and personal here. It was more than the pity of nobility or hatred of injustice. In the short time they had worked together, Darius had developed a deep respect and love for this eighty-year-old administrator.

Love demanded forgiveness. Justice demanded retribution. There was no way of escape for Darius. As brilliant as he must have been, human wisdom could not untangle this dilemma. But just to make sure, the conspirators gathered again to press the law. "So the king gave the order, and they brought Daniel and threw him into the lions' den. The king said to Daniel, "May your God, whom you serve continually, rescue you!" Recognizing he was powerless, Darius did the only thing left. He hoped against all his sixty-two years of pagan experience that the God in whom Daniel had absolute confidence did exist.

Typically, Daniel remained quiet. While everyone else was screaming and accusing, Daniel let his integrity speak for him. Sometimes silence speaks louder than any shout, and calmness is more compelling than any argument. After all, the name Daniel means "God is my judge." He humbled himself under the mighty hand of God and waited, just like Christ: "And while being reviled, He did not revile in return; while suffering, He uttered no threats, but kept entrusting Himself to Him who judges righteously" (1 Peter 2:22, NASB).

As the huge stone was rolled into position covering the mouth of the den, Darius must have felt the weight of the world roll onto his heart. In silence the king and his nobles officially sealed the den, imprinting their signet rings into the hot wax of the seal. The seal alerted anyone who might open the den before morning that they were interfering with Persian justice and were subject to immediate death. With Daniel's fate in God's hands, the conspirators went home to celebrate. Darius went to his palace to mourn: "Then the king returned to his palace and spent the night without eating and without any entertainment being brought to him. And he could not sleep."

How long has it been since you laid awake at night worrying about someone you loved? Darius's response was an indication not only of a tender heart and a deep friendship, but also of a fledgling faith. A thousand thoughts must have crowded the king's mind. As an ancient Near Eastern monarch, he was no stranger to execution. The thing that distressed him was Daniel's welfare. "Is he safe, or dead already? Is his God really who Daniel says He is? Is He able to save him?" Catching himself, Darius must have marveled that this man so affected him in the few months they had worked together.

SLEEPLESS IN BABYLON

As Darius stared at the ceiling, his budding faith did battle with deep-rooted reason: "Have I ever seen anyone emerge from the lions' den? No! Have I ever seen this God whom Daniel worships? No. Have I seen anything that would make me believe He exists at all? Not to my knowledge. But this man Daniel is absolutely committed to Him. Daniel is such an incredible man. He is enough to make me wonder—to make me hope his God really does exist."

It's not inconceivable that Darius uttered his first prayer to God that sleepless evening. It might have gone something like this:

Most High God of Daniel and the Hebrew exiles, I don't even know if You exist. Daniel says You rescue and save, and he trusts You implicitly. He says Your dominion reaches throughout the earth even into this palace, and I guess into the lions' den. If You are who Daniel believes You to be, rescue my friend from the power of the lions.

Knowing his religious heritage and man's natural tendency to want to offer something to bargain with God, I'm sure Darius added, "And if You do, I will proclaim Your greatness throughout my kingdom and call on men everywhere to fear and reverence Your name."

Dawn came like molasses in January, but the first light of the next day found Darius at the mouth of the lions' den: "At the first light of dawn, the king got up and hurried to the lions' den. When he came near the den, he called to Daniel in an anguished voice." Personally, I think that there was some delay in Daniel's reply—partly because God has a sense of the dramatic, and partly because Darius woke Daniel from a sound sleep. Since the Bible follows Darius rather than Daniel, we know what happened in the palace, but we are left to our imagination as to Daniel's night. Doubt brought disquiet and anxiety to the palace, but faith brought rest to the lions' den. Faith is something Daniel had plenty of. In fact, the "Hall of Fame of Faith" in Hebrews 11 probably refers to Daniel, "who through faith . . . shut the mouths of lions." James Graham imagines what might have happened in the lions' den:

> As the guards closed the aperture and went their way, Daniel slid gradually to the floor of the den. The big lions that had come bounding from their caverns at the inflow of light all stopped suddenly short as a steed reined up by powerful hands on the bridle. The initial roars died away as they formed a solid phalanx and looked toward this man who stood in their caverns. Others of the great beasts yawned and lay down on the floor, but not one made a move to advance toward their visitor. "Thanks be unto Jehovah," breathed the prophet. "He hath stopped the mouths of these fierce beasts that they will do me no harm."
>
> He sat down on the floor of the den and leaned his back against the wall to make himself comfortable for the night. Soon two cub lions moved in his direction, not stealthily or crouching as though to attack, but in obvious friendliness, and one lay on each side of Daniel as though to give him warmth and protection in the chilly dungeon. Presently their mother, an old lioness, crept over and lay in front of the prophet. He gently stroked their backs as they each turned

their heads and licked his hand. . . . Enclosed by the lioness
and her cubs, the head of the patriarch was gradually pil-
lowed on the back of one of the cubs as the four slept
soundly in perfect peace and tranquility.[2]

As the king called out at the top of his lungs, "Daniel, servant of
the living God, has your God, whom you serve continually, been able
to rescue you from the lions?" Daniel rose from his rest and replied
with grace and the deepest respect for his earthly master, "O king,
live forever! My God sent his angel, and he shut the mouths of the
lions. They have not hurt me, because I was found innocent in his
sight. Nor have I ever done any wrong before you, O king." Overjoyed,
Darius ordered Daniel lifted out of the den. They didn't find a scratch
on him because "he had trusted in his God."

Personally, I wish the next event had been lost in history, but it
wasn't and it is here in the Bible for a reason. After examining Daniel,
the king exercised swift justice on those who had betrayed his confidence. According to Near Eastern custom dominated by pagan
values, not only the conspirators but their wives and children were
thrown into the lions' den.

Two reasons press my mind as I ask why this grisly scene is
recorded here. There is no sadistic pleasure in God's justice. But
He wants us to see that these men were judged by their own treach-
ery. They were the ones who "paid no attention to the king" and by
their own law their lives were forfeited. The fact that blameless wives
and children were also killed reminds me clearly that innocent
people are often hurt as a result of my sin. It is one thing to bear
my own judgment. But worst of all is realizing that the consequences
of my sin spilled over onto innocent people I love.

THE IMPACT OF A MAN OF INFLUENCE

Daniel 6 is the last historical chapter of the book and includes an
amazing tribute to this man of faith. It is not a commendation of
Daniel, outlining his feats of faith and service to the king. Instead
we find a royal decree from a man whom Daniel influenced greatly,
praising the character and wonders of Daniel's God, and calling on
all men to do the same:

Then King Darius wrote to all the peoples, nations and men of every language throughout the land:

"May you prosper greatly!

"I issue a decree that in every part of my kingdom people must fear and reverence the God of Daniel.

"For he is the living God
and he endures forever;
his kingdom will not be destroyed,
his dominion will never end.
He rescues and he saves;
he performs signs and wonders
in the heavens and on the earth.
He has rescued Daniel
from the power of the lions." (Daniel 6:25-27)

In a few short months of working together, how had Daniel so influenced this man's life? The message of Daniel's life was clear, the print unblurred. He was a man of competence, character, consistency, and courage. As a result, his faith infected kings and changed the course of history for God's people. But don't misunderstand. Daniel's primary goal was not to change the culture but to be faithful to the King of kings. Because of his faithfulness, another king turned from lifeless idols to worship the living God.

As a person who wants to make an impact on the people around me, some serious questions arise that I need to ask myself. Is the message of God's grace and majesty written clear and crisp in my life, or is it blurred and cryptic? Do people know me to be a person of competence and character? How about when the lions roar? Am I a person of consistency and courage, able to stand for what I believe, even when it costs me dearly?

SURVIVING THE LIONS

Daniel provides an excellent paradigm for not only facing and surviving the attack of unprincipled people, but for influencing those around us in the process.

Do Quality Work

Both our ability to positively impact others and our ability to survive attack depend on our competence. A great deal of confusion exists in America today about the place of our everyday work in God's plan. As far as God is concerned, our most basic responsibility in serving Him is doing our work with excellence. Whether our work finds us in a church building, a business office, a manufacturing plant, a retail store, an educational institution, a hospital, a home, or a government office, as in the case of Daniel, God wants us to do excellent work. He makes that clear in Colossians 3:22-23:

> Slaves, obey your earthly masters in everything; and do it not only when their eye is on you and to win their favor, but with sincerity of heart, and reverence for the Lord. Whatever you do, work at it with all your heart, as working for the Lord, not for men.

"Nothing is more dangerous to the faith of youth than for them to make the disconcerting discovery that the men who have advocated their faith are men of mediocre ability," warns Frank Gabelein, leading Christian educator and longtime headmaster of Stonybrook School. What is true of youth is also true of anyone else. Nothing is more discrediting to your Christian witness and mine than mediocrity in our work. The first thing the men and women around us will notice is the quality of our work. If they see shoddy or mediocre work, they will fail to respect our faith and will not be able to see beyond what we produce. In essence, our work becomes a giant barrier keeping them from God.

On the other hand, when we do our work with excellence and an attitude of always giving it our best shot—delivering more than we promise—we gain respect in the eyes of those around us, even when they disagree with us. Competence not only musters allies from unexpected quarters in times of crisis, it gives us a platform from which to speak. It can open incredible opportunities for you and me to speak openly of our faith and build bridges rather than barriers.

One of the best bridge builders I know is Bill McCartney, head football coach at the University of Colorado at Boulder, a city not known for its warmth toward biblical Christianity. In fact, it can be a war zone for Christians. Yet McCartney has not only survived but flourished living in the lions' den. He has even been permitted to host the world's largest gathering of Christian men on the university's campus. His dream to fill Folsom Field in Boulder with 50,000 men was reached in July 1993, at the Promise Keepers National Convention. In McCartney's twelve seasons as coach of the Buffaloes, the quality of his work is evident to all. Since 1988, the Buffaloes have consistently been one of the top twenty-five teams in the U.S., posting a 47-12-4 record. During that time, McCartney led his team to three Big Eight championships and the National Championship in 1990.

Coach McCartney's solid winning record as a coach has built a bridge of respect that has given him the freedom to make controversial stands in an atmosphere that would not be so hospitable to a less successful coach. This is not to say that critics are nonexistent. Virtually no season goes by without some attack on McCartney's faith. However, the detractors of this outspoken man of God find little sympathy among avid Colorado Buffalo fans and school administrators. Even though not everyone agrees with him, they respect both his ability and his character. They have allowed him to fulfill his dream of calling men to Christ in a local culture that more readily calls people to the world.

Make Faithfulness to God Your Highest Priority

Not only is this the second key to surviving the lions, no other goal is lofty enough or compelling enough to energize you to keep going when you can't see any progress in transforming the culture. If making an impact on our culture is our highest priority, we have "baptized" a worldly view of success. Chuck Colson warns us,

> If the church is to fulfill its role, if the church is to do anything at all useful for the culture, if the church is to resist and conquer the barbarian invaders, the church must first disregard all these objectives and concentrate on being faithful to its identity in Jesus Christ. . . .
>
> Our goal is to be faithful to the holy God who calls us to be the church, whether we actually make a difference in our

world or whether it falls to pieces around us and dissolves into a stew of secularism.[3]

Peter wrote these instructions to the early Church that still make good advice today:

> For it is God's will that by doing good you may silence the ignorant talk of foolish men. Live as free men, but do not use your freedom as a cover-up for evil; live as servants of God. . . . But how is it to your credit if you receive a beating for doing wrong and endure it? But if you suffer for doing good and you endure it, this is commendable before God. To this you were called, because Christ suffered for you, leaving you an example, that you should follow in his steps.
> "He committed no sin,
> and no deceit was found in his mouth."
> (1 Peter 2:15-16,20-22)

Don't Be Surprised When Attacked

Lions don't just live in dens. They work in offices and live in neighborhoods and even go to churches just like yours. C. S. Lewis reminds us, "The greatest evil is not done in those sordid 'dens of crime' that Dickens loved to paint. . . . But it is conceived and ordered (moved, seconded, carried, and minuted) in clean, carpeted, warmed, and well-lighted offices, by quiet men with white collars and cut fingernails and smooth-shaven cheeks who do not need to raise their voices."[4]

Maintain an Attitude of Thanksgiving

One of the items so easily missed in this dramatic chapter is found in verse 10. Daniel continued giving thanks to his God. What would we have done? Knowing the plot was hatched, knowing they were watching, knowing there was no way anyone could save you or me. Would we be occupied with the goodness of God toward us? Colossians 3:15 tells us, "Let the peace of Christ rule in your hearts, since as members of one body you were called to peace. And be thankful."

Thanksgiving is not only an act of gratitude, but an expression of faith. There are many times when I have to give thanks for what God has given even though I am not experiencing it at the moment. I thank the Lord for His peace and protection when I feel afraid, because I know He has given these things even though I may not feel them or see them at the moment. This is not a matter of pretending, but of acknowledging spiritual reality. So I thank the Lord for strength and endurance when I feel like I can't go on because He can do exceeding abundantly beyond what I ask or dream. I thank the Lord for the ability to love when I am being attacked and want to attack in return, because I know His love is ready to flow through me at that very moment, and I need to remember Jesus' words: "Father forgive them for they do not know what they are doing." Thanksgiving turns my attention to the Source of my life and reminds me of the abundance I have in Christ. It frees my mind and emotions from the resources of this world and lifts me into the abundant storehouse of God.

Never Let the Enemy Set the Agenda
Don't play by the enemy's rules. Play by God's rules. I am convinced that Daniel could have eaten his opponents alive, but he refused to live by their rules of engagement where anything goes and the ends justify the means. Peter reminds us of the Christian's rules of engagement when he writes,

> Do not repay evil for evil or insult with insult, but with blessing, because to this you were called so that you may inherit a blessing. For,
> > "Whoever would love life
> > > and see good days
> > must keep his tongue from evil
> > > and his lips from deceitful speech.
> > He must turn from evil and do good;
> > > he must seek peace and pursue it.
> > For the eyes of the Lord are on the righteous
> > > and his ears are attentive to their prayer,
> > but the face of the Lord is against those who do evil."
> > > (1 Peter 3:9-12)

Put Your Safety and Reputation in God's Hands
If you don't defend yourself, what can you do? Again Peter reminds

us just a few verses later that the safest place we can be is in God's hands: "So then, those who suffer according to God's will should commit themselves to their faithful Creator and continue to do good" (1 Peter 4:19).

Maintain Consistency

Changing your routine makes you look guilty whether you are or not. Under pressure, I've found that it's easy to trim back a little on integrity. Faced with criticism, it's natural to conform. E. B. White describes the tendency pretty well: "People remodeled their ideas too—took in their convictions a little at the waist, shortened the sleeves of their resolve, and fitted themselves out in a new intellectual ensemble copied from a smart design out of the very latest page of history."[5]

Don't Resist the Enemy Alone

This strong pattern of godly living runs consistently through the book of Daniel. Even here where it appears Daniel must stand alone, a second look will reveal a compatriot—King Darius. It's very likely that Daniel had outlived Shadrach, Meshach, and Abednego, and most of the other men of faith who had come from Judah seventy years before. But as we see in this chapter, Daniel was consistently making new acquaintances and expanding his friendships. Unlike many older individuals whose circle of friends and supporters gets smaller, Daniel's was growing. Not only did they need Daniel, he needed them as well. Christians should lean on each other, carry each other, and even stand on each other's shoulders, together becoming what God wants us to be and bringing glory to His name.

All of us stand on the shoulders of giants like Daniel, men and women who stood tall for Christ in previous generations; individuals who were absolutely honest, worked hard, and remained faithful to their convictions. In his book *I Almost Missed the Sunset*, Bill Gaither relates the effect of one such man:

> Gloria and I had been married a couple of years. We were teaching school in Alexandria, Indiana, where I had grown up, and we wanted a piece of land where we could build a house. I noticed the parcel south of town where cattle grazed, and I learned it belonged to a 92-year-old retired

banker named Mr. Yule. He owned a lot of land in the area, and the word was he would sell none of it. He gave the same speech to everyone who inquired: "I promised the farmers they could use it for their cattle."

Gloria and I visited him at the bank. Although he was retired, he spent a couple of hours each morning in his office. He looked at us over the top of his bifocals.

I introduced myself and told him we were interested in a piece of his land. "Not selling," he said pleasantly. "Promised it to a farmer for grazing."

"I know, but we teach school here and thought maybe you'd be interested in selling it to someone planning to settle in the area."

He pursed his lips and stared at me. "What'd you say your name was?"

"Gaither. Bill Gaither."

"Hmmm. Any relation to Grover Gaither?"

"Yes sir. He was my granddad."

Mr. Yule put down his paper and removed his glasses. "Interesting. Grover Gaither was the best worker I ever had on my farm. Full day's work for a day's pay. So honest. What'd you say you wanted?"

I told him again.

"Let me do some thinking on it, then come back and see me."

I came back within the week, and Mr. Yule told me he had the property appraised. I held my breath. "How does $3,800 sound? Would that be okay?"

If that was per acre, I would have to come up with nearly $60,000! "$3,800?" I repeated.

"Yup. Fifteen acres for $3,800."

I knew it had to be worth at least three times that. I readily accepted.

Nearly three decades later, my son and I strolled that beautiful, lush property that had once been pasture land. "Benjy," I said, "you've had this wonderful place to grow up through nothing that you've done, but because of the good name of a great granddad you never met."[6]

As we stand on the shoulders of other men and women of integrity, it's important to realize that generations after us will stand on our shoulders as well. I wonder what they will be able to see from that perspective?

THE BIG IDEA

Anyone who attempts to make a difference in his world will encounter personal enemies. If we face our foes on their level and use their tactics, we've already lost the battle. As Christians, we have the ability not only to survive but to rise above the attacks of our enemies to glorify our Lord.

Use the following thoughts and ideas to stimulate your thinking about influence.

We work hard with our own hands.
When we are cursed, we bless;
when we are persecuted, we endure it;
when we are slandered, we answer kindly.
1 CORINTHIANS 4:12-13

Dear friends, do not be surprised at the painful trial
you are suffering, as though something strange were happening
to you. But rejoice that you participate in the sufferings
of Christ, so that you may be overjoyed when his glory
is revealed. If you are insulted because of the name of Christ,
you are blessed, for the Spirit of glory and of God rests on you.
1 PETER 4:12-14

Be self-controlled and alert.
Your enemy the devil prowls around like a roaring lion
looking for someone to devour. Resist him,
standing firm in the faith, because you know that your brothers
throughout the world are undergoing the same sufferings.
1 PETER 5:8

*If it is possible, as far as it depends on you,
live at peace with everyone. Do not take revenge,
my friends, but leave room for God's wrath,
for it is written: "It is mine to avenge; I will repay," says the
Lord. On the contrary:*

*"If your enemy is hungry, feed him;
if he is thirsty, give him something to drink.
In doing this, you will heap burning coals on his head."*

*Do not be overcome by evil,
but overcome evil with good.*
ROMANS 12:18-21

"But I say to you, love your enemies."
MATTHEW 5:44, NASB

*Wars on earth are but tremors felt from
an earthquake light years away.
The Christian's war takes place at the epicenter
of the earthquake. It is infinitely more deadly
while the issues that hang on it make earth's most momentous
question no more than village gossip.*
JOHN WHITE

*We are all ready to be savage in some cause.
The difference between a good man and a bad one
is the choice of the cause.*
WILLIAM JAMES

It is a rough road that leads to the heights of greatness.
LUCIUS ANNAEUS SENECA

Being powerful is like being a lady.
If you have to tell people you are, you aren't.
MARGARET THATCHER

On lifting the oppression of Christians in the former USSR:

Why do we oppress the very people
who do not absent themselves from work,
who are not alcoholics and who give us a productive day's
work? We need their strength.
MIKHAIL GORBACHEV

CHAPTER EIGHT

The Road to Restoration
DANIEL 9:1-17

✤

As the story goes, a very dejected Satan once came before God and wailed, "Almighty God, I want you to know that I am bored—bored to tears! I go around with nothing to do all day long. There isn't a stitch of work for me to do!"

"I can't understand you," replied God. "There's plenty of work to be done, only you've got to have more imagination. Why don't you try to lead people into sin? That's your job."

"Lead people into sin!" Satan said incredulously, "Why Lord, even before I can get a chance to say a blessed word to anyone, he has already gone and sinned!"

Mark Twain was right: "We are all like the moon; we have a dark side." Even without Satan's help we are quite capable of sin. Unfortunately most men and nations tend to trivialize the problem of sin.

- ◆ We call it chance; God calls it a choice.
- ◆ We call it fascinating; God calls it fatal.
- ◆ We call it a trifle; God calls it a tragedy.
- ◆ We call it a mistake; God calls it madness.

We not only minimize the problem, we go through elaborate mental gymnastics to cover its manifestation. None of us wants to admit

167

we are wrong—ever. And if you wonder how far we'll go to avoid admitting our wrongs, just read the following traffic accident explanations listed on actual insurance forms.

♦ Coming home, I drove into the wrong house and collided with a tree I didn't have.
♦ The guy was all over the road. I had to swerve a number of times before I finally hit him.
♦ I pulled away from the side of the road, glanced at my mother-in-law, and headed over the embankment.
♦ In my attempt to kill a fly, I drove into a telephone pole.
♦ I had been driving my car for forty years when I fell asleep at the wheel and had an accident.
♦ The pedestrian had no idea which direction to go, so I ran over him.
♦ The telephone pole was approaching fast. I was attempting to swerve out of its path when it struck my front end.[1]

Why is it so much easier for us to invent an excuse than to tell the truth? Every man and woman knows we were not made for sin. We know we were born for a higher plane of existence. Yet finding ourselves here in "Sin City" with no idea of how to restore ourselves, it is easier to try to convince ourselves that everything is okay, than come face to face with the horror of our situation. So we pack our troubles in a trunk, sit on the lid, and smile as if there is no problem. But there is. Every man and woman alive on this planet feels the rumbling deep inside the trunk and fears the lid will come flying open any moment.

Fortunately the gracious sovereign Ruler of our universe has offered a way of escape from the darkness through Jesus Christ. Rather than covering our sin, when we openly acknowledge our rebellion against God, He offers to light the dark side for both men and nations. But until then, the darkness hangs like a heavy cloak on our shoulders.

For generations, Daniel's people had lived in sin. They had repeatedly violated divine law, ignored their agreement with God, and refused to be accountable. The very ones God intended to be a light to the nations had trafficked in the twilight of compromise, assimilating the ways of the pagan world around them—all the while, dabbling at their worship with God. Repeatedly God sent the prophets to warn them that they were committing spiritual adultery. They turned their heads. They wanted to pursue the excitement that the worship of other gods had to offer, but they wanted to be able to go home to a loyal "husband" (God), who would unquestioningly provide for their needs no matter how disloyal they were to Him.

After repeated warnings, God allowed the Jews to make a full diet of the life of paganism they sampled in Palestine. Nebuchadnezzar came as God's chastening tool, destroying Jerusalem and the Temple, and deporting most of the survivors to Babylon. The first to suffer for his nation's sin was Daniel. For sixty-eight years he had been in Babylon, serving God and the rulers of Babylon in that order. Then in 539 BC, Babylon fell under the forces of Cyrus, just as Isaiah had prophesied years before.

Daniel's advancement in the new Persian government had been meteoric, culminating in the plot by his peers, his deliverance from the lions' den, and the conversion of King Darius. Although God is always at work in the affairs of men, there are times when His activity becomes much more apparent to godly men—usually just before some nexus of great events.

Things were happening to Daniel that were beyond coincidence. He could have easily been left in retirement. After all, he was well into his eighties. Instead, the king selected him for the highest level of government service. Then there was the lions' den. Daniel was ready to be with his Lord in eternity, but God had delivered him from the mouths of the lions. Why? There must have been some reason. So Daniel began to search the Scriptures to see if he could uncover what God was up to. He tells us what he discovered in chapter 9:

> In the first year of Darius son of Xerxes (a Mede by descent), who was made ruler over the Babylonian kingdom—in the first year of his reign, I, Daniel, understood from the Scriptures, according to the word of the Lord given to Jeremiah the prophet, that the desolation of Jerusalem would last seventy years.

Daniel had discovered this timetable in the twenty-ninth chapter of the book of Jeremiah: "This is what the LORD says: 'When seventy years are completed for Babylon, I will come to you and fulfill my gracious promise to bring you back to this place. For I know the plans I have for you,' declares the LORD, 'plans to prosper you and not to harm you, plans to give you hope and a future'" (Jeremiah 29:10-11).

Studying this passage, Daniel realized that God scheduled the captivity in Babylon for seventy years. Calculating the years, he saw the time was virtually up, and that God had already set political pawns in motion to accomplish His sovereign purpose. But as Daniel read the passage further, he saw something that made him sick to the pit of his soul. There was a condition placed on the restoration—a condition that the Jews had not met.

> "Then you will call upon me and come and pray to me, and I will listen to you. You will seek me and find me when you seek me with all your heart. I will be found by you," declares the LORD, "and will bring you back from captivity. I will gather you from all the nations and places where I have banished you," declares the LORD, "and will bring you back to the place from which I carried you into exile." (Jeremiah 29:12-14)

The journey to restoration was to begin on the path of confession and repentance. This had been the one condition God had consistently placed on His people for restoration. In the remarkable instructions God gave His people while they were wandering nomads in the Sinai Desert (Deuteronomy 28-29), He promised them blessing if they followed His law. He also promised them severe discipline and ultimately loss of their homeland if they continued to rebel against Him.

And then in chapter 30 of Deuteronomy, He made another promise should they turn their hearts toward Him, repent of their evil ways, and follow His law: "Then the LORD your God will restore your fortunes and have compassion on you. . . . Even if you have been banished to the most distant land under the heavens, from there the LORD your God will gather you and bring you back"

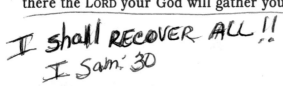

I shall RECOVER ALL !!
I Sam. 30

(Deuteronomy 30:3-4). It was the same condition for God's blessing He restated at the dedication of the Temple:

> When I shut up the heavens so that there is no rain, or command locusts to devour the land or send a plague among my people, if my people, who are called by my name, will humble themselves and pray and seek my face and turn from their wicked ways, then will I hear from heaven and will forgive their sin and will heal their land. (2 Chronicles 7:13-14)

Unfortunately, the Jews in Babylon were not seeking God. This was their home now. Most of the generation that had lived in Palestine had died. Those still living or born in Babylon were comfortable and well established in their communities and didn't really care about returning to the hardships of rebuilding a culture. As Daniel pondered the captivity, God's promise, and the prerequisite of repentance, he fell to his knees in profound grief, realizing that this condition had not been met. Remarkably, this righteous man did not pray that his fellow Jews would come to the place of repentance. Feeling the weight of his people's sin, he repented himself, pleading with God, "in prayer and petition, in fasting, and in sackcloth and ashes."

RENEWING THE UNITED STATES

It seems that we desperately need this same kind of response in the U.S. today. Comfortable, established, and shy about hardship and sacrifice, we need men and women who are willing to shoulder the weight and lead the way to national repentance. As we close the twentieth century, it is apparent to any astute observer that the U.S. isn't working anymore. Investigate any area of society, and you will find that this nation, which once led the world in almost every area of endeavor, is now leading the world in decline.

As I am writing this chapter, President Bill Clinton is touring the country pushing his plan to "reinvent government." But is the rearrangement of the Washington bureaucracy really the solution to this nation's problems? Can the Democratic Party or any other political party offer a solution to America's crisis? Can any form of government really solve the problems eating away at the soul of the U.S.?

Over two hundred years ago a group of—for the most part—godly men sat down to construct a document that would serve as the framework of government for the new nation occupying the center of the North American continent. For almost two hundred years, that document has served us well. But what has happened? Why do we need to "reinvent" government today? Has this document failed to be adequate? Is it now irrelevant as we close the twentieth century?

You will not find the reason that government doesn't work in the contents of documents, but in the hearts of people—we've turned our backs on God. As the twentieth century dawned, a spiritual controversy was brewing in North America. At issue were unbiblical beliefs about God and man that had already emasculated the Church in Europe. Man was not so bad, God was not so big, the Bible was not so reliable as the Christian faith had taught for nearly two thousand years, and Christ was not God. Recognizing that these beliefs struck at the heart of the Christian faith, many men and women fought violently to restrain these "modern" ideas from infiltrating the Church. The conflict was, for all intents and purposes, lost by the mid-1930s. Winning many battles, we lost the war. Perhaps E. M. Bounds, a contemporary pastor, put his finger on the cause when he wrote about current preachers, "The pulpit today is weak praying. The pride of learning is against the dependent humility of prayer. Prayer is with the pulpit too often only official—a performance for routine service."[2] Licking its wounds, evangelical Christianity circled its wagons and focused on itself, leaving the culture to the "new secular faith."

As men felt less responsible before God, government began to move into the vacuum. The role of the church became more and more restricted to the souls of men, leaving the rest to government. By the end of the 1940s, the U.S. had become a materialistic society. By the 1950s the U.S. was beginning to believe in its own strength, and the church was becoming as materialistic as the culture. Then in the early 1960s the U.S. Supreme Court began a trend of hostile decisions toward biblical faith, reversing an almost-two-hundred-year trend of supporting biblical principles.

Please don't think I'm blaming this nation's problems on the government. Though crises exist in Washington, I do not believe the real problem with our nation is political in nature. Veteran Washington insider Chuck Colson agrees:

> I spent the first half of my professional life in politics and public service. . . . I really believed that people could be changed by government being changed. I never looked beyond the structures and the institutions and legislation into the hearts of people.
>
> But when I became a Christian, I gained a new perspective on the actual influence political structures have over the course of history. I began to see that societies are changed only when people are changed, not the other way around. The crisis is not political; it is moral and spiritual.[3]

Writing three centuries ago, Blaise Pascal warned,

> It is vain, O men, that you seek within yourselves the cure for your miseries. Your principal maladies are pride, which cuts you off from God, sensuality, which binds you to the earth. Either you imagine you are gods yourselves, or, if you grasp the vanity of such a pretension, you are cast into the other abyss, and suppose yourselves to be like the beasts of the field and seek your good in carnality.[4]

America's problem is us—you and me. We cannot cure our own miseries, because our disease is something we have chosen as, step by step, our nation has walked away from God. Our leaders, the government, the courts we see today are products of our desire to rule ourselves. What we have is what we asked for.

These choices have a cost, however—the very vitality of the U.S. Addressing the Militia of Massachusetts on October 11, 1798, President John Adams made the necessity of shared moral values clear: "We have no government armed in power capable of contending in human passions unbridled by morality and religion. Our constitution was made only for a moral and religious people. It is wholly inadequate for the government of any other."[5]

If the U.S. doesn't change, we will have to reinvent government—

government for people unbridled by principle and common moral values. Actually, it's already been invented. It is called totalitarianism. Quite frankly, the steady slide toward collectivism and more government control is frightening. People in the former Eastern Block and Soviet Union must wonder why we want to go where they have already been. Colson describes the process:

> First a program is created, then a bureaucracy; in the process, the state takes on more and more power. As government swells, so does its tendency toward repression. Before long, civil rights and liberties are eliminated in an effort to control the citizenry. And thus decadent societies can pave the way for totalitarian governments.[6]

That's where we're headed—unless we repent. I don't know how widespread repentance was on the part of the Jewish nation. I do know, though, that at least Daniel repented. How many does it take to turn things around? However few the number, there were enough to get the Jews moving back to Jerusalem. How many would it take for America? I don't know. But there's one thing I do know. Each of us can add one more to the number by following Daniel's example.

PREREQUISITES OF REPENTANCE

If we think that repentance is something we can approach casually, Daniel sets us straight right from the start. Two things strike me immediately about his prayer.

A Singular Focus on God

First, Daniel focused his entire being singularly upon God. He turned away from his other responsibilities and "turned to the Lord." Literally the phrase means he "set his face." Daniel willfully, emotionally, and intellectually gave his full attention, his full focus to God. In our fast-paced, stress-filled world, rarely does one particular item have our attention. It seems that life demands that we think about and often do two things (or more) at once. Repentance, however, is a single-minded activity. God will have no other thing but His face crowding our attention.

A Humble Heart

The second thing that jumps out at me is Daniel's humble heart. He was deeply penitent. He recognized that he and all his people must give account to God, and they had come up quite a bit short on their balance sheet. Fasting, sackcloth, and ashes were the external symbols of internal grief in the ancient Near East, indicating the profound remorse Daniel felt over his people's sin and rebellion against God. There was no self-righteousness here, though Daniel was a godly man. You will not find a judgmental attitude toward sinners—nor contentment with his own niceness. Daniel knew all men stand on level ground before a righteous God.

DANIEL'S CONFIDENCE IN CONFESSION

Standing without defense and without excuse before a Holy God is not exactly what most men and women consider a fun day's activity. It's a little like walking into the IRS office and saying, "Hi, I'm turning myself in. I've cheated on my income tax for the last ten years." You can expect some rather serious consequences. So what in the world would possess a man to do such a thing? It's something that each of us needs to recognize—that God already knows. Even secret sins are open scandal in Heaven. But we still need something to overcome our natural fear of judgment—a prospect that keeps us living in the dark where we can hide our sins if only from ourselves. These things motivated Daniel to repent.

An Intimate Friend

Daniel's relationship with God was personal. An intimacy existed that allowed him to say, "I prayed to the Lord my God." He was not some distant deity, but an intimate Friend to Daniel. After eighty years of walking with God, Daniel knew that he could draw near to Him with confidence and find grace and mercy at His throne.

An Almighty Sovereign

Daniel knew God to be more than a sympathetic listener. There was no doubt in Daniel's mind that God could handle what he was about to ask. He is the Almighty God of the universe, a "great and awesome God." He is not some "nice" deity who would love to help but is too busy or is incapable of really solving the problem. He is the God who is able—able to accomplish anything our small minds can conceive.

A Promise Keeper

A third certainty drew Daniel to the Lord—God's character, specifically, His faithfulness. He is not only the "great and awesome God," He also "keeps his covenant of love with all who love him and obey his commands." Writing in his first letter, the Apostle John reminded his followers, "There is no fear in love. But perfect love drives out fear, because fear has to do with judgment" (1 John 4:18). Daniel had complete assurance both he and his people were absolutely secure in God's love. Far from bringing judgment, repentance would remove the disciplining hand of God on their country. Daniel had everything to gain by coming, and everything to lose by continuing to lurk in the shadows.

Because God is faithful, there was another thing that Daniel was absolutely sure of. Hundreds of years before, God made a unilateral covenant with Abraham promising that the land of Palestine would belong to his descendants. God had repeated this promise to Moses, Solomon, Isaiah, and Jeremiah. Daniel knew that God would keep His word. His love and commitment to His people would not change. However, the enjoyment of His fellowship and the experience of His blessing was conditioned on their obedience. In the covenant He made through Moses, God made it clear that He would not reward the insurrection of rebel hearts. Though the land of Palestine belonged to them, they could not enjoy it apart from a submissive relationship to God. That submission began with repentance—coming clean about sin and selfish living.

God's faithfulness, power, and love all say, "Come!" The real danger is remaining in the dark, not walking into the light.

A PARADIGM FOR REPENTANCE

Repentance is more than acknowledging and confessing our sin. It is a radical change of mind. The New Testament word for repentance, *metanoia*, means just that—to change one's mind. Repentance is a change of perspective in how we see ourselves, the world, and most of all, God Himself. Rather than talk about it theoretically, we can examine elements of repentance firsthand in Daniel's prayer. They provide not only a paradigm for individual repentance, but a pattern for national repentance as well. Just how does my mind need to change?

From Blame to Confession: An Admission of Personal Guilt

Drawn by God's faithfulness, power, and love, Daniel immediately got to the point: "We have sinned and done wrong. We have been wicked and rebelled." Without a doubt, one of the hardest phrases to utter in any dialect is, "I am wrong." Although Freud made it fashionable, men and women have loved to blame others for their sin since the Garden of Eden. However, the uniform testimony of the Bible is clear—sin is my choice. No one else can make me decide to do the wrong thing. It is my choice and my responsibility.

Therefore, genuine repentance requires that I brazenly see myself as I am, without excuse, reservation, or self-justification. Sin is not my friend's fault, my parents' fault, my mate's fault, my boss's fault, or society's fault. *I* sinned. If I choose to hit someone in the face with a brick, it's not society's fault—it's my fault. If I choose to commit adultery, it's not my wife's fault for being cool toward me—it's my fault. If I choose to cheat someone in business, it's not because it's a dog-eat-dog world—it's my choice.

I don't know about you, but I find Daniel's use of the first person here totally unexpected. It is true: If one player jumps offside, the whole team is penalized. But if anyone was "onside" in the Jews' calamity, if anyone didn't deserve to be penalized, it was Daniel. Yet we never find him accusing, pointing the finger, or plagued with bitter feelings toward his fellow countrymen who blatantly rebelled against God's law. In fact, he readily, almost eagerly, heeds the call to repentance. And he did more than simply identify with the sins of his people. As a fellow sinner, he felt the shame. He knew that in his heart lurked the same dark propensities as in everyone else. He knew he needed grace like everyone else. He knew that he had not followed the Lord his God as fully as he could.

Every one of us knows that we don't follow God fully either. While I long for repentance in Washington, I know that it must come to my street before it comes to Pennsylvania Avenue. Until good people acknowledge their need of grace, there will be no restoration. Only those who recognize the darkness within themselves know their need of grace. Only those who have tasted God's grace have the courage to walk in the full light of God's truth and freely admit the darkness of their own souls.

From General to Specific: A Specific Admission of Guilt

Genuine repentance specifies the sin. God has no regard for blanket confessions. Most of the time they simply cover the dirt or "sweep it under the rug." In effect, we are asking God to forgive sin without personally dealing with the problem that caused it. General confessions like this may cause us to feel sentimentally religious, but they don't force us to get to the darkness of our soul—which is the stuff genuine repentance dirties its hands with. Daniel's confession included a catalog of offenses, which he uncovered before God:

- ◆ We have turned away from your commands and laws. (verse 5)
- ◆ We have not listened to your servants the prophets. (verse 6)
- ◆ We are covered with shame . . . because of our unfaithfulness to you. (verse 7)
- ◆ The Lord our God is merciful and forgiving, even though we have rebelled against him. (verse 7)
- ◆ We have not obeyed the LORD our God or kept the laws he gave us through his servants the prophets. (verse 10)
- ◆ All Israel has transgressed your law and turned away, refusing to obey you. (verse 11)
- ◆ We have not sought the favor of the LORD our God by turning from our sins and giving attention to your truth. (verse 13)

When I am confessing my personal sin, I need to be brutally specific. God knows exactly what I did. He was there. He saw every detail and monitored every thought. Confession is not for His benefit; it's for my benefit. I need to lay bare that putrescent part of my inner being and bring it into the light. Only then can the healing power of Jesus Christ bring wholeness. The promise of forgiveness is as specific as the command to confess.

This is the message we have heard from him and declare to you: God is light; in him there is no darkness at all. If we claim to have fellowship with him yet walk in the darkness, we lie and do not live by the truth. But if we walk in the light, as he is in the light, we have fellowship with one another, and the blood of Jesus, his Son, purifies us from all sin.

If we claim to be without sin, we deceive ourselves and the truth is not in us. If we confess our sins, he is faithful and just and will forgive us our sins and purify us from all unrighteousness. (1 John 1:5-9)

When we confess national sins, we need to use the same kind of specificity. We must do more than ask for God to forgive the sins of our nation. We need to ask ourselves these questions:

- ◆ What are the specific sins that are ravaging our nation, and our communities?
- ◆ What rebellious thinking is driving our culture? What erroneous assumptions are guiding our leaders?
- ◆ What destructive results are these attitudes and actions producing in our people?

When we come face to face with the ugliness of our society, then we can join godly men and women in genuine repentance for our nation.

From Resistance to Acceptance: A Complete Submission to God's Discipline

Genuine repentance acknowledges that God is perfectly just in bringing discipline into the life of a person or a nation. We might expect Daniel to waffle or complain about the tremendous calamity God allowed to fall on him and his people, but read what Daniel says:

All Israel has transgressed your law and turned away, refusing to obey you. Therefore the curses and sworn judgments written in the Law of Moses, the servant of God, have been poured out on us, because we have sinned against you. You have fulfilled the words spoken against us and against our rulers by bringing upon us great disaster. Under the whole heaven nothing has ever been done like what has been done to Jerusalem. Just as it is written in the Law of Moses, all this disaster has come upon us, yet we have not sought the favor of the Lord our God by turning from our sins and giving attention to your truth. The Lord did not hesitate to bring disaster upon us, for the Lord our God is righteous in everything he does; yet we have not obeyed him. (Daniel 9:11-14)

In so many words, Daniel affirmed, "God warned us it would hurt; we didn't listen. It hurts and we have no one to blame but ourselves. God is absolutely right in doing what He did." If anything, I would have to say God's mercy tempered His justice toward the Jews. After generations of rebelling against God and chasing other deities, they deserved nothing less than rejection.

When I look at the tremendous privileges Americans (myself included) enjoy and take for granted as if we were entitled to them no matter how we behave, I know we have an extremely merciful God. We are definitely not getting what we deserve. We are receiving grace—a lot of grace. We not only don't deserve God's blessing, any people as privileged as we are and yet so ungrateful, deserves discipline.

We can be sure, however, that God's mercy will not get in the way of His desire for our spiritual welfare. One day, if not already, we will feel the sting of our deserved ends. Personally, I believe we are starting to experience the beginnings of God's discipline on America. As Christians, we will be affected too, and must accept what God sends rather than blame others.

From Pride to Pain: A Deep Sense of Shame

In verse 7 Daniel says, "Lord, you are righteous, but this day we are covered with shame. . . . our kings, our princes and our fathers are covered with shame because we have sinned against you." When we violate God's law, the result is guilt. Guilt is a judicial matter. Shame, on the other hand, is a personal, emotional matter.

Because I was a "lively" child, the words, "You should be ashamed of yourself, Bill Peel!" were not foreign to my ears. Inherent in the rebuke was the implication that I was not living up to my potential.

My accusers were calling on me to evaluate the distance between my behavior and the person I could or should be in their estimation. Shame is the emotional grief we feel when we miss our potential. It is the internal pain we feel for disgraceful behavior. I am ashamed when I know that I have done something beneath me.

Shame is a natural feeling for sinful man. Each of us knows we were made for better. If there was no sense of what we should be, there would be no sense of shame. Shame is the evidence that we have felt the sting of sin and know we are wrong. It is the grief of knowing we have taken God's best and given Him what we could spare, rather than what He deserves—our best. It is the anguish of knowing what we could have been by God's grace, compared to what we have chosen to be. American poet John Greenleaf Whittier said it well in the poem "Maud Miller": "For all the sad words of tongue or pen, the saddest are these: 'It might have been!'"

From Self-Sufficiency to Dependence: An Honest Intention to Forsake Sin

Genuine repentance involves a change of mind about sin, something Daniel confessed had not happened for his people at the time of his prayer. He acknowledged in 9:13, "Yet we have not sought the favor of the LORD our God by turning from our sins and giving attention to your truth."

Perhaps we should ask how our mind needs to change. Ultimately, sin is our attempt to take care of our needs in this world apart from God. He gears His discipline precisely to confront this lie and teach us the absolute futility of this kind of thinking. Repentance is more than simply turning from sinful behavior. It is a change of mind that changes our focus from the world to God as the one true Source of fulfillment, safety, and meaning in life. Repentance involves acknowledging the truth that God is the Source of life. It is to seek His favor and forsake all strategies that depend on anything or anyone else.

Interestingly, by the time the Jews returned to Palestine, they had indeed turned from their adulterous hunger for other gods. As a nation, they never had a problem with idolatry again.

Repentance does not mean we will never sin again. But it does mean that we intend to walk in the light of the truth of God's Word. When we walk in the light, we are able to see sin for what it is and confess it immediately, maintaining an unbroken fellowship with the Source of life.

From My Ability to God's: An Appeal to God's Mercy
The basis of genuine repentance is always God's character, not my ability to please God or change my ways. Repentance rests squarely on His mercy, not my merit. Listen as Daniel completes his prayer:

> Now, O Lord our God, who brought your people out of Egypt with a mighty hand and who made for yourself a name that endures to this day, we have sinned, we have done wrong. O LORD, in keeping with all your righteous acts, turn away your anger and your wrath from Jerusalem, your city, your holy hill. Our sins and the iniquities of our fathers have made Jerusalem and your people an object of scorn to all those around us.
> Now, our God, hear the prayers and petitions of your servant. For your sake, O Lord, look with favor on your desolate sanctuary. Give ear, O God, and hear; open your eyes and see the desolation of the city that bears your Name. We do not make requests of you because we are righteous, but because of your great mercy. O Lord, listen! O Lord, forgive! O Lord, hear and act! For your sake, O my God, do not delay, because your city and your people bear your Name. (9:15-19)

As I come to God, my hope is in His character. Repentance rests squarely on God's willingness to forgive, not my penitence. As a truly repentant person, I come to God with nothing in my hands, not even my own willingness to be on my knees.

From My Prestige to God's: A Desire for God's Glory
As we come before our gracious God, what is it that we really want? The ultimate desire behind genuine repentance is God's glory. Daniel ends his prayer by saying, "O Lord, listen! O Lord, forgive! O Lord, hear and act! For your sake, O my God, do not delay, because your city and your people bear your Name."

Often I find myself coming before God motivated by a strong

desire to get out from under the circumstances I am in. It would be unnatural for me to desire anything less. Certainly no one enjoys the pain of God's discipline, and yet there is something more that we should want. Beyond relief from our circumstances, a love for God that desires His glory more than our comfort fuels genuine repentance.

SIGN ME UP: WHERE DO I BEGIN?

Study Scripture and Your Culture

The amazing testimony of men and women who immerse themselves in God's Word is that it is amazingly contemporary. After two thousand years, the Bible still speaks to our culture. In his second letter to Timothy, Paul writes, "All Scripture is God-breathed and is useful for teaching, rebuking, correcting and training in righteousness, so that the man of God may be thoroughly equipped for every good work" (2 Timothy 3:16-17). More than ever before we need God's Word to light our path into and through the darkness folding around us. How can we know God and the blessings He wants us to experience? How can we know what offends Him and is destructive to the spiritual and physical health of our bodies and our nation? How can we know how He wants us to respond in a given situation? How can we see Him at work, if we have not seen how God works in the pages of the Bible?

Without God's Word, we stumble through the events of life as a person lost at night in a dark forest. We need light, but we also need to understand the forest. We need to study the culture we are in. Students of the Bible often note the reference to the men of Issacar who followed David. They "understood the times, and knew what Israel should do" (1 Chronicles 12:32). Scripture is not applied in a vacuum. Understanding our times is crucial to good decision-making. As Daniel studied God's Word, his world began to make sense to him and he knew how to respond.

Like Daniel, Abraham Lincoln was both a student of his culture and the Scriptures. As President, when he called the nation to repentance, he specified the problem. He knew God and what offended Him in the culture. Listen to Lincoln's words from "Proclamation of a Day of National Humiliation, Fasting, and Prayer."

We have been the recipients of the choicest bounties of Heaven; we have been preserved these many years in peace and prosperity; we have grown in numbers, wealth, and power as no other nation has ever grown. But we have forgotten the gracious hand which preserved us in peace and multiplied and enriched and strengthened us, and we have vainly imagined, in the deceitfulness of our hearts, that all these blessings were produced by some superior wisdom and virtue of our own. Intoxicated with unbroken success, we have become too self-sufficient to feel the necessity of redeeming and preserving grace, too proud to pray to the God that made us.

It behooves us, then, to humble ourselves before the offended Power to confess our national sins and pray clemency and forgiveness upon us.

Get Serious with God Yourself

Without a doubt, America needs to come to the place of repentance before God. But if revival comes to our culture, it will be because good people, men and women like Daniel, become humble enough to repent. Can we openly go before God and say the following with David?

> Search me, O God, and know my heart;
> test me and know my anxious thoughts.
> See if there is any offensive way in me,
> and lead me in the way everlasting. (Psalm 139:23-24)

The greatest failure in the Christian life is not failure itself—no matter how large the sin or how many times we repeat it. The biggest failure is to hide our sin and refuse to accept God's forgiveness. God satisfied His righteous demands in Christ. He is ready, even eager to forgive through the blood of Jesus Christ. We have every reason to walk into the light.

Repentance Must Begin with Us

If we want to change our culture, we've got to take a good look at ourselves. It is obvious that Christians must lead the way in repentance. Christ asks us some rather penetrating questions in the Sermon on the Mount:

> "Why do you look at the speck of sawdust in your brother's eye and pay no attention to the plank in your own eye? How can you say to your brother, 'Let me take the speck out of your eye,' when all the time there is a plank in your own eye? You hypocrite, first take the plank out of your own eye, and then you will see clearly to remove the speck from your brother's eye." (Matthew 7:3-5)

As I understand this verse, the fact that you or I want to confront sin in someone else before we deal with ourselves is a bigger problem to Christ than the other person's sin. Not only are we hypocritical, we can't see to do the job well. This is true individually and corporately.

As I look at many Christians and churches, I have to ask, "Why would someone want what we have?" Are we more at peace, more courageous, more competent, more moral, with more character than the culture around us? Any honest Christian has to recognize that judgment must begin with the house of God. If I have one criticism of evangelical Christians, it is that we are not a very gracious people as a whole. We are rigid and critical toward those who don't buy our line. We look at them as enemies rather than victims of the enemy and fellow strugglers who might be a little behind where we are. We seem hard, full of pride, and demanding to the world, when in fact we should be the most gracious people in the world. When we recognize that we also need grace when we need to repent ourselves, a winsome humility will replace our repulsive pride.

Criticize Leaders Less and Repent More

It doesn't take long—usually about five minutes—for conversations to drift toward "the mess" in Washington. If you are like me, you get involved in a leader-bashing conversation at least once a day. By 8:30 this morning I had already reached my quota.

Although there are many wonderful public servants in government, corruption, immorality, incompetence, and confusion are epidemic in the seats of power in our country. Stop a minute to ask yourself why it is that we have these kinds of men and women in office. In a democracy the obvious reason is that we put them there. But perhaps there is a less obvious reason.

Agonizing over the corruption of Ferdinand Marcos's Philippine government, Jaime Cardinal Sin, Archbishop of Manila, spent hours in prayer asking God to change the plight of his nation. The assassination of Marcos's political rival, Benigno Aquino, seemed to call for something more. As Cardinal Sin studied the Bible for a plan of action, he discovered a pattern that seemed to explain the presence of corrupt leaders: When God wants to punish a people, He gives them unjust rulers.

Cardinal Sin reasoned that what the people of the Philippines needed was not a call to revolution, but a call to repent of their own unjust hearts. He spent months traveling through his country calling the people to prayer, fasting, and repentance. A wave of revival swept through the Philippines and hundreds of thousands began to meet in small groups and fast and pray for their nation. In due time, Marcos's regime came to an end.[7]

There is, of course, no formula that will guarantee God's blessing, but when we become the people we need to be, God has no need to chasten us through corrupt leaders.

When confronted with an opportunity to participate in a Washington-bashing, perhaps we should sometimes add, "Yes, we have gotten exactly what we deserve. God gives corrupt people corrupt leaders. I wonder what that says about what we should really be talking about if we want to make a difference?" A little humility might go a long way toward softening the religious right's image as sinister, rigid, and exclusionary.

Don't Step Back from an Opportunity for Impact

Courage is a rare commodity in a materialistic society. Most Christians I know are willing to be little more than hit-and-run drivers; they hit with their words and run from involvement. I'm not suggesting that everyone should run for public office or seek positions of authority. I am saying that when you receive an opportunity to make a difference, think long and hard before you turn it down. Ask yourself why you would want such a position. Ask yourself why you would want to avoid it. Act courageously on what you know is right. Pray for courage and change your mind about the value of the comfortable life.

Maintain an Ever-Increasing Intimacy with God

Knowing God will give you the confidence to walk into the light. His love will cast out any fear of rejection you might harbor. His might and faithfulness will also bring you the courage to do His will in a world hostile to His ways. Because He is here, you will be able to bear the pain and rejection that will come as a result of following Him. Because He is holy, rigid arrogance and pride will give way to an attractive humility. You will be able to say with Paul,

> But we have this treasure in jars of clay to show that this all-surpassing power is from God and not from us. We are hard pressed on every side, but not crushed; perplexed, but not in despair; persecuted, but not abandoned; struck down, but not destroyed. We always carry around in our body the death of Jesus, so that the life of Jesus may be revealed in our body. (2 Corinthians 4:8-10)

Far from being frightening, the place of repentance is the safest place any man, woman, or nation can be. And perhaps, as we admit our weakness, we become more powerful than ever before; while openly confessing our failure, we plant ourselves more squarely on the path of success than ever before.

Years ago a small town in Texas was dominated by a man who had been fortunate enough to discover oil on his property and accumulate a large fortune. Since the town had been hard hit economically, the new millionaire announced that he would bring all of the businessmen of that small town out of bankruptcy if they would simply write a letter acknowledging the certainty of their failure. Upon receiving the letter he promised to pay their debts and supply them with new capital to start afresh in their business. Many accepted the generous offer, but those individuals who were too proud to accept this gift remained insolvent and were forced to pay the penalty of their pride.

THE BIG IDEA

Repentance is the initial step toward both personal and national renewal. God graciously invites us to come clean about our sin so He can deal with it. We have everything to win by coming, and everything to lose by keeping a "safe" distance.

Use the following thoughts and ideas to stimulate your thinking about repentance.

*If at any time I announce that a nation or kingdom
is to be uprooted, torn apart and destroyed,
and if that nation I warned repents of its evil,
then I will relent and not inflict the disaster I had planned.
And if at another time I announce that a nation or kingdom
is to be built up and planted,
and if it does evil in my sight and does not obey me,
then I will reconsider the good I had intended to do for it.*
JEREMIAH 18:7-10

*I have considered my ways
and turned my steps to your statutes.
I will hasten and not delay
to obey your commands.*
PSALM 119:59-60

*Let us examine our ways and test them,
and let us return to the LORD.*
LAMENTATIONS 3:40

*"Yet I hold this against you: You have forsaken your first love.
Remember the height from which you have fallen!
Repent and do the things you did at first."*
REVELATION 2:4-5

Submit yourselves, then, to God. Resist the devil,
and he will flee from you. Come near to God and he will come
near to you. Wash your hands, you sinners,
and purify your hearts, you double-minded.
Grieve, mourn and wail. Change your laughter to mourning
and your joy to gloom. Humble yourselves before the Lord,
and he will lift you up.
JAMES 4:7-10

Let us then approach the throne of grace with confidence,
so that we may receive mercy
and find grace to help us in our time of need.
HEBREWS 4:16

The most pessimistic attitude anyone could possibly take today
would be to suggest that a way of life based
on materialistic values, on laying up treasure on earth
in the shape of an ever-expanding Gross National Product,
and a corresponding ever-increasing consumption stimulated
and fostered by the fathomless imbecilities of advertising,
could possibly provide human beings
made in the image of their Creator,
sojourners in time, but belonging to eternity,
with a meaningful basis for existence.
MALCOLM MUGGERIDGE
Living Through an Apocalypse

This is the bitterest of all—
to know that suffering need not have been;
that it has resulted from indiscretion and inconsistency;
that it is the harvest of one's own sowing;
that the vulture which feeds on the vitals is a nestling of one's
own rearing. Ah me! This is pain!
F. B. MEYER
Christianity in Isaiah

*The process (of the fall of man) was not, I conceive,
comparable to a mere deterioration as it may now occur in
a human individual; it was a loss of status as a species.
That condition was transmitted by heredity to all later
generations, for it was not simply what biologists call
an acquired variation. It was the emergence of a new kind
of man; a new species, never made by God,
had sinned its way into existence. . . . It was a radical
alteration of his constitution.*
C. S. LEWIS

*With the discovery of the atom, everything changed,
except for man's thinking.
Because of this, we drift toward unparalleled catastrophe.*
ALBERT EINSTEIN

*Our society finds Truth too strong a medicine
to digest undiluted. In its purest form
Truth is not a polite tap on the shoulder;
it is a howling reproach.
What Moses brought down from Mount Sinai
were not the Ten Suggestions . . . they are commandments.
Are, not were.*
TED KOPPEL

CHAPTER NINE

How to Change Your World

DANIEL 9

It was one of those conversations between a man and his son that you wait thirty years for, when fathers suddenly grow wise and sons finally recognize how foolish they have been. Dad was a year away from retirement. I was two years into my first job, feeling a little frustrated with my effectiveness. When Dad walked into the room, I was on the floor rummaging through some old books he kept close at hand in the spare bedroom. I guess for the first time I was ready to listen to the wisdom he had picked up in sixty-eight years of life. As we talked, he rather abruptly said, "That book you have in your hands changed my life." I looked down and introduced myself for the first time to E. M. Bounds and a book now published under the title *Power in Prayer*. Later I found out just how profoundly this book had affected my dad's life. He prayed daily for fifty other people.

That night as I opened that tattered copy of Bound's 1911 classic, his profound words jumped out at me.

We are constantly on a stretch, if not a strain, to devise new methods, new plans, new organizations to advance the Church and secure enlargement and efficiency for the gospel. . . . Men are God's method. The church is looking for better methods; God is looking for better men. . . . What the church needs today is not more machinery or better, not new organizations or more and novel methods, but men whom the Holy Ghost can use—men of prayer, men mighty in prayer. The Holy Ghost does not flow through methods, but through men. He does not come on machinery, but on men. He does not anoint plans, but men—men of prayer.[1]

As hard as we may work, and as much influence as we may acquire, nothing happens without prayer. Prayer is the key that unlocks the storehouse of God's riches. It is the call that moves Heaven to act on behalf of earth. If we want to have an impact on our world, we must learn to pray. Christ made it very simple in John 15:5: "Apart from me you can do nothing." Prayer is the key to effectiveness in every enterprise of life.

WHAT HAPPENS WHEN WE PRAY?

The Apostle Paul certainly understood the importance of prayer. If ever there was an individual who could have made his way by sheer force of the will, by pure dint of personal force, by brute intensity of intellectual competence, it was Paul. But we find Paul consistently requesting that prayer be offered for his effectiveness. For example, we find Paul the courageous evangelist requesting, "Pray also for me, that whenever I open my mouth, words may be given me so that I will fearlessly make known the mystery of the gospel, for which I am an ambassador in chains. Pray that I may declare it fearlessly, as I should" (Ephesians 6:19-20).

William Wilberforce, a member of the English parliament in the nineteenth century, understood the importance of prayer. In his fifty-year struggle to end slavery in the British empire, Wilberforce knew that all his political power, personal wealth, and persuasive talent could not dent his society. Together with a small group of his peers, known as the Clapham sect, he stormed the gates of Heaven with his requests for change in the hearts of his countrymen.

Jeremiah Lanphier, a New York layman, understood the importance of prayer. Concerned for the spiritual welfare of his country during a financial panic in 1857, Lanphier advertised a prayer meeting at noon in the Old Dutch Reformed Church in Manhattan. Noon came and found Lanphier praying alone. Then 12:15. Then at 12:30 six people showed up to join him. The next week, fourteen came, and then the next week, twenty-three.

With a growing sense of urgency, this small group decided to meet every day. Soon the crowd filled the building and spilled over to the Methodist Church on John Street, and then to every public building in downtown New York. Horace Greely's newspaper reporter counted 6,100 men praying, but he could make it to only twelve of the prayer meetings in one hour. Then a landslide of prayer began, and men and women came to Christ. Ten thousand per week in New York trusted Christ. The awakening spread, and in one year more than a million people came to Christ. Eventually, the revival crossed the Atlantic and made itself felt throughout the world for a generation.

At the turn of the twentieth century, men and women again began to pray for an outpouring of God's Spirit. At special prayer meetings held at Moody Bible Institute in Chicago, the Keswick Convention in New England, Australia, India, and Korea, men and women prayed for revival. In 1904 it began in Wales, where 100,000 came to Christ in five months. But not only were the churches filled with new converts, the social impact on Wales was astounding. Judges received white gloves because there were no cases to try: no rapes, no robberies, no murders, no burglaries. Officials even met to discuss what to do with the unoccupied police force.

From Great Britain, revival recrossed the Atlantic. At Yale University twenty-five percent of the student body participated in prayer and Bible study groups. In Portland two hundred forty stores signed an agreement to close from 11 to 2 for prayer. The headline in the *Denver Post* on January 20, 1905, read "Entire City Pauses for Prayer Even at the High Tide of Business—Remarkable outburst of gospel sentiment . . . noonday meetings draw congregations unprecedented in numbers." The article went on to report,

> For two hours at midday all Denver was held in a spell. . . .
> The marts of trade were deserted between noon and two
> o'clock this afternoon, and all worldly affairs were forgotten,
> and the entire city was given over to meditation of higher
> things. The Spirit of the Almighty pervaded every nook.
> Going to and coming from the great meetings, the thousands

of men and women radiated this Spirit which filled them, and the clear Colorado sunshine was made brighter by the reflected glow of the light of God shining from happy faces. Seldom has such a remarkable sight been witnessed—an entire great city, in the middle of a busy weekday, bowing before the throne of heaven and asking and receiving the blessing of the King of the Universe.

Valdemar Hvidt, a Danish attorney, knew the importance of prayer. He tackled the biggest problem he could imagine in the 1930s—unemployment at the height of the Great Depression, which was much more severe in Europe than in the United States. With little prospect of success, Hvidt convened a group of associates to tackle the problem. They began by praying for guidance about how to solve an impossible situation. As a result, they implemented new ideas that resulted in thousands of new jobs. In addition, old political adversaries buried the hatchet for the sake of the country, and great progress was made until the Nazi occupation ended their efforts in 1939. When Denmark faced a far darker problem than unemployment, Hvidt's prayer group assumed a new role as part of the Christian Resistance Movement.[2]

Benjamin Franklin understood the importance of prayer. At a juncture in the Constitutional Convention, which was fraught with controversy, Franklin rose and recommended that the delegates convene with daily prayer and commit their work to the Lord. He cautioned them,

I have lived a long time, and the longer I live the more convincing proof I see of this truth, that God governs in the affairs of men. If a sparrow cannot fall to the ground without His notice, is it probable that an empire can rise without His aid? We have been assured in the Sacred Writings that "Except the Lord build the house, they labor in vain that build it." I firmly believe that without His concurring aid we shall proceed in this political building no better than the builders of Babel.[3]

Most recently the United States understood the importance of prayer. Even with all of our sophisticated military technology, we had no assurance that we could beat Sadam Hussein's army in desert warfare. As American forces went to the desert, we went to church and prayed. As a result, tens of thousands of body bags came back from the Persian Gulf—empty.

Daniel understood the importance of prayer. In chapter 9 of Daniel we discover why he threw caution to the wind and prayed so urgently even though he faced the lions' den. Something much more important than his personal safety was at stake. The restoration of the Jewish homeland lay in the balance. Even though he had significant political sway, Daniel knew that no man's influence was enough to accomplish God's grand purposes for Israel. So Daniel added the power of prayer to all his personal effort. Daniel's prayer in chapter 9 provides a paradigm for effective prayer for anyone who longs to change his or her world.

HOW TO PRAY EFFECTIVELY

Immerse Yourself in God's Word

Some men and women tend to look at God like a celestial genie. Rub Him the right way and you get what you want. Effective prayer is not manipulating God to do our bidding. It is not asking a reluctant God to do our will. Instead, it is asking a generous God to accomplish His purposes. We discover His purposes in the Bible— His ways, His likes and dislikes, His concerns, and His promises. The more we understand His Word, the more confidence we will have as we pray. Christ says in John 15:7, "If you remain in me and my words remain in you, ask whatever you wish, and it will be given you." Christ's promise is a call for us not only to know, but to internalize the life-giving Word of God.

The Word of God and prayer go hand in hand. Andrew Murray said it like this:

> Little of the Word with little prayer is death to the spiritual life. Much of the Word with little prayer gives a sickly life. Much prayer with little of the Word gives emotional life. But a full measure of both the Word and prayer each day gives a healthy and powerful life.[4]

Daniel must have understood this principle. As busy as he was with government affairs, Daniel found time to pray several times a day and study the Word of God: "Three times a day he got down on his knees and prayed, giving thanks to his God" (6:10). When Daniel prayed, according to God's Word, he asked God to fulfill the promises He had made to Israel: "I, Daniel, understood from the Scriptures, according to the word of the Lord given to Jeremiah the prophet, that the desolation of Jerusalem would last seventy years. So I turned to the Lord God and pleaded with him in prayer and petition" (9:2-3).

Let's face it. There is never enough time, and I personally am constantly juggling priorities to get everything done. But developing the spiritual disciplines of prayer and study are not as much a matter of priority as a matter of recognition. In my own life, when I recognize my desperate need of guidance and wisdom, and understand God's eagerness to give, then I have no trouble giving prayer and Bible study a priority in my life. Until I do that, no sense of duty will consistently motivate me over the long haul. Abraham Lincoln felt this necessity many times during the dark days of the war between the states. He wrote, "I have been driven many times upon my knees by the overwhelming conviction that I had nowhere else to go. My own wisdom, and that of all about me, seemed insufficient for that day."

Coming face to face with our own limitations and honestly assessing the needs of the day will also drive us to prayer. When a colleague asked Martin Luther about his schedule for the following day, Luther told him, "Work, work from early until late. In fact, I have so much to do that I shall spend the first three hours in prayer." Rather than detracting from our daily work, whether it is translating Scripture or transplanting hearts, prayer makes us more effective. In fact, when we realize we can do nothing apart from Christ, prayer will become as natural to us as breathing.

Believe in the Power of Prayer

Daniel did something amazing when he discovered God's promise to restore Palestine to the Jews. He prayed. Daniel rested securely in God's sovereignty, but far from sitting back immobilized, Daniel leaped to action and prayed, sensing he could play a part in the fulfillment of God's promise.

When God calls us to action, prayer is not the only thing, but it is the first and most important thing we need to do. Men and women who pray effectively have confidence in the fact that God is forever listening to the cry of His children. Even though they believe that God is sovereign, they believe that prayer moves the hand that moves the world.

Do we really believe that prayer changes things? If we do, we will pray about everything, trusting God to use our prayer to accomplish His will. Knowing God has promised to return, I still pray, "Thy kingdom come." Knowing God has chosen mates for my boys, I still pray for them to make godly choices. Knowing that God already knows how you will respond to this book, I still pray for its effect on your life. Knowing God has sovereignly chosen the fate of our nation, I still pray for another spiritual awakening. My hope is that my prayers, along with thousands of others, are all part of God's sovereign plan to bring it about. I feel tremendously privileged to play some small part in that plan.

Give God Your Full Attention

Effective prayer involves our whole being. Great men and women of prayer get wrapped up in their prayers. Note that when Daniel chose to intercede for his nation, he was single-mindedly engaged, emotionally distraught, volitionally active, and physically alert. Effective prayer is serious business that deserves the totality of our being. It is not for lazy or half-hearted Christians. On the contrary, prayer is hard work. This being the case, we need to select times to pray when we can be alert and focused. Mind, will, and emotions must all be engaged.

[handwritten margin note: MIND WILL EMOTIONS NEEDED TO PRAY]

In my own life, I must confess with embarrassment that many times I am only half there, like the little boy whose mind was on hold while his mouth was on automatic: "Now I lay me down to sleep. I pray Thee Lord my soul to keep. If he hollers, let him go. Eeny, Meeny, miney, mo." If that happens to you, apologize as though you were talking face to face with someone. You are. Then focus your mind or come back later when you can think clearly about what you are doing.

Don't Give Up

When God calls on us to wait for His answer, there is a tremendous tendency to doubt God's goodness. Christ, however, reminds us that God's willingness to answer our prayers far eclipses our willingness to give good things to our own children (Matthew 7:9-11). So why does He make us wait? Many times He is preparing us to receive our request. Perhaps our faith needs enlarging or our hope transferred to God from the circumstances we requested. Maybe it is to intensify our earnestness in seeking God. For whatever the reason, the Bible tells us not to give up, but to keep praying. Instead of causing us to diminish our efforts in prayer, delay should intensify our asking. If asking does not get it, we should send out a search party, earnestly seeking the Lord. If seeking does not do it, we need to move to noisy knocking, earnestly persevering until we have what we want.

Watch where you put your hope. Though God loves to answer the prayers of His children, there are times when we ask for things that would not be good for us or the world. From our limited perspective, it seems so crystal clear what should be done. But we should always remember to hold our perspective with some degree of suspicion. Only God sees the whole. Only He has the wisdom to know exactly what is the best way to accomplish His good purpose for us.

> At the Promise Keepers Conference in July 1993, Wellington Boone gave the men in attendance an excellent formula for praying with perseverance:
>
> P-U-S-H
> Pray Until Something Happens.

If you're like me, you have a tendency to latch hold of the answer you desire rather than the One who answers. This is dangerous. I've learned it's all too easy for my delight to move subtly from God to the circumstance I desire. When this happens, God may delay His answer to my prayer so that my hope will return to Him. He may also see that what I request is not best, or that there is a better way to accomplish what I really desire.

When my four-year tour of duty in grad school came to a close, I began the interview process. As my classmates and I interviewed with potential employers, one particular position stood out to Kathy and me as we considered our future. The situation looked perfect—great people, great place, and great pay. So Kathy and I began to pray. Days turned into weeks as we waited to hear. Nothing.

As graduation neared, we became more anxious, wondering not only if God would answer our prayer, but if I would even have a job. By April I was depressed. Then, out of the blue, another position opened up. We interviewed, liked the people, and three days before graduation, I had a job. Two weeks after graduation, I was offered the first position we had prayed for so intently, and wanted so desperately. I thanked them and said that I had taken another job. As it turned out, I did get the best position offered that spring. I got everything I wanted, but it was not the particular thing I asked for.

If I become fixated on the answer to my prayer rather than God, my faith will be shaken. We need to constantly be on guard and remember that God is our only hope. David prayed, "Keep me safe, O God, for in you I take refuge. I said to the LORD, 'You are my Lord; apart from you I have no good thing'" (Psalm 16:1). David ends Psalm 16 with this word of praise: "You have made known to me the path of life; you will fill me with joy in your presence, with eternal pleasures at your right hand" (verse 11). Our hope is in the God who answers, not in the answer.

Make God's Glory Your Ultimate Goal

When we follow great men and women of prayer through the Bible and history, we find that they concern themselves with God's glory. They want others to recognize God's greatness and power. That's a servant's concern, isn't it—not the glory of the servant but the exaltation of his master. Perhaps that is why so many of our prayers are ineffective. We have our roles reversed. I have prayed many prayers that were motivated by what people think of me rather than by concern for God's reputation. It's not that my requests were out of line or even selfish by nature. It's just that I was more concerned about my glory than God's.

The consuming motive behind every prayer request we make should be God's glory. James pins us to the motive mat pretty tightly in his letter. He says, "You do not have, because you do not ask God. When you ask, you do not receive, because you ask with wrong motives, that you may spend what you get on your pleasures" (James 4:2-3). God has nothing against pleasure. He invented it. But pleasure is a gift from God, not a goal. God is the goal. If my own interests or status consume me, it's a sure bet I'll never get what I want. And what I do get will never be enough to satisfy me.

One of the interesting paradoxes of life is that we can totally immerse ourselves in the Master's work and be totally consumed with our glory and status before men at the same time. The fact that God tolerates our disloyalty and consents to use unrighteous vessels is an incredible testimony to His grace, humility, and power.

It seems to me that our motives would be a safe object of scrutiny if we were praying for the spiritual revival of the U.S. Personally, I find that all kinds of motives, which have nothing to do with God's glory, try to creep into my mind as I pray—to be able to say I was right, to play a prominent role, to be known as one of the ones who prayed revival in, not to have to feel as if I am climbing uphill against the culture all the time. When these things drive my prayers, I am asking to spend what I get on my pleasures. I might as well ask God to make me rich so I can indulge all my fantasies. No. It's worse than that.

God made us by nature servants, and we can never know fulfillment seeking our own glory. We were made for God's pleasure and His glory. God's glory is not only the motive behind effective prayer; it is always in our best interest as well.

Make Knowing God Your Highest Priority

God made it clear, in no uncertain terms, through the prophet Jeremiah, that He feels strongly about an intimate relationship with His children.

This is what the LORD says:

> "Let not the wise man boast of his wisdom
>   or the strong man boast of his strength
>   or the rich man boast of his riches,
> but let him who boasts boast about this:
>   that he understands and knows me,
> that I am the LORD, who exercises kindness,
>   justice and righteousness on earth,
>   for in these I delight," declares the LORD.
>   (Jeremiah 9:23-24)

Having an impact on the world is a collaborative effort in which God allows us to participate and play a vital role, especially through prayer. There's no doubt that our knowledge of God and understanding of what He desires us to do tempers our prayers. How often we miss God's best because we fail to ask according to the greatness of His character and might! Simply consider the following things we know about God. He is

◆ Eager to answer, without reluctance (Isaiah 65:24)
◆ Able to do more than we can imagine (Ephesians 3:20-21)
◆ Incredibly generous, giving more than we ask or deserve (Jeremiah 33:3, Psalm 86:5)
◆ Absolutely good (Matthew 7:9,11)
◆ In total control (Ephesians 1:11)
◆ Utterly faithful to fulfill His promises (Numbers 23:19)

So how should knowing these things affect our prayers? E. M. Bounds challenges us,

> We tread altogether too gingerly on the great and precious promises of God and too often we ignore them wholly. The promise is the ground on which faith stands in asking of God. This is the one basis of prayer. We limit God's ability. We measure God's ability and willingness to answer prayer by the standards of men.[3]

Prayer is like a window of the spirit, and what we are able to see by faith to a large extent depends on the size of our God. Knowing who God is will allow us to visualize and ask the impossible. *INTIMATE* Could God's Spirit fall upon this nation again? Could businesses close their doors to allow men and women time to call upon God in prayer? Could millions come to Christ? Could Washington come up with a solution to resolve the national debt crisis? Could policemen wonder how to spend their time because of a crash in the crime rate? Could democracy replace communism in China? Could Croatians and Serbs live in peace? Not without Christ and not without prayer.

Just a few years ago, we would have listed the fall of the Berlin Wall and the crash of communism in the former USSR in the preceding list. I'm not sure I would have been able to pray with real confidence in 1988 that the Berlin Wall would fall. But someone did. The more we learn about the events in Eastern Europe, the more we see that the sovereign hand of God moved at the request of God's children. He is able to do exceeding abundantly beyond all we ask or think. How I wish I knew this better. Nancy Spiegleberg describes my frustration with myself so well.

> Lord,
> I crawled across the barrenness to you
>   with my empty cup,
> Uncertain
>   in asking any small drop of refreshment.
> If I had only known you better,
> I'd have come running with a bucket.[4]

If you and I knew God better, what would we have the courage to ask?

HOW TO PRAY FOR THE UNITED STATES

Hopefully, one of the things we would pray early, late, and long for is the spiritual renewing of the U.S. We would not just sit by as passive observers watching the pied pipers of secularism lead our nation down the road to certain destruction. We are not powerless. We can pray. In fact, our nation's future depends more on your prayer and mine than the quality of leaders we have in Washington.

Pray for Our Government's Leaders
In Paul's correspondence with Timothy we find these essential instructions:

> I urge, then, first of all, that requests, prayers, intercessions and thanksgiving be made for everyone—for kings, and all those in authority, that we may live peaceful and quiet lives in all godliness and holiness. This is good, and pleases God our Savior. . . . I want men everywhere to lift up holy hands in prayer, without anger or disputing. (1 Timothy 2:1-3,8)

Paul uses some of the strongest language in the New Testament to emphasize his point. He is not suggesting a good idea here. He is

pleading with us as if our lives depended on it. And to further emphasize his point, he grabs the thesaurus and commandeers every word
the Greeks used for prayer in this one sentence: "requests, prayers,
intercessions and thanksgiving." I'd say he was pretty serious.

We should cover every leader in our country with an avalanche
of prayer. If we did this, I wonder what would happen. Truthfully, I
don't wonder—I know. Our nation would change. God may or may
not give you and me the responsibility to occupy public office, but
He has given every child of God the power to influence those who do.
Charles Stanley suggests nine ways to pray for our leaders:

- Pray that they would realize their personal sinfulness and
  their daily need for cleansing of their sins by Jesus Christ.
- Pray that they would recognize their personal inadequacy to
  fulfill their tasks and that they would depend upon God for
  knowledge, wisdom, and the courage to do what is right.
- Pray that they would reject all counsel that violates spiritual
  principles, trusting God to prove them right.
- Pray that they would resist those who would pressure them
  to violate their conscience.
- Pray that they would reverse the trends of socialism and
  humanism in this nation, both of which deify man rather
  than God.
- Pray that they would be ready to sacrifice their personal
  ambitions and political careers for the sake of this nation, if
  yielding them would be in the best interest of their country.
- Pray that they would rely upon prayer and the Word of God
  as the source of their daily strength, wisdom, and courage.
- Pray they would remember to be good examples in their
  conduct to fathers, mothers, sons, and daughters of this
  nation.
- Pray that they would be reminded daily that they are
  accountable to Almighty God for the decisions they make.[5]

Pray for those who influence culture. Although we all influence
culture to some degree, certain career fields have been afforded a
larger sphere of influence: educators, including teachers, administrators, and writers; both print and broadcast media professionals,

including, reporters, editors, and writers; entertainment figures, including musicians, vocalists, actors, and television personalities; sports figures, including athletes and coaches. The people have conferred incredible power to individuals in these fields to define and direct culture—toward truth or error. Unfortunately, men and women who have no moral anchor, or even worse, who are openly hostile toward biblical Christianity occupy many of these positions of public trust. Take Ted Turner for example.

Turner's creation, CNN, is the most-listened-to news source in America, with an increasing global impact. Speaking to newspaper executives in Atlanta, Turner said that the Ten Commandments are out of date: "When Moses went up on the mountain, there were no nuclear weapons. There was no problem with the ozone layer or these other problems." Turner suggested that the Ten Commandments be replaced with his own version that he calls the "Ten Voluntary Initiatives." The first is, "I love and respect planet Earth and all living things thereon, especially my fellow species, mankind." The second, "And I promise to treat all persons everywhere with dignity, respect, and friendliness."[6]

Praying diligently that God would turn individuals like Ted Turner to the truth is very important. When we turn on the news, go to a movie, pick up a book or magazine, go to class, or attend a sporting event, we should take the opportunity to pray that God would turn every individual involved toward the truth. We should also pray that He would protect our minds from falsehood and evil, and for courage and protection for godly individuals in these fields who are attempting to stand for what is right. We must also pray that God would reveal to the public the true spiritual nature of those persons hostile to the truth and break up evil's monopoly in these fields, so that new individuals committed to serving Christ will have the opportunity to serve Him there.

Pray for Our Spiritual Leaders

It has become apparent through their moral failure that our nation's spiritual leaders are ordinary men and women just like you and me. This would have been no surprise, had we read the Bible thoroughly. Unfortunately, the effect of their fall is not ordinary at all. We need to pray that God will protect all spiritual leaders from

Satan's attacks and enticements, and that their commitment to the truth might extend beyond their words deep into their hearts. We need to pray that each of them will provide a model of integrity and humility that will bring glory to God.

Pray for Business Leaders and Specifically Your Place of Work
In his booklet *Winning Back the Soul of American Business*, Os Guinness states,

> Anyone who delves deeply into the American situation in the 1990s comes up against a conundrum and a challenge. The conundrum lies in the fact that American business is close to the heart of both the American crisis and the necessary answer to that crisis. The challenge lies in the fact that far too few business leaders have recognized the nature of the problem and far too few Christian leaders have stepped forward to offer a constructive response.[7]

The fact is that the values that dominate the marketplace—power, possessions, and position—also dominate American culture. Guinness and many others are doubtful that this culture will change until American business reorients its compass away from materialism toward biblical values. But not only is this country at stake, capitalism itself is fueled by the character traits that only Christ can produce consistently: hard work, self-denial, thrift, saving, and moral living. Selfish materialism cannot supply the kind of leadership needed to energize a free market economy. Eventually government will feel compelled to curtail the greed, label it "obscene profit," and redistribute wealth—unless something more than hedonistic accumulation drives the marketplace.

We need to pray that Christians everywhere will recognize that Jesus Christ is Lord of the marketplace. Pray that they will exercise the discipline of craftsmanship in their work, doing their best work for God and their fellow man, and that God will expand their sphere of influence. Pray that business leaders would hear the high calling of God to serve Christ in meeting the physical needs of their fellow man. Pray that God would expand the profit and influence of businesses run on godly principles of business.

Pray for Unbelievers
The United States has the fourth largest nonChristian population
in the world. The latest figures indicate that there are 164 million
Americans who do not have a personal relationship with Jesus
Christ. We should ask God to free these individuals from their sin
through Jesus Christ. Pray that as they become Christians there
will be someone or some church close by to guide them further into
the truth.

Pray for Believers
Americans are the most spiritually blessed people in the world, yet
we have so little to show for it. We need to ask for courage to stand
for what we know is right and to get involved when called to action.
We need wisdom to recognize and take advantage of the opportunities we have for impact. We must pray for commitment to the truth,
to righteous living, and to solid relationships, and for compassion
to replace judgmental attitudes toward those caught in sin.

What an incredible privilege God has given us! How can we
remain pessimistic about America when God has given us the ability to pray? Keep these words of E. M. Bounds in mind:

> God's greatest movements in this world have been condi-
> tioned on, continued and fashioned by prayer. God has put
> Himself in the great movements just as men have prayed.
> Persistent, prevailing, conspicuous and mastering prayer has
> always brought God to be present.
>
> How vast are the possibilities of prayer! How wide its
> reach! It lays its hand on Almighty God and moves Him to do
> what He would not do if prayer was not offered. Prayer is a
> wonderful power placed by Almighty God in the hands of His
> saints, which may be used to accomplish great purposes and
> to achieve unusual results. The only limits to prayer are the
> promises of God and His ability to fulfill those promises.[8]

THE BIG IDEA

God uses prayer to accomplish His sovereign purposes. We
can use prayer to change our culture.

Use the following thoughts and ideas to stimulate your thinking about prayer.

The greatest thing we can do for God and man is pray.
It is not the only thing, but it is the chief thing.
The great people of the earth are the people who pray.
I do not mean those who talk about prayer;
nor those who say they believe in prayer;
nor yet those who can explain about prayer;
but I mean those people who take time to pray.
S. D. GORDON

Sixteen key individuals affect your life every day if you live in the United States. Pray for them by name.

◆ The President
◆ Two senators from your state
◆ One congressman from your district
◆ The governor of your state
◆ The state senator from your district
◆ The state representative from your district
◆ Nine Supreme Court judges

Prayer may not change things for you,
but it for sure changes you for things.
SAMUEL M. SHOEMAKER

We tread altogether too gingerly upon the great and precious
promises of God, and too often we ignore them wholly.
The promise is the ground on which faith stands
in asking of God. This is the one basis of prayer.
We limit God's ability. We measure God's ability and willingness
to answer by prayer by the standard of men.
E. M. BOUNDS
Possibilities in Prayer

*Men may spurn our appeals, reject our message,
oppose our arguments, despise our persons, but they
are helpless against our prayers.*
J. SIDLOW BAXTOR

*The one concern of the devil is to keep saints from prayer.
He fears nothing from prayerless studies,
prayerless work, prayerless religion.
He laughs at our toil, mocks at our wisdom,
but trembles when we pray.*
SAMUEL CHADWICK

*Hearty, heroic, compassionate,
fearless martyrs must the men be who take hold of and shape
a generation for God. If they are timid timeservers,
place seekers, if they be men pleasers or men fearers,
if their faith has a weak hold on God or His Word,
if their denial be broken by any phase of self or the world, they
cannot take hold of the Church
nor the world for God.*
E. M. BOUNDS

*God shapes the world through prayer.
Prayers are deathless. The lips that uttered them may be closed
in death, the heart that felt them may have ceased to beat,
but the prayers live before God,
and God's heart is set on them and prayers outlive
the lives of those who uttered them; outlive a generation,
outlive an age, outlive a world.*
E. M. BOUNDS
Purpose in Prayer

A desire for God which cannot break the chains of sleep
is a weak thing and will do but little good for God
after it has indulged itself fully.
The desire for God that keeps so far behind the devil
and the world at the beginning of the day will never catch up.
E. M. BOUNDS
Power Through Prayer

❖

Revival—the inrush of the Spirit of God into a body
that threatens to become a corpse.
D. M. PANTON

❖

When we are praying about a result,
say, of a battle or a medical consultation,
the thought will often cross our minds that,
if we only knew it, the event is already decided one way
or the other. I believe this to be no good reason
for ceasing our prayers. The event certainly has been decided.
In a sense, it was decided before all the worlds.
But one of the things taken into account in deciding it,
and therefore one of the things that really causes it to happen,
may be this very prayer that we are now offering.
C. S. LEWIS

CHAPTER TEN

The Power of One
DANIEL 1–6

N o one even remotely in touch with current events could have missed the news coverage of "Magic" Johnson's announcement that he is HIV positive in 1991. It was a media circus. The morning of November 9, CNN coverage aired successive clips of Johnson's press conference, Pat Riley praying for Johnson with his team before their game, President Bush's public statement of personal concern, and a report that the Center for Disease Control in Atlanta had been deluged with 10,000 calls an hour about AIDS since the Thursday announcement.

Why does one person's tragedy affect so many people? Certainly AIDS is no backwater issue. It seems almost every star in Hollywood is either a spokesperson or fund-raiser for this cause. But everyone, from Health Department officials to those lobbying for AIDS research funding, predicted a massive increase in awareness because of the plight of one person. The reason is that Earvin Johnson is in a truly influential position. And whether we like it or not, Johnson is influencing the moral values of our nation—perhaps even more than the Church.

The withdrawal of the evangelical Church from significant interaction with our culture during the greater part of this century has had a devastating result. The separatism that flowed from the

Scopes Trial in the 1920s left a vacuum of influence in our culture that secular thinking has eagerly filled. George Gallup quantified the loss of influence in his research. He found that the percentage of those who believe "religion" is losing its influence in America has grown from fourteen percent to forty-nine percent in the last thirty years.[1]

Although Gallup concluded that the U.S. is still a religious country, the sincerity of faith evidenced in his research did not impress him. He wrote, "While religion is highly popular in our country, survey evidence suggests that it is only superficial—it does not change people's lives to the degree one would expect from the level of professed faith."[2] As we consider how to regain lost ground, the book of Daniel gives us some clear insights. In his seventy-plus years of service, Daniel exerted a consistent influence in the Babylonian and Persian governments that not only changed the lives of individuals but the course of history as well.

We often think of individuals like Daniel, David, Alexander the Great, Martin Luther, and Joan of Arc as men and women of destiny. They seem to have appeared almost magically in history at precisely the right time. In recent history, figures such as George Washington, Abraham Lincoln, William Wilberforce, Winston Churchill, John Kennedy, and Martin Luther King, Jr., come to mind.

A close examination of their lives, however, reveals that they were just ordinary people exercising the disciplines of influence on a micro level. They had a destiny for influence before God dropped them in a bigger pond for macro impact. Very likely, if we had approached them during their lifetime and told them they were having a cultural impact, they would have incredulously said, "I'm just doing my job." Billy Graham, Mother Teresa, and others still living would say the same thing.

In God's plan, each of us has a destiny. Though the world may never know your name or mine, we have a calling to influence our generation for Christ. The individuals in the early Church understood this well. By the end of the first century, the followers of Christ had grown from a few hundred to an estimated 500,000. What explains such a remarkable growth in a day glaringly devoid of any means of mass communication?

The prime agents in the spread of the gospel were not a *few* men and women gifted in communication using extraordinary means to reach *thousands*, but rather *thousands* reaching a *few* at a time. It was the little man and the unknown woman who used the every-day opportunities of life to speak of Christ to others. As early as the eighth chapter of the book of Acts, we discover that it is the amateur missionary who began to take the gospel out of Jerusalem and even-tually to the far reaches of the Roman empire. For the most part it was not by means of formal presentations, but "gossiping the gospel" with friends, associates, and acquaintances, over meals, on the high-ways, and during the course of ordinary commerce.

From this group, God elevated a few we can call by name: Peter, Paul, Barnabas, and John. But even these were ordinary men who took the will of God seriously, no matter how big a pond their rip-ples disturbed.

WHAT IS INFLUENCE?

Influence is the power or capacity to produce a desired result, to impact or to cause some change to take place. The power of influ-ence is very different from the power of legislation pursued so fer-vently by evangelicals during the 1980s. Rather than focusing on laws, influence focuses on hearts. Although both involve power, the power of influence is granted rather than imposed. The power of influence given to Magic Johnson, for instance, was not legislated, but was conferred by willing people from their heart.

Influence changes people from the inside out. It sways their thoughts, their perceptions, and their values. As a result, influ-ence also has the power to subtly change behavior. Recognizing this, Madison Avenue has paid Johnson millions of dollars to influ-ence the public's behavior to buy certain products. Interestingly, shares of Carter-Wallace stock, maker of Trojan condoms, went up $3.00 at the news that Johnson would become a spokesper-son for safe sex.[3]

THE SOURCE OF INFLUENCE

Where does this kind of power come from? What is the source of influence? Why does Magic Johnson hold the power to sway our thinking and behavior? Obviously, sports figures in the U.S. are among the most highly esteemed heroes of our culture. We afford them authority to influence us far beyond their expertise. Professional football players, for example, endorse everything from sports equipment to panty hose. Is there something beyond just being in an influential career? Was the fact that Daniel worked in the king's court the only reason he exerted the influence he did over the years?

Throughout the book of Daniel, God's formula for impact unfolds. Far from resting on one factor, several elements emerge that must come together. The foundational first requirement for impact is obvious competence—the pursuit of excellence in one's daily work. Scripture lends credence to this idea. Proverbs 22:29 states, "Do you see a man skilled in his work? He will serve before kings; he will not serve before obscure men." Nehemiah is a good example of this truth. He based his appeal to the king on the excellence of his service: "If it pleases the king and your servant has found favor in his sight, let him send me to the city in Judah where my fathers are buried so that I can rebuild it" (Nehemiah 2:5). Paul commanded us, "Whatever you do, work at it with all your heart" (Colossians 3:24).

Dorothy Sayers, a colleague of C. S. Lewis, wrote,

In nothing has the church so lost her hold on reality as in her failure to understand and respect the secular vocation. She has allowed work and religion to become separate departments, and is astonished to find that, as a result, the secular work of the world is turned to purely selfish and destructive ends, and that the greater part of the world's intelligent workers have become irreligious, or at least, uninterested in religion. But is it so astonishing? How can anyone remain interested in a religion which seems to have no concern with nine-tenths of his life? The church's approach to an intelligent carpenter is usually confined to exhorting him not to be drunk and disorderly in his leisure hours, and to come to church on Sundays. What the church should be telling him is this: that the first demand that his religion makes on him is that he should make good tables.[4]

Professional athletes provide an excellent paradigm of influence, because we immediately see not only the importance of excellent work, but also its source. The public does not give the power of influence to everyone who plays basketball or football. The factor that confers the power of influence is excellence. Certain players stand out because of their ability to produce excellence, even among the talented ranks of the NBA. Bench sitters do not interest Madison Avenue—it's the standouts that do. It is the prodigious ability some men and women have that makes them so influential. Their amazing talent makes them extremely valuable to those who want to influence the buying power of the American public. A cultural value system that elevates sports stars provides them the opportunity. The disciplined exercise of their gifts enables them to take advantage of that opportunity, giving them the platform to speak.

The power of influence is not merely a matter of having an influential career, but also a matter of giftedness. The disciplined exercise of God-given talents gives authority to a person, regardless of the breadth of influence he or she may have been given.

The opposite is also true. No matter how strategic the career, without the gift, there is no power. In fact, there is a negative effect. Many people believe that Jimmy Carter, while being one of the finest men in the White House in our lifetime, did not possess the gifts needed to accomplish his goals as President. The words *born again* became a term of derision during the late 1970s due in some degree to his administration. It is, however, intriguing that today, while still regarded as a poor president, some call him "the best former president we have ever had." It is fascinating how much respect Carter commands today compared to his time in office. He is more positively influential now in a less influential career. The crucial difference is a matter of giftedness. The following parable illustrates the devastating results of moving outside your core competence.

Once upon a time, the animals decided they should do something meaningful to meet the problems of the new world. So they organized a school. They adopted an activity curriculum of running, climbing, swimming and flying. To make it easier to administer the curriculum, all the animals took all the subjects.

The duck was excellent in swimming; in fact, better than his instructor. But he made only passing grades in flying, and was very poor in running. Since he was slow in running, he had to drop swimming and stay after school to practice running. This caused his web feet to be badly worn, so that he was only average in swimming. But average was acceptable, so nobody worried about that—except the duck.

The rabbit started at the top of his class in running, but developed a nervous twitch in his muscles because of so much make-up work in swimming.

The squirrel was excellent in climbing, but he encountered constant frustration in flying class because his teacher made him start from the ground up instead of from the tree-top down. He developed charley horses from over-exertion, and so only got a C in climbing and a D in running.

The eagle was a problem child and was severely disciplined for being a non-conformist. In climbing classes he beat all the others to the top of the tree, but insisted on using his own way to get there.[5]

What is true of these forest creatures is also true of us. When individuals operate in the realm of their core competencies, they excel because they are energized and receive a great deal of satisfaction from what they do. On the other hand, when they ignore their design, there is a predictable scenario of mediocrity and burnout. If the impact were merely personal, it would be bad enough. But it is not. Mediocrity drastically affects our impact on others. Frank Gaebelein, one of the premier Christian educators in the U.S., is said to have once warned, "Nothing is more dangerous to the faith of youth than for them to make the disconcerting discovery that the men who have advocated their faith are men of mediocre ability."

Consider the impact Daniel would have had on Nebuchadnezzar or Darius had Daniel been mediocre at what he was doing. Neither of these men would have been inclined to listen to his witness, had he not been an excellent administrator. But when Nebuchadnezzar tested his new servants, "he found none equal to Daniel, Hananiah, Mishael, and Azariah. . . . In every matter of wisdom and understanding about which the king questioned them, he found them ten times better than all the magicians and enchanters in his kingdom" (1:19-20). Seventy years later, Darius confronted the same competence: "Now Daniel so distinguished himself among the administrators and the satraps by his exceptional qualities that the king planned to set him over the whole kingdom" (6:3).

The emerging paradigm then seems to be: Giftedness coupled with opportunity produces a positive influence. Opportunity coupled with incompetence results in a negative impact. The gift provides the true authority. The opportunity given by culture provides the breadth of the expression of authority.

Another factor crucial to the paradigm of influence is responsible action. God may give the gift, but the individual must still choose to discover, develop, and employ that gift. Culture may provide the opportunities for us to touch vast numbers of people, but we must still choose to take that path. Chuck Swindoll writes, "Soaring never just happens. It is the result of a strong mental effort—thinking clearly, courageously, confidently. No one ever oozed his way out of mediocrity like a lazy slug."[6]

I've often wondered how many gifted athletes have chosen not to take the hard road of discipline that could have led them to professional status. How many highly intelligent students coasted through school, never stretching for their potential? How many young people gifted in scientific discovery have shied away from that field because it is dominated by nonChristians? Whether a result of laziness, or honest misunderstanding, individuals waste their gifts when they fail to accept the discipline of training and craftsmanship. We are responsible for developing what God gives us.

We came face to face with this fact in our initial introduction to Daniel. He and his friends were gifted—intellectually superior. But that was not enough. Their gift had to be developed, and they faithfully endured three grueling years of disciplined study. Daniel was faithful to develop what God had given him. No wonder we read at the end of Daniel 1, "And Daniel remained there [in the king's court] until the first year of King Cyrus."

But giftedness and discipline make up only two-thirds of the influence equation. Another equally important factor of influence comes to mind, especially as we think of political figures such as

Daniel. Character follows hard on the heels of ability in the influence equation. Great character must govern great gifts if we want to maintain influence gained by competent work. Lack of integrity has aborted the influence of many a leader. Notable modern examples include Richard Nixon and Jim Wright. In business, names like Michael Milken and Charles Keeting come to mind. In the religious realm, Jimmy Swaggart and Jim Bakker are memorable examples of influence lost. Every one of these men was brilliant at what he did. But no amount of brilliance could overcome the character flaws that brought their downfall.

On the other side are figures of virtue like Billy Graham, Jack Eckerd, C. Everett Koop, and Margaret Thatcher. Their integrity over the years has made even their toughest critics respect and admire them.

Character, however, involves much more than integrity. As Christians, we need to think of the full range of attributes contained in the concept of Christlikeness. Characteristics such as love, joy, peace, patience, kindness, goodness, faithfulness, gentleness, and self-control (Galatians 5:22-23) are attributes that God wants the world to see in His family. Authentic Christlikeness consistently impresses men and women. Unfortunately, the shoddy caricatures all too often presented by Christians, not only misrepresent reality, they repulse people. But the man or woman who is growing in Christ and becoming more like Him every day is the most powerful influence for the Kingdom in our time. In Paul's words, godly character "adorns the doctrine of God" (Titus 2:10, NASB). The clear paradigm of influence that emerges from Daniel's life is simply this:

COMPETENCE + CHARACTER = INFLUENCE

Although some careers have more strategic impact, every job is an opportunity for influence. Whether we engage in daily tasks that are strategically influential or not, our influence will emerge when we perform the common tasks of our work and life uncommonly well and back them with extraordinary character. There are no "spiritually neutral" tasks or careers. In every situation there is an opportunity to honor Christ. Paul makes this clear in Colossians 3:17. He writes, "And whatever you do, whether in word or deed, do it all in the name of the Lord Jesus, giving thanks to God the Father." Of work he specifically commands, "Whatever you do, work at it with all your heart, as working for the Lord, not for men" (3:23). This is our destiny. As influential as we may become on earth, we will never rise above the significance of being Christ's servant.

As a person accepts the discipline of development and craftsmanship, greater opportunities of influence may incrementally open up. In some instances, God may catapult men and women to totally new levels of influence they never dreamed of. Joseph was a young man who graduated from the school of incarceration to become prime minister of Egypt. Esther was a nice Jewish girl whom God had gifted with an abundance of grace and beauty. Suddenly she found herself as queen of Persia and had the opportunity to intervene in her people's annihilation. Daniel was a faithful man abruptly yanked from his home, and eventually he found himself the chief official in the courts of Nebuchadnezzar and Darius. In each case, these individuals were being faithful to the Lord right where they were. There was no aspiration of grandeur, only a desire to serve God.

Each of these acts of service required a large measure of courage to respond to the opportunity presented. I shudder to think what would have happened to the nation of Israel if men and women like these had followed the modern trend toward a "privatized faith"—personally engaging, but culturally irrelevant. We must reengage the culture on its turf, master its wisdom, face its challenges, and better it. As it did for Daniel, Esther, Joseph and anyone who has been in a similar situation, this will take a major dose of courage. It takes courage because we are entering the big time, and Satan will not sit by and offer merely token resistance. We can expect opposition as we have never seen it before. Only one thing stands at that point between us and our destiny—fear.

As a speaker for the 1993 Promise Keepers Conference, I was overwhelmed at being part of the largest peacetime gathering of men in United States history. My fear and anxiety only mounted as the time for my workshop approached. The question that Satan kept bombarding me with was, "What are you doing here? What do you have to offer these people?" The implication was that the other speakers had something much more significant to offer than I did. As I shared my feelings, I discovered that many of the other speakers felt the same way I did. Men who I was sure must be cool and calm, who had traveled all over the world, and spoken to thousands, were asking the same question I was asking: "What am I doing here?" It took courage for all of us to face the lie and believe that God had selected us and brought each of us to that place.

Courage comes from a close walk with God. He is the only antidote to fear. As Paul says, "If God is for us, who can be against us?" I have a Post-it note stuck to my computer that reads, "Be strong and take heart, all you who hope in the LORD" (Psalm 31:24). The Lord told Joshua, "Have I not commanded you? Be strong and courageous. Do not be terrified; do not be discouraged, for the LORD your God will be with you wherever you go" (Joshua 1:9).

God is the One who gives courage, but sometimes we need to hear those words from someone else. That's what encouragement is all about. It's putting courage into someone else's heart. I can't count the times in men's small groups that someone has had just the right word or passage of Scripture that brought courage to another person's heart. I know this chapter is about the power of one, and rightly so. But more times than not, the one who had the courage to stand and change history had someone or a group that encouraged him or her when fear came in like a thief stealing all sense of God's presence.

I was fortunate enough to have my nineteen-year-old son with me at Promise Keepers to remind me of the truth. I told him about my fear and that the stakes were high. He contemplated what he would tell me for some time. Then, just before I spoke as we sat quietly together, he leaned over and told me, "Dad, you're holding four aces and a trey, and threes are wild." God had gifted me to speak, He had given me a message, He had brought me to that place, I was prepared, and He was with me. Not a bad hand to face the devil's call. I stepped to the podium with courage, thanks to John.

The complete paradigm of influence looks like this:

**COMPETENCE + CHARACTER + COURAGE = GREAT
INFLUENCE**

God does NOTHING but IN ANSWER TO PRAYER !!

John Wesley said, "Give me one hundred preachers who fear nothing but sin, and desire nothing but God, and I care not a straw whether they be clergy or laymen; such alone will shake the gates of hell and set up the kingdom of heaven on earth. God does nothing but in answer to prayer." Wesley was right. But like most preachers, he exaggerated the numbers. All God needs is one. That one is you or me.

DISCOVERING OUR DESTINY

If we want to fulfill our destiny, it is apparent that we must follow hard after three things.

Discover Our Core Competencies and Strive for Excellence

Interestingly, today when we think of men and women doing God's work, we assume that spiritual activities such as prayer, Bible study, and evangelism will capture God's interest and pleasure. We might stretch it to include anything done for the church, or perhaps more broadly to family life or to some humanitarian activities. But how many people see their daily work as something valuable to God?

More often than not, we find men and women laboring under the assumption that their daily work means very little to God. One physician told me he grew up in a church that had a clear ranking system that looked like this:

    ★★★★ Missionaries
      ★★★ Pastors
        ★★ Christians who went to Bible college

If you were working in a "secular job" and had not been to Bible college, you were a lowly "one-star Christian."

If Christ is calling us to make an impact on our world, where is He leading? Many people feel that if they really get serious about serving God, they must leave the work world and go to seminary. Unfortunately, 2 Peter 3:10 is often misapplied, causing men and women to feel as if their work has absolutely no value to God. The argument usually goes like this: "You spend your life building temporal things and God comes along behind you and burns them up! Why would anyone pour their life into something so temporary?"

The argument goes on to suggest two things that God will not burn up: the Word of God and the souls of men and women. It is not difficult to see why people who buy this line of thinking make a mid-life job change and choose a vocational ministry.

Take a moment to think through what this means: Any job outside ministry is a colossal waste of time. Not only that, but anyone who chooses a vocation outside ministry is choosing God's second best. This thinking is not only unbiblical but also damaging to the cause of Christ, as well as to one's personal faith.[7] The sad fact is that many leave their work to discover that they not only abandoned their greatest sphere of influence but also lost the source of authority for their ministry. I'm glad Daniel and millions of others down through history have resisted this tripe. When Wilberforce made a serious commitment to Christ, he went to John Newton to discuss whether he should leave Parliament and go to seminary. Newton wisely reminded Wilberforce, "Maybe God has you there for a purpose." Indeed, He did. Wilberforce became one of the strongest forces for Christ in his generation, and millions live as free men and women today because of his personal crusade to end slavery in the British empire. Something that could have never been accomplished from a pulpit.

Over the years we have developed some rather strange ideas about God's will. If we think that the only way we can follow God fully is by going into vocational ministry, most of us will miss our destiny. We please God primarily by being what He designed us to be and acting in a way that He designed us to act. Following God's will is essentially and fundamentally being what He made us to be.

Man cut himself off from the universal chorus of praise offered by all creation by choosing to step outside his design and take his destiny into his own hands. Thwarted by our blinding sinfulness that obscures who we are, and a world system that asserts the prerogative of determining our function, men and women find it difficult to find their way back to their rightful place in creation. Redeemed men and women must learn to praise God not only in ritual, but fundamentally in the ordinary activities of their daily work. Think about it. Everything in nature does what God designed it to do but man. We are the only creatures who choose to attempt to be something we are not.

Most of us were brought up to believe that we could become anything we wanted to be. If we wanted it badly enough and were willing to work hard, we could open any door of opportunity. The world around us, for the most part, assumes the same thing. Businesses, schools, churches, and—sadly—even parents many times assume that they can mold and shape a person into something they want him or her to become. Businesses believe that they can take their top salesperson, send her to management training, and make her the sales manager. Schools believe that they can transform students who love to compete for grades into students who learn for the joy of learning. Churches assume that they can recruit a volunteer, put him through teacher training, and make a competent Sunday school teacher. The folly of this philosophy is apparent in the results: consistently poor performance and a plague of burnout.

Dr. Ann McGee-Cooper, a leading creativity expert, expressed this tendency like this:

> I grew up as a classic people pleaser. "Nice girls do as they are told. Nice girls don't hurt others' feelings." I learned my lesson well, so well that as an adult, I was so concerned about the feelings and needs of others that I had little awareness of my own. Saying yes to every request that came along was a classic symptom I displayed. I was so eager to please and be needed that I tried to do everything for everybody.[8]

Many young preachers have tried to mimic Chuck Swindoll, but listen to his own admission from *Growing Strong in the Seasons of Life*:

> Having been exposed to a few "greats" in various churches and an outstanding seminary, I (like some of the other guys in the class) tried to be like them. You know, think like, sound like, look like. For over ten years in the ministry I—a rabbit— worked hard at swimming like a duck or flying like an eagle. I was a frustrated composite creature . . . like that weird beast in the second chapter of Daniel. And my feet were slowly crumbling beneath me. The worst part of all, what little bit of

originality or creativity I had was being consumed in that false role I was forcing. One day my insightful and caring wife asked me, "Why not just be you? Why try to be like someone else?" Well, friends and neighbors, this rabbit quit the swim team and gave up flying lessons and stopped trying to climb. Talk about relief! And best of all, I learned it was OK to be me . . . and let my friends and family members be themselves. Originality and creativity flowed anew![9]

The question I need to ask is, "What am I designed to be?" If our lives have meaning and purpose, it is reasonable to assume that God shaped our being to accommodate our purpose. Ephesians 2:10 states this as strongly as I know: "For we are God's workmanship, created in Christ Jesus to do good works, which God prepared in advance for us to do."

God uniquely designed each person for a specific part of His work. As God created each of us with our unique inventory of abilities, He had our function in mind. By discovering our design, we uncover the mystery of our purpose. Understanding our design is the only reliable means of defining our specific purpose outside the audible voice of God.

Obviously, for a person to know true success and fulfillment, he needs to align himself with the creative purpose of God, discovering, accepting, developing, and using the abilities He has given. When we do, the effects are dramatic. In *Finding a Job You Can Love*, Ralph Mattson and Arthur Miller write,

When a man takes his correct position in creation, divine ecology falls into place and praise naturally emerges. Competence then manifests itself in work and play. . . . The incompetency we see everywhere is not because people lack gifts, but because they are not in the right place for their gifts. They are the stewards of what God has given them. There are plenty of gifts to do all the work that needs to be done everywhere and to do it gloriously well—so well, in fact, that people would go rejoicing from day to day over how much was accomplished and how well it was accomplished. But the world's systems, corrupted by the sin of man, place enormous obstacles in the way of each person who attempts to find his rightful place in creation. Such systems assume that people are fodder for their intentions.

In short, most Christians as well as nonChristians do not understand what a job means and cannot address the world on the matter of widespread waste of human resources. Therefore they cannot make a redemptive difference....

The result is too many Christians performing incompetent, second-rate work, replacing the biblical command to redeem the time with an intention to "put in some time," an unsatisfactory result for the world and for the Kingdom.[10]

If we are going to influence our world for Jesus Christ, we must understand and obey what God gifted us to do. Many of us, though, wonder how we discover our design. The clearest path is found by following the scent of joy in our life. When we do what God designed us to do, His energy flowing through us leaves an aroma of deep satisfaction in our mind not present in other activities. I've found it helpful to follow the joy in my life all the way back to my earliest memories and recall the things I have done. I asked myself, "What was I doing? Where was I doing it? Who, if anyone, was I doing it with? What did I accomplish?" When I found consistency, I knew I'd hit pay dirt.

Accept the Discipline of Character

Without character, the most gifted man or woman in the world will ultimately fail to influence anyone positively. God's goal for us as Christians is very clear—to conform us into the image of Christ. He achieves this goal in a number of ways, the most important of which is through intimacy with Christ Himself. Simply put, the more time I spend in intimate communication with Christ, the more He rubs off on me. Technically, I am dying, and more of Christ is coming to life in me. My old life is being exchanged for His new life. The more this balance shifts, the more like Christ I become.

Just as we have seen repeatedly in the life of Daniel, God uses difficult circumstances to shape our character. Of particular importance in our present discussion is what God does with our gifts. In my experience, the very last thing most of us want to surrender to God is the use of our gifts. It is the most potent and personal thing about us. Willful person that I am, I want to be able to do my thing when I want to do it. Of all the evil things in me, this intent must die for me to be like Christ.

The most devastating thing God can do to my old self is to put me in a position where I cannot use my gifts. There God reminds me, "These are My gifts. I can use them, or not use them, as I see fit." I can honestly say that the misery of waiting is the most painful thing that I have ever experienced. This claiming of my gifts is the most necessary part of my sanctification. Apart from it, I cannot be like Christ. Apart from Christ's control, my gifts can be the most incredibly destructive potential I can imagine. Only when they are in His hands and under His direction are they safe to use and able to accomplish His purposes.

Have the Courage to Swim Where God Places You

My friend Rick Kingham, who is on the board of Promise Keepers, likes to compare two rides at the water park in Denver. One is called "The Lazy River." As you might imagine, it's a low-impact, low-threat floating trip on an inner tube. Some people love to plop down and just drift. Rick, on the other hand, loves the Bonzai. It's a screaming fall of 150 feet and looks like a straight drop from the top. It doesn't take a lot of courage to ride the Lazy River. Not so with the Bonsai.

Likewise, it doesn't take a lot of courage to follow the safe route, the predictable path in life. Follow Jesus Christ and you will find yourself at times looking down from the top of the Bonsai. Without courage, you'll turn and tell Christ, "I think I'll sit this one out. Tell You what, Lord. Why don't You meet me at the Lazy River."

In our study of the book of Daniel we have seen that a life following Jesus Christ fully is not always a safe venture. It requires courage. You will meet opportunities, as well as face obstacles that will challenge you to the edge of your faith. The problem is, playing it safe might be the most dangerous route to take if it is not where Jesus leads.

Courage in career choice. Since our culture elevates some careers as more valuable than others, affording them more influence, we should accept the opportunity of influence without being sucked into the value system if God has gifted us to do the work. Consider the impact Earvin Johnson could have for good had he expressed his sorrow over his promiscuous lifestyle rather than simply confessing his "naiveté."

As long as a career meets legitimate human needs, and does not require compromises of Christian values, we should encourage people gifted by God to do the work required to enter that field. Even entering fields dominated by nonChristians and pagan thought should not be discouraged. We should also encourage individuals to climb as high in those fields as their capacity will take them and they feel led by God. We should not encourage them to take a lower course because the road is easier or paved by less moral failure. We need to aim as high as God and our gifts will carry us.

Courage in public responsibility. Another arena where we need courage to step out of the safety zone is our political responsibility. Although we must jettison any philosophy of government that believes political power can solve America's dilemmas, as citizens of a democratic system we are all responsible to play a role in our nation's direction. Just as in Daniel's day, the participation of godly men and women at all levels of political and governmental affairs is essential to our nation's health—morally and economically as well as spiritually.

God calls us to pray for the welfare of our leaders, especially men (1 Timothy 2:1-8). He will call some of us to be those leaders, serving on community task forces or committees. He will create opportunities for others to run for the school board, city counsel, state legislature, congress, and even the presidency. When these opportunities arise, we dare not retreat within the walls of personal privacy for fear of personal consequences. The cost of retreat is almost always greater than the cost of advance in such cases. A life spent protecting itself is not only tragic, it is one of the greatest wastes imaginable.

Where does the courage come from for soaring? Norman Vincent Peale found the answer in the little Swiss village of Bergenstock, near Lucerne. He writes,

> Bergenstock is pervaded by the spirit of a remarkable man named Frederick Frey, who developed it. Born a peasant, Frey became an important figure in the Swiss power industry and then one of the greatest hotelkeepers in the world. His son Fritz once surprised me with the statement that his

when the heart is gripped by God, it is free to soar!!

father's greatness arose out of a youthful sickness that required him to spend a year in the hospital. When I asked Fritz how that experience led to greatness, he said, "During that year my father read the Bible six times."

From that, Fritz said, his father developed such a faith that, if he were to walk a ridge with steep precipices on both sides, he would do it absolutely without fear: "He was never afraid after the time he poured the Bible down inside himself."[11]

When the heart is gripped by fear, the soul is frozen by inertia. When the heart is gripped by God, it is free to soar. Perhaps the greatest key to courage is the Word of God. As Joshua led Israel into the land of Palestine, God told him three times in so many verses, "Be strong and courageous." He also told him, "Do not let this Book of the Law depart from your mouth; meditate on it day and night" (Joshua 1:8). There is a direct relationship between courage and Scripture. God's Word fortifies us with the truth. It gives us the mental ammunition to do battle with the lies of Satan that would make us fall back in fear. Like Frederick Frey, we will know we have nothing to fear. Knowing that God is with us wherever we might go will give us the courage to resist the fear and discouragement that Satan will doubtless throw in our path as we pursue God's will.

As you finish this book, I would like you to consider the impact of the person who pursues competence, character, and courage:

- ◆ He has a vision for what God might do through him, and has a specific, strategic plan for having an impact on the world around him.
- ◆ She knows who she is, where she fits, and is moving toward the harmony that God intends to exist between woman and her work.
- ◆ He does not make an artificial distinction between the secular and sacred, approaching all work that requires his gifts as a holy task and as an expression of his uniqueness.
- ◆ She knows her resources, opportunities, and gifts come from God and are not of her own making, so she exhibits

both gratitude toward God and graciousness toward others in her life.

♦ He assumes the discipline of craftsmanship, making his work increasingly attractive to others around him.

♦ She does her work with delight, exhibiting an infectious joy. After finding what God created her to do, she experiences the pleasure and significance of alignment with the Author of meaning and purpose.

♦ He is able to make choices based on who he knows himself to be, resisting systems of influence in the world that call him to make decisions based primarily on values such as the measure of fame, prestige, wealth, or safety.

♦ She is confident that God will elevate her to the position of leadership where she can best serve her fellow man and glorify God.

♦ He has the ability to remain calm in the midst of fluctuations in the economy or the instability of the government, because he knows he is in the hands of a faithful and unchanging God who placed him in those circumstances for a purpose.[12]

No matter where this person might be on the spectrum of cultural influence, he or she will be influential in some sphere within the culture.

I don't know what God has put on your heart, but I will join Charles Cohn in challenging you, "Whatever it is, however impossible it seems, whatever the obstacle that stands between you and it; if it is noble, if it is consistent with God's kingdom, you hunger after it. You must stretch yourself to reach it." To do less would be tragic, both for you and our generation.

THE BIG IDEA

God created all of us for impact, but not in the same realm or for the same capacity. By faithfully fulfilling the responsibilities before us, we place ourselves in "ready position"—to be used by God in future matters we may not be able to see today. The next step is up to Him.

Use the following thoughts and ideas to stimulate your thinking about the impact God may want you to have on your generation.

Whatever your hand finds to do,
do it with all your might.
ECCLESIASTES 9:10

I am only one; But still I am one. I cannot do everything,
but still I can do something;
I will not refuse to do the something I can do.
HELEN KELLER

Every man's work, whether it be literature, or music,
or pictures, or architecture, or anything else,
is always a portrait of himself.
SAMUEL BUTLER

Genius is nothing but a greater aptitude for patience.
BENJAMIN FRANKLIN

Talent develops itself in solitude; character in the stream of life.
GOETHE

Give me a man who sings at his work.
THOMAS CARLYLE

Nature arms each man with some faculty which enables him
to do easily some feat impossible to any other.
RALPH WALDO EMERSON

We're all born under the same sky,
but we don't all have the same horizon.
KONRAD ADENAUER

He is a wise man who wastes no energy
on the pursuits for which he is not fitted.
GLADSTONE

Build on your strengths
and your weaknesses will be irrelevant.
PETER DRUCKER

According to the experts,
80% of workers in this country are under-employed.
RICHARD BOLLES

If a man is called to be a street sweeper,
he should sweep streets even as Michelangelo painted,
or Beethoven composed music, or Shakespeare wrote poetry.
He should sweep streets so well that all the hosts of heaven
and earth will pause to say,
here lived a great street sweeper who did his job well.
MARTIN LUTHER KING, JR.

The credit belongs to the man who is actually in the arena,
whose face is marred by dust and sweat and blood;
who strives valiantly; who errs and comes short again
and again, who knows the great enthusiasms,
the great devotions, and spends himself on a worthy cause;
who at the best, knows the triumph of high achievement;
and who, at the worst, if he fails, at least fails while daring
greatly, so that his place shall never be with those cold
and timid souls who know neither victory nor defeat.
THEODORE ROOSEVELT

Those who aim at great deeds must suffer greatly.
PLUTARCH

Before James Garfield was President of the United States, he was principal of Hiram College in Ohio. The father of a student approached him to ask if the course of study couldn't be simplified so that his son might be able to complete his work in a shorter amount of time. "Certainly," Garfield replied. "But it all depends upon what you want to make of your boy. When God wants to make an oak tree, He takes a hundred years. When He wants to make a squash, He requires only two months."

I would rather fail in a cause that will someday triumph than triumph in a cause that will someday fail.
WOODROW WILSON

The only place where success comes before work is in the dictionary.

Press on! Nothing can take the place of persistence.
Talent will not. Nothing is more common than
unsuccessful men with talent.
Genius will not. Unrewarded genius is a proverb.
Education will not. The world is full of educated derelicts.
Persistence and determination
alone are overwhelmingly powerful.
CALVIN COOLIDGE

The heights by great men reached and kept
were not attained by sudden flight
But they, while their companions slept
were toiling upward in the night.
ANONYMOUS

Laziness means more work in the long run.
Or look at it this way. In a battle,
or in mountain climbing,
there is often one thing which it takes a lot of pluck to do;
but it is also, in the long run, the safest thing to do.
If you funk it, you will find yourself,
hours later, in far worse danger.
The cowardly thing is also the most dangerous thing.
C. S. LEWIS
Mere Christianity

I am beginning to suspect that the common transactions
of life are the most sacred channels
of the spread of the heavenly leaven.
There was ten times more of the divine
in selling her that [fabric] in the name of God as you did
than there would have been in taking her into your pew
and singing out of the same hymnbook with her.
GEORGE MACDONALD
The Curate's Awakening

As I grow older, I pay less attention to what men say.
I just watch what they do.
ANDREW CARNEGIE

We never know what minor act of hopeless courage,
what word spoken in defense of truth,
what unintended consequence might swing the balance
and change the world.
CHARLES COLSON
Against the Night

History pivots on the actions of individuals
both great and ordinary.
CHARLES COLSON
Against the Night

One man with courage makes a majority.
ANDREW JACKSON

The price of greatness is responsibility.
WINSTON CHURCHILL

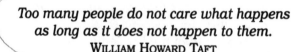

Too many people do not care what happens
as long as it does not happen to them.
WILLIAM HOWARD TAFT

If one advances confidently in the direction of his dreams,
and endeavors to live the life which he has imagined,
he will meet with a success unexpected in common hours.
HENRY D. THOREAU

The saints are the sinners who keep on going.
ROBERT LOUIS STEVENSON

Find out where you can render service, and then render it.
The rest is up to the Lord.
S. S. KRESGE

It would be no surprise if a study of secret causes
were undertaken to find that every golden era in human history
precedes from the devotion and righteous passion of some
single individual. This does not set aside the sovereignty

*of God; it simply indicates the instrument through
which he uniformly works. There are no bona fide mass
movements; it just looks that way.
At the center of the column there is always one man who knows
his God, and knows where he is going.*
RICHARD ELLSWORTH DAY

Turn Up the Light

All great systems, ethical or political,
attain their ascendancy over the minds of men
by virtue of their appeal to the imagination; and when they
cease to touch the chords of wonder and mystery and hope,
their power is lost, and men look elsewhere for some set
of principles by which they may be guided.
RUSSELL KIRK

In April of 1912, the Titanic, the largest ocean liner ever built, sailed from Southampton on her maiden voyage from England to New York City. Some 882 feet long, the new flagship of the White Star Line was the crowning achievement of ocean-going technology and the new standard of luxury and safety for those traveling between Europe and North America. At last passengers could travel the treacherous ice fields of the North Atlantic without fear. Double-hull construction and sixteen watertight compartments virtually insured that the ship was unsinkable.

But on April 14, shortly before midnight, the unthinkable happened. While steaming at high speed about 1,600 miles northeast of New York, the Titanic hit an iceberg in heavy fog, slashing a 300-foot gash in her hull that flooded six of the watertight compartments. The ship sank into the icy depths of the North Atlantic in less than three hours. "In one of the 20th century's first major lessons on the limits of faith in technology, the ship proved tragically inadequate when it collided with reality."[1]

Two mistakes compounded the tragedy. First, the management of the White Star Line was so confident of the invulnerability of their ship that they failed to place sufficient lifeboats aboard for the number of passengers and crew. Second, another vessel, the Californian,

237

had stopped because of the fog and lay just twenty miles away from the sinking Titanic. Unfortunately, no one was at the Californian's radio to pick up the distress call. By the time she did receive the message, it was too late to do anything except join in the rescue of the fortunate few who fit in the lifeboats. Of the 2,227 on board, 1,522 perished that night.

Many of us grew up thinking that our nation was unsinkable. Like the Titanic, the greatness of our country makes the thought of our sinking almost unimaginable. Unfortunately, the U.S. altered its course to sail through the treacherous sea of relativistic thinking and hit an iceberg. Today a number of our "watertight compartments" are flooding rapidly. Essential elements that keep a country afloat, such as leaders of integrity, stable families, strong common cultural beliefs, moral values, and a commitment to individual responsibility are all taking in water fast. The U.S. is listing to port and will sink unless something changes our present course.

Fortunately, there is hope. As we have learned from our study of Daniel, a person of competence, character, commitment and courage can make a tremendous difference. That difference, however, will not be made if that person is floating idly around twenty miles away and is nowhere near the radio to hear the call for help.

As I see it, Christians have two choices. We can either sleep through the disaster, hiding and waiting until the ship has sunk, then pick up a few survivors. Or we can sail full speed ahead toward the disaster before the ship goes to the bottom and we hope to steer her into safer waters where repairs can be made. Unfortunately, changing the course of a nation is not as simple as changing the course of a ship. Whoever controls the helm determines where the ship will go. To change the course of a nation, millions of minds must be captured by an idea that compels them to change.

CHANGING OUR COURSE

The man or woman who makes a lasting difference in this world is not one who masters the world's ways of influence and power wielding, but one who allows himself or herself to be mastered by Jesus Christ—a process that begins with the mind. Paul makes this clear in Romans 12:1-2—

> Therefore, I urge you, brothers, in view of God's mercy, to offer your bodies as living sacrifices, holy and pleasing to God—this is your spiritual act of worship. Do not conform any longer to the pattern of this world, but be transformed by the renewing of your mind.

We have a problem, though. Many Christians have attempted to give Christ their body before giving Him their mind. This simply does not work. We can only submit our members to the extent that our control center is committed to Christ. The real battle for our culture begins within you and me—first and foremost—before it spills into the streets.

I am saddened by much of what I see as well-intentioned public demonstrations by Christians. By their attitudes, many protesters have often polarized people who could have been marshaled to their side. As a result, Christians are viewed as raving fanatics. The national press corps has not helped—to say the least. They have a strong agenda to destroy evangelical Christianity and angry Christians have played right into their hands. We are losing the battle, but not because of negative media attention. We are losing because we're fighting in the wrong arena—the streets.

We need to be careful of letting the enemy set the agenda of warfare. I think that we have majored on battles that it is almost impossible to win by direct frontal assault. By massing his troops, Satan has distracted us from the real battle for the hearts of Americans. Colonel S.L.A. Marshal writes, "It is one of the commonplaces of war that we see good troops fight bitterly for worthless ground which the enemy is strongly contesting and in the next round treat carelessly the really worthwhile object simply because the enemy momentarily does not seem to regard it as worth a contest."[2] We need to be very careful about letting the enemy set the agenda.

TURN UP THE LIGHT AND TURN DOWN THE HEAT

Increasingly thoughtful leaders are beginning to realize that the war is not for the streets, but for the minds of Americans. Minds are not changed by bullhorns, but by the espousal of thoughtful arguments backed up by lives of integrity. We must turn up the light and turn down the heat, if we expect people to listen. Television spots run by the DeMoss Foundation are a case in point. They are turning up the light by producing and funding television time for thoughtful, emotionally appealing vignettes that emphasize the sanctity of life. The productions end by saying, "Life, isn't it a beautiful choice!" No one can argue with that statement, and it leaves a seed that over time may do more to change a person's mind and actions than any bullhorn-driven protest. Please don't misunderstand me. We should be angry and outraged about a number of issues. But if we want to see things change, we must stop to ask if anything of lasting value will happen as a result of angry, confrontational methods. We must also be challenged by James' pronouncement, "The anger of a man does not achieve the righteousness of God" (James 1:20, NASB).

Since life is so relentless, Americans run from anyone shouting or challenging them to do anything—no matter how right or wrong it may be. It is true—protest can alter a person's behavior, but not his or her mind. Unless a person changes the way he or she thinks, there will be no real change.

In its inception, MADD, Mothers Against Drunk Drivers, was a belligerent organization. It was founded by Candy Lightner, a mother who became outraged and rightly so at the way the court merely slapped the hand of a drunk driver who killed her daughter. Soon Lightner was joined by other angry individuals who were sick and tired of a society that looked the other way while intoxicated individuals took to the roads to kill and maim innocent people. A few years ago MADD turned up the light, and turned down the heat, focusing on ad campaigns written to change the way we think about drinking and driving. The result has brought a radical change not only in the way our legal system handles individuals charged with "driving under the influence," but also in the attitude of average Americans. It is no longer funny to see a drunk staggering to his or her car.

CHANGE IDEAS—CHANGE A CULTURE

Change a person's ideas, and you change a person. Change a person, and you change a culture. The person or group that controls ideas controls the culture. It is that simple. That is why seizure and control of the media was so central to the agenda of the Communist

Party. They knew that if they controlled the stream of images moving into the minds of the people, they could control the masses. People like Alexander Solzhenitsyn were a tremendous threat because they had the potential of seizing the imagination of the people. Chuck Colson is right: "Societies are not held together by rules and laws; order cannot be enforced by swords or guns alone. People must find their motivation and meaning in powerful ideas— beliefs that justify their institutions and ideals."[3] If the U.S. changes course, it will be because the powerful ideas of the Christian faith seize the imagination of the American people.

SEIZING THE AMERICAN IMAGINATION

In the early part of this century, the Christian faith ceased to touch the chords of wonder, mystery, and hope, and thus lost the imagination of the United States. At war with itself over the heretical beliefs of liberalism imported from Europe, the Church forgot to build people. Suffice it to say, there was a lot more heat than light. By the 1920s, the U.S. began to look for guidance elsewhere. In the malaise of the Great Depression, Franklin Roosevelt gave people a new hope—that government could solve our problems and create a new society. For the last fifty years, our feeling of safety has risen and fallen in direct proportion to the strength of our government.

Although our international enemies are neutralized by the internal failure of their own ideologies, today, the U.S. feels insecure. Even propped up by the liberal media, the U.S. is skeptical of Washington. The time is ripe for something new to seize the American imagination. Many political leaders want us to believe that more government is the answer, kind of a let-Momma-take-care-of-it-for-you philosophy. Small wonder we're insecure—Momma can't take care of us any more.

If the Christian faith is going to once again recapture the imagination of our nation, several things must characterize our message of light.

Our Message Must Be Positive
Christians today are much better at defining what we are against than what we are for. When many Americans think of Christians,

they define us in terms of what we don't do. We are for life, not just against abortion. We are for mutual respect between men and women, not just against pornography. We are for healthy productive families, not just against the myriad of forces attempting to tear families apart.

The Christian faith is by and large a positive faith. Its true power both for the individual and society comes from the positive proclamation of the truth. William E. Gladstone warned, "To be engaged in opposing wrongs affords, under the condition of our mental constitution, but a slender guarantee for being right."

Our Message Must Be Winsome

Surely an uncompassionate Christian is one of the greatest oxymorons of the universe. More often than not, it seems we have a greater concern for getting our point across than we do for the other person. Abraham Lincoln said, "If you would win a man to your cause, first become his friend." It is true that people don't care how much you know, until they know how much you care.

The most compelling idea we have to impart to anyone is that Jesus Christ, the Sovereign Ruler of the universe, loves each of us and wants to deliver us to a new plane of existence. If we want people to believe this higher life really exists, we must live there ourselves and demonstrate the same unselfish compassion toward others that Christ demonstrates toward us.

Our Message Must Be Personal

The light we want to bring to others must shine in us first. The reason Darius wanted to listen to Daniel was because he held Daniel in such high regard. Similarly, if we want society to listen to us, it must first hold us in high regard. Too often today, people look at Christians as just another special interest group, clamoring for its rights. The light must change us before we can expect the light to change society. We must do more than proclaim the light. We must be the light ourselves. Oswald Chambers gives a valuable warning in *My Utmost for His Highest*:

> True earnestness is found in obeying God, not in the inclination to serve Him that is born of undisciplined human

nature. It is inconceivable, but true nevertheless, that saints are not bringing every project into captivity, but are doing work for God at the instigation of their own human nature which has not been spiritualized by determined discipline.

We are apt to forget that a man is not only committed to Jesus Christ for salvation; he is committed to Jesus Christ's view of God, of the world, of sin, and of the devil, and this will mean that he must recognize the responsibility of being transformed by the renewing of his mind.[4]

As we allow God to transform us, perhaps God will be gracious to use us as He did Daniel, to bring light to this darkened world.

Notes

INTRODUCTION

1. Alexander Solzhenitsyn, quoted by William J. Bennett, *Index of Leading Cultural Indicators* (New York: Simon & Schuster, 1994), pages 9-10.
2. Walker Percy, quoted by Bennett, page 9.

CHAPTER ONE—OPPORTUNITY KNOCKS

1. Tim Hansel, *You Gotta Keep Dancin'* (Elgin, IL: David C. Cook, 1985), page 55.
2. George MacDonald, *The Curate's Awakening*, Michael Phillips, ed. (Minneapolis, MN: Bethany House, 1985), page 60.
3. Dorothy L. Sayers, *Christian Letters in a Post-Christian World* (Grand Rapids, MI: Eerdmans, 1969), page 14.
4. Quoted by Charles R. Swindoll in *Living on the Ragged Edge* (Waco, TX: Word, 1985), page 177.
5. C. S. Lewis, *Mere Christianity* (New York: Macmillan, 1952), pages 172, 174.
6. Joni Earickson-Tada, quoted by Philip Yancey in *Where Is God When It Hurts?* (Grand Rapids, MI: Zondervan, 1984), page 119.

7. Quoted by Richard Soume, *Nehemiah: God's Builder* (Chicago: Moody Press, 1978), page 20.

CHAPTER TWO—KEEPING YOUR MIND OUT
OF THE GUTTER WHEN YOU LIVE IN A SEWER

1. *National and International Religion Report*, May 20, 1991, vol. 5, no. 11.
2. Leighton Ford, *The Christian Persuaders* (New York: Harper & Row, 1966), pages 71-72.
3. Joseph C. Aldrich, *Lifestyle Evangelism* (Portland, OR: Multnomah, 1982), pages 15-16.
4. Robert E. Slocum, *Maximize Your Ministry* (Colorado Springs, CO: NavPress, 1990), page 287.
5. Oswald Chambers, *My Utmost for His Highest* (New York: Dodd, Mead & Co., 1935), page 209.
6. Walter Moberly, *The Crisis in the University* (London: SCM Press, 1949), page 52.

CHAPTER THREE—HOLDING LIFE TOGETHER
WHEN HELL BREAKS LOOSE

1. C. S. Lewis, *A Grief Observed* (New York: Seabury Press, 1961), page 9.
2. A. W. Tozer, *Knowledge of the Holy* (New York: Harper & Row, 1961), page 1.
3. C S. Lewis, *The Screwtape Letters* (New York: Macmillan, 1968), pages 21-22.
4. Tozer, pages 10-11.

CHAPTER FOUR—THE ROCK IN THE SWAMP

1. *National and International Religion Report*, vol. 5, no. 11, May 20, 1991.
2. Robert Slocum, *Maximize Your Ministry* (Colorado Springs, CO: NavPress, 1990), pages 121-122.
3. Slocum, pages 124-125.
4. S.L.A. Marshal, *Men Against Fire* (Gloucester, MA: Peter Smith, 1978), pages 42-43.

5. Oswald Chambers, *My Utmost for His Highest* (New York: Dodd, Mead & Co., 1935), page 242.

CHAPTER FIVE—THE SLIPPERY SLOPE OF SUCCESS

1. Quoted by Philip Yancey in *Where Is God When It Hurts?* (Grand Rapids, MI: Zondervan, 1984), page 53.
2. Joyce Lain Kennedy, "Many Professionals Discover that Success Does Not Bring Happiness," *Dallas Morning News*, February 18, 1990, no page.
3. Michael Korda, *Success* (New York: Random House, 1977), pages 4,6.
4. Stanley W. Angrist, "Selling to the Rich—and to Regular Folk," *The Wall Street Journal*, September 21, 1992.
5. Faith Popcorn, *The Popcorn Report* (New York: Doubleday, 1991), page 191.
6. Quoted by Charles R. Swindoll, *Improving Your Serve* (Waco, TX: Word Books, 1981), pages 190-191.
7. Ben L. Abuzzo with Maxie L. Andersen and Larry Newman, "'Double Eagle II' Has Handed!" *National Geographic Magazine*, December 1978, vol. 154, no. 6, page 864.

CHAPTER SIX—THE TRUTH ABOUT CONSEQUENCES

1. Charles Colson, *Against the Night* (Ann Arbor, MI: Servant Publications, 1989), pages 10-11.
2. "Hugh Fumes: '20/20' Host Slashes at GOP," *Mediawatch*, January 20, 1993.
3. Russell Kirk, *Confessions of a Bohemian Tory* (New York: Fleet Publishing, 1963), page 222.
4. James Dobson, Focus on the Family monthly letter, March 1993.
5. Joseph Stowell, *The Dawn's Early Light* (Chicago: Moody Press, 1990), page 16.
6. Dallas Willard, *The Spirit of the Disciplines* (San Francisco: Harper & Row, 1988), appendix.
7. Colson, page 135.
8. Oswald Chambers, *My Utmost for His Highest* (New York: Dodd, Mead & Co., 1935), page 250.

CHAPTER SEVEN—LIVING IN THE LIONS' DEN WITHOUT BEING EATEN

1. Tim Hansel, *When I Relax I Feel Guilty*, quoted by Charles R. Swindoll, *Strengthening Your Grip* (Waco, TX: Word Books, 1982), page 141.
2. James Graham, *The Prophet Statesman*, quoted by Donald K. Campbell in *Daniel: Decoder of Dreams* (Wheaton, IL: Victor Books, 1977), pages 74-75.
3. Charles Colson, *Against the Night* (Ann Arbor, MI: Servant Publications, 1989), page 135.
4. C. S. Lewis, *The Screwtape Letters* (New York: Macmillan, 1961), page x.
5. E. B. White, *One Man's Meat* (New York: Harper Colophon, 1982), page 135.
6. Bill Gaither with Jerry Jenkins, *I Almost Missed the Sunset* (Nashville, TN: Thomas Nelson, 1992), pages 17-19, 163.

CHAPTER EIGHT—THE ROAD TO RESTORATION

1. Tim Hansel, *You Gotta Keep Dancin'* (Elgin, IL: David C. Cook, 1985), page 84.
2. E. M. Bounds, *Power Through Prayer* (Grand Rapids, MI: Baker Book House, 1972), page 13.
3. Charles Colson, *Against the Night* (Ann Arbor, MI: Servant Publications, 1989), page 11.
4. Blaise Pascal, Pascal's Pense'es (New York: E.P. Dutton & Co., 1958).
5. John Adams, "Address to the Officers of the First Brigade of the 3rd Division of the Militia of Massachusetts," October 11, 1798.
6. Colson, page 69.
7. Colson, pages 141-142.

CHAPTER NINE—HOW TO CHANGE YOUR WORLD

1. E. M. Bounds, *Power Through Prayer* (Grand Rapids, MI: Baker Book House, 1972), pages 5,7.

2. Quoted by Robert Slocum in *Maximize Your Ministry* (Colorado Springs, CO: NavPress, 1990), pages 247-249.

3. E. M. Bounds, *The Possibilities of Prayer* (Grand Rapids, MI: Baker Book House, 1979), page 106.

4. Nancy Spiegleberg and Dorothy Purdy, *Fanfare: A Celebration of Belief* (Portland, OR: Multnomah Press, 1981), no page.

5. Robert Flood, ed., *The Rebirth of America* (Philadelphia: DeMoss Foundation, 1986), no page.

6. Cal Thomas, "Ted Turner Stars in Own Divine Tragicomedy," Los Angeles Times Syndicate, no date.

7. Os Guinness, *Winning Back the Soul of America* (Washington DC: Hour Glass Publishers, 1990), page 3.

8. Bounds, no page.

CHAPTER TEN—THE POWER OF ONE

1. Robert Bezilla, ed., *Religion in America: 1990 Report* (Princeton, NJ: The Princeton Religion Research Center, 1990), pages 60-61.

2. Bezilla, page 8.

3. Charles Leerhsen, "Magic's Message," *Newsweek*, November 18, 1991, page 59.

4. Dorothy L. Sayers, *Creed or Chaos?* (New York: Harcourt & Brace, 1949), page 56.

5. Quoted by Charles R. Swindoll, *Growing Strong in the Seasons of Life* (Portland, OR: Multnomah, 1983), page 312.

6. Charles R. Swindoll, *Living Above the Level of Mediocrity* (Waco, TX: Word Books, 1987), page 17.

7. For further reading on God's perspective of work, see *Your Work Matters to God* by Doug Sherman and William Hendricks (NavPress, 1987).

8. Ann McGee-Cooper, *Time Management for Unmanageable People* (Dallas, TX: Cooper & Associates, 1983), page 131.

9. Swindoll, *Growing Strong in the Seasons of Life*, pages 313-314.

10. Ralph Mattson and Arthur Miller, *Finding a Job You Can Love* (Nashville, TN: Thomas Nelson, 1982), page 41.

11. Norman Vincent Peale, *My Favorite Quotations* (San Francisco:

Harper and Row, 1990), page 36.

12. Adapted from Mattson and Miller, pages 55-57.

CONCLUSION—TURN UP THE LIGHT

1. Robert D. Ballard, "Epilogue for Titanic," *National Geographic Magazine*, October 1987, vol. 172, no. 4, page 459.
2. S.L.A. Marshal, *Men Against Fire* (Gloucester, MA: Peter Smith, 1978), page 98.
3. Charles Colson, *Against the Night* (Ann Arbor, MI: Servant Publications, 1989), page 170.
4. Oswald Chambers, *My Utmost for His Highest* (New York: Dodd, Mead & Co., 1935), page 253.

Author

✤

Bill Peel is the mid-south regional director of the Christian Medical and Dental Society, a discipleship ministry among health-care professionals. Also the president of Foundations for Living, Peel champions the cause of lay ministry and helps men and women discover how they can impact their world for Jesus Christ in the midst of everyday life—especially through their careers. Peel teaches leadership seminars for corporations, and he travels frequently speaking at churches and conferences. He pioneered work with men in the 1970s and has been responsible for hundreds of men being in small groups.

Peel is a member of the Promise Keepers Speakers Team. He is the author of the first Promise Keepers study guide, *What God Does When Men Pray* (NavPress/Promise Keepers, 1993), and was involved in a nationwide radio campaign in 1993 calling men to prayer.

Peel is a graduate of Southern Methodist University and Dallas Theological Seminary. He and his wife, Kathy, live in Nashville, Tennessee. They have three sons.